THE FALL AND ʳ
OF MAN

How Genesis Supports Darwin

Joseph Fitzpatrick

University Press of America,® Inc.
Lanham · Boulder · New York · Toronto · Plymouth, UK

Then the Lord God said, "Behold, the man has become like one of us, knowing good and evil; and now, lest he put forth his hand and take also of the tree of life, and eat, and live for ever" – therefore the Lord God sent him forth from the garden of Eden, to till the ground from which he was taken. He drove out the man; and at the east of the garden of Eden he placed the cherubim, and a flaming sword which turned every way, to guard the way to the tree of life.

Genesis 3: 22-24

(Revised Standard Version of the Bible)

"A non-Catholic philosopher once said to me: 'You know – I just can't stop myself reading and re-reading and thinking over the first three chapters of Genesis.'"

Karol Wojtyla (Pope John Paul II)

The first three chapters of Genesis form "the immutable basis of all Christian anthropology."

(Pope John Paul II)

"As soon as it is realized that the Garden of Eden is a myth, it is seen to be a very good myth, curiously congruous with evolution, because the Fall is (in the myth itself) a 'fall upwards' seeing that by it the knowledge of good and evil is obtained."

William Temple (Archbishop of Canterbury)

"The doctrine of original sin is not found in any of the writings of the Old Testament. It is certainly not in chapters one to three of Genesis."

Herbert Haag
(former president of the Catholic Bible Association of Germany)

"Old Testament scholars have long known that the reading of the story (in Genesis 3) as the 'Fall of Man' in the traditional sense, though hallowed by St Paul's use of it, cannot stand up to examination through a close reading of the Genesis text. But though this has long been evident, scholars have not, on the whole, succeeded in formulating a general picture of the purpose and impact of the story which could rival the traditional one and could carry equal force or similar relevance over so wide a range of biblical materials and theological considerations."

James Barr (Professor of Hebrew Bible at Vanderbilt Divinity School)

Some sections of the Book of Genesis are still "waiting for interpreters with the right constellation of interpretive interests to exploit the text's potential to be read in a new way."

David M. Carr (author of *Reading the Fractures of Genesis*)

"No man ...who knows nothing else, knows even his Bible."

Matthew Arnold

"The Church has abandoned its spiritual leadership insofar as it has left post-medieval man without guidance in his endeavours to find meaning in a complex civilisation which differs profoundly in its horizons of reason, nature and history from the ancient that was absorbed and penetrated by the early Church."

Eric Voegelin

For Eileen

and all our grandchildren, present and future

Contents

Acknowledgements

Over the years in which I have been preoccupied with the challenges posed by chapter 3 of the Book of Genesis, I have been supported and sustained by the encouragement I have received from a number of friends who reassured me that my reasoning was convincing, evidence-based and on the right tracks. I owe them a genuine debt of gratitude. I am not by temperament an iconoclast and the fact that the case I was arguing ran counter to centuries of tradition, with at its source the towering figure of Augustine, has been at times almost overwhelming. That I have pursued my self-imposed task to a reasonably satisfactory conclusion owes much to their positive responses and approval. So let me thank my friends Vivienne Blackburn, John Dunne, Dick Weaver and Roderick Johnston, each of whom read complete drafts or portions of the text at various stages of its composition and provided thoughtful comments as well as their indispensable encouragement and enthusiasm. I also wish to thank Fergus Kerr for enabling me to try out my ideas in the form of five articles published in *New Blackfriars*, the theological journal he edits. A particular debt of gratitude is owed to James O'Connell, Emeritus Professor of Peace Studies at the University of Bradford. My interest in Genesis 3 and in the whole issue of Original Sin grew out of conversations I had with him some years ago, and he also read an early draft and made some critical suggestions that reduced the work's flaws and imperfections. To my wife Eileen go my greatest thanks of all. She has had to put up with my alternating periods of silent abstraction and voluble exposition, and has done so with great patience, humour and love. Without doubt, she has been my Muse, amusing and amused, but always positive, warm and encouraging.

Introduction

Everybody knows the story of Adam and Eve in the Garden of Eden; and everybody appears to know what the story *means*. In the words of the *The Lion First Bible*:

In the very beginning, when God made the world and everything was good, there were no sad days. God made the beautiful garden of Eden for Adam and Eve to enjoy and take care of... God said they could eat any of the juicy fruit from the trees in the garden—all except one. That would not be good for them. If they ate it, bad things would happen.

But there is always someone who wants to spoil things. One sunny day, the sneaky snake came and hissed in Eve's ear:

"Take no notisss of what God sayss. He's jussst being mean. The fruit of the tree iss good to eat. It will make you as clever asss God."

Eve looked at the tree with its rosy, juicy fruit. She wanted to be as clever as God. So she reached up to pick it. And she ate. Eve gave some to Adam. And he ate the fruit too.

But that very evening, when God came to talk to them, they both hid.

"Why are you hiding from me?" God said. "Have you eaten the fruit of the tree I told you not to touch?"

"Don't blame *me*," Adam said, ashamed. "It's all Eve's fault."

"Don't blame *me*," Eve said, making excuses too. "It's all the snake's fault."

God looked stern and very sad.

"Then the snake will be punished," God said. "But you have not
done as I told you. You wanted your own way, and now everything is
spoiled. I meant you always to be happy. But now things will hurt you
and make you sad. I wanted you to live here with me always, but now
you must go away—and you can't come back. You will have to work
hard. You will grow old. And one day you will die."
    And so it was.[1]

This version of the story, which with some stylistic variations can be
found in any number of children's publications, is the one that is believed throughout the Western world and, as we shall see in Chapter
One, in its essential outline the one taught by the most influential Christian thinker in the West, St Augustine of Hippo. Indeed, I have found
that most people today tend to believe that there has only ever been one
single interpretation of the Genesis tale, the one propagated by
Augustine, and are surprised to learn that among the Fathers of the
Church there were multiple interpretations; and that the Eastern Orthodox Church has historically responded to the story recounted in Genesis
chapter 3 in a manner markedly different from the Christian West.[2]
    I have no intention of providing a history of the doctrine of the Fall
and Original Sin from before Augustine to the present day, but it can be
said without fear of contradiction that it was Augustine's interpretation
that was disseminated widely within the Catholic tradition throughout
the twentieth century by means of the textbooks of theology used in
seminaries for the training of priests and the catechisms used in Catholic
schools during that period[3] as well as by the authoritative *Catechism of
the Catholic Church*, published in 1994 under Pope John Paul II.[4] And
the doctrine of Original Sin in its Augustinian garb has been from the
outset a central tenet of Reformed Christianity, in both its Lutheran and
its Calvinist forms. Indeed Luther and Calvin went much further than
traditional Catholicism in their accounts of the dire consequences for
humanity brought about by Man's first sin.[5] It is not surprising, therefore, that the theme of *Paradise Lost* was the preoccupation of the Protestant Puritan poet, John Milton, whose great epic poem's opening lines
convey Augustine's central teaching with admirable economy:

Of Man's First Disobedience and the Fruit
Of that Forbidden Tree, whose mortal taste
Brought Death into the World, and all our woe...[6]

However, while this interpretation—a first or original sin of disobedience leading to the introduction of death, all further sin and immense human suffering and misery—is solidly rooted in the Western literary canon and well worn by custom and use, it has been under attack for some time now, and over the past thirty or forty years there has been a growing consensus among biblical scholars of all Christian denominations that this version can no longer stand up to the kind of detailed scrutiny that developments in biblical scholarship have made possible.[7] The same scholars have gone on to draw the conclusion that the traditional Christian doctrine of the Fall of Man, and the associated doctrine of Original Sin, cannot be found in the Hebrew Old Testament or cannot be supported by a reasonable interpretation of chapter 3 of Genesis.

The destructive demolition work is well in hand, but there has not been found a constructive alternative interpretation of Genesis 3 that might account for the data of the story told there while also affording readers an insight into the nature of the moral evil that we see all around us in the world we inhabit. It would be nice to "tidy away" the notions of the Fall or original sin and to restrict our focus to the pleasant and beautiful things we meet with in our lives, but the moral evil we encounter in the world is all too palpable and its existence cries out for some kind of theological explanation as well as the kind of insight that the traditional doctrine of original sin sought to provide.

In this book I attempt to do what some have believed to be an impossible task: I argue in the first chapter against the traditional understanding of original sin, as set out, as far as possible in his own words, by St Augustine, and I then provide in the following five chapters an alternative interpretation of Genesis 3, one that I believe does more justice to the biblical data than Augustine's. This alternative interpretation maintains that the story told in chapter 3 of Genesis is, in fact, a symbolic account of the ascent of a hominid couple to full human consciousness; it is about hominisation, about Man's becoming Man, the transformation or mutation of proto-humans into fully recognisable human beings. The couple's acquisition of reason certainly makes them capable of sin—there is no ducking the fact that sin pervades the human world—but it also makes them capable of responding to God's offer of salvation, wholeness and fulfilment. (The equivalence of *divine* salvation and *human* fulfilment is an underlying motif.) My interpretation has a strong "detective story" element, as I attempt to support it by recent developments in biblical studies and anthropology as well as by well established positions in Christian theology. In this way I hope to provide some intellectual and spiritual assistance to those who are unhappy with the traditional teaching, for whatever reason, but who remain alert to the existence of sin in the world and seek to understand it and, indeed, to overcome it.

In the course of my argument I also uncover a feature of human nature that the traditional interpretation of Genesis 3 has caused to be overlooked or undervalued, at least in the West, a feature that casts light on the divine-human relationship and one that I believe holds great promise for Christian theology and spirituality, linking as it does with the Wisdom tradition binding the Old and New Testaments. I have attempted to suggest some of the theological benefits that follow from this interpretation but these are really only hints that others more competent in the field might care to develop and bring to fruition.

It is my hope that readers will find that the book takes them on a stimulating and rewarding intellectual and spiritual journey, enabling them to gain a fresh insight into some very ancient problems besetting our common humanity without in any way conflicting with their modern scientific outlook. If I succeed in my efforts the only ones likely to be put out will be certain fundamentalist Christians and others, mostly dogmatic atheists, who love to insist on the incompatibility of religion and science, and in particular on the incompatibility of Genesis 3 with Darwin's theory of evolution. In my opinion, that will be no bad thing.

If I might attempt to state briefly at the outset what I hope to have achieved, it is *not* to have substituted an optimistic understanding of Genesis 3 for a pessimistic one, nor primarily to have provided an interpretation of Genesis 3 that is compatible with evolution—important as these two features are for theology and human self-understanding—but rather to have argued persuasively for the replacement of a relatively impoverished understanding of the history of salvation by an enriched one: one that copes better with the data of scripture, in both Old and New Testaments, is theologically more fruitful, and more convincing in accounting for human nature and human behaviour.

NOTES

1. Pat Alexander, *The Lion First Bible*, (Oxford: Lion Hudson plc, 1997) pp. 20-27.
2. N. P. Williams, *The Ideas of the Fall and of Original Sin: a historical and critical study*, 1924 Bampton Lectures, (London: Longman, Green & Co.,

1927) provides an authoritative overview of the various interpretations and responses.

3. See, for example, Herbaert Haag, *Is Original Sin in Scripture?*, (New York: Sheed and Ward, 1969) chapter 2.

4. *Catechism of the Catholic Church*, (London: Geoffrey Chapman, 1994) paragraph 397 ff.

5. See N.P. Williams, op. cit., pp. 322, 426. I have attempted to use inclusive language in this book, referring to "humankind," "human beings" and "humanity" etc., but there are times when these phrases become cumbersome and I have fallen back on the simpler generic monosyllable "man." However, to indicate its generic character I have capitalized the letter "M" so that the reader can see clearly that it is human beings in general and not the male person that is being referred to. English unfortunately does not have a word corresponding to the Latin "homo" which is clearly different from the gendered word "vir."

6. John Milton, *Paradise Lost*, I, 1-3 (1681).

7. This point is referred to by Marguerite Shuster, *The Fall and Sin: What we have become as Sinners*, (Grand Rapids: Eardmans, 2004) p. 4. See also Herbert Haag, op. cit., p. 19; James Barr, *The Garden of Eden and the Hope of Immortality*, (London: SCM Press, 1992) p. ix; and Raymond E. Brown, *An Introduction to the New Testament*, (New York: Doubleday, 1996) p. 580-581.

Chapter One
Augustine on Original Sin

My reason for beginning with Augustine of Hippo is because it was largely through his influence that the term "original sin" was introduced into Christian discourse and it is his interpretation of original sin that tends to be discussed whenever Western theologians ponder the meaning of the story of Adam and Eve in Eden. As I said in the Introduction, so dominant has Augustine's interpretation become that most Westerners, Christian and non-Christian alike, tend to think that there has only ever been one interpretation and that this is the only interpretation possible.

Aurelius Augustine (354-430 AD) was a convert to Christianity, deeply influenced by Neoplatonic philosophy, who became the Catholic bishop of Hippo in his native North Africa in 396. A scholar whose vast written output was preserved by a combination of good luck and good management,[1] Augustine is without doubt the most influential "Doctor" of the Church in the West. The West has to a large extent built its theology on the foundations laid by Augustine. Standing on the frontier separating classical antiquity from the Middle Ages, Augustine was a powerful influence behind the rise of scholastic philosophy and theology in medieval Europe and was one of Thomas Aquinas's main sources. Unlike Aquinas, Augustine was also adopted by the Protestant Reformers; Martin Luther was an Augustinian friar. Pre-Reformation reformers such as John Wyclif and John Hus also claimed Augustine on their side as did the Catholic Jansenists in France in the seventeenth century. In a way that is unique to him, Augustine is claimed by just about every major religious denomination in the West and many Christian religious movements have looked back to him as their inspiration and guide.

Many of Augustine's writings were hammered out in controversies with views he considered heretical and, in the case of original sin and the associated doctrine of grace, Augustine's main opponent was Pelagius, a British monk, who for some time exerted considerable influence among Christians in Rome and further afield. Pelagius is said to have taught that Adam had been created mortal, that the sin of Adam injured nobody but himself, that while Adam set a bad example for posterity the guilt for his sin is not inherited by those who have come after him, and that infants today are born in the same state as Adam before the fall.[2] On all of these points the Pelagians were opposed by Augustine.

Augustine wrote about original sin on more than one occasion and his numerous writings make frequent references to aspects of this doctrine as well as to the general sinfulness of human beings. I have elected to present here the account he gives of original sin in Books 12-14 of *The City of God,* supplemented with references to some other works, because this represents the views of the mature Augustine who has had time to think of the problems raised by his account of original sin and time also to develop responses to these problems.

In *The City of God* Augustine works out his theology in the context of what he understands to be the history of humanity and he frames his reflections on original sin likewise in the general history of humankind. So in Book 12, chapter 10, for example, he gives us his opinion on those who think that the human race, like the world itself, always existed, and in the following chapter he writes "On the mistaken history which ascribes many thousands of years to times past." As so often, Augustine works at a fairly speculative level and before he begins his treatment of original sin in chapter 6 of Book 12, he dwells for a time on the nature of angels and on the fall of the angels in heaven. This is no incidental preamble to his reflections on the original sin of the human race since in the mind of Augustine it is very clear that the fall of the angels, of those who chose darkness in preference to the light, is closely linked to the fall of Man. The big question Augustine addresses in this chapter is how it was possible for evil to have a beginning and, since God made all things good, how it was possible for something good to be the cause of evil. "How can a natural being that is good though changeable, before he comes to have an evil will, create something that is evil, I mean, the evil will itself?" (CG 12: 6; 33)[3] Here Augustine is addressing the problem in its most acute form. It is not difficult to see how moral evil is the product of an evil will, but how can an evil will emerge from one that is good?

LAPSATION OF THE WILL

Augustine gives his answer to this problem in the next chapter, chapter 7, saying that we should not seek "an efficient cause of an evil will, for the cause is not one of efficiency but of deficiency even as the evil will itself is not an effect but a defect." (Ibid., 33) Augustine clearly believes that this notion that evil is not something positive, something real, but rather an absence of the real, a deficiency, the privation of what is good—*privatio boni*—puts a stop to the search for the efficient cause of evil, a search that threatens to engulf God himself since the question can be asked how evil could have begun if God himself had not willed that it begin. For Augustine there can be no question of God being implicated in the origin of moral evil and he believes that the notion of evil as deficiency, as literally non-being, creates a firewall between evil and God. There can be no efficient cause of nothing. Rather nothing is the absence of being rather as darkness is the absence of light and silence the absence of sound (Ibid., 33). "To be sure, each of these two things is known to us, and one only through our eyes, the other only through our ears, yet clearly we know them not by their definite shape, but by the absence of shape or form. Hence let no one seek from me" (and here we encounter Augustine the rhetorician) "to know what I know that I do not know, except it be in order to learn how not to know what we should know cannot be known." (CG 12:7; 35)

So Augustine's view is that sin or moral evil is the result of an evil will and original sin is no exception, being the result of Man's evil will. There is no anterior cause, however, of the evil will itself, nothing beyond the evil will causing itself to turn bad. The evil will is the result of a lapse of the will itself, it brings about its own corruption. "The lapse is not to what is bad, but to lapse is bad. In other words, the natural objects to which there is a lapse are not bad, but to lapse is bad because the will lapses against the natural order from what has supreme being to what has less being." (CG 12:8; 37) Sin is not a consequence of anything in the natural world—such as gold or beautiful bodies or whatever—but resides in the soul of man who comes to love such things to excess at the expense of righteousness and moderation. An evil will, the only source of sin there is, is the result of the will's own lapse, nothing more and nothing less.

ONTOLOGY VERSUS PSYCHOLOGY

As an account of evil as a philosophical concept, Augustine's argument here is good but it is not clear that he provides an adequate account of original sin, of the first morally evil human action. When viewed *psychologically* it is difficult to see how a good will can lapse in the context of the Garden of Eden. It is the nature of the will to seek the good and a good will seeks the truly good. What motivation could anyone have to lapse if his will were already thoroughly good, where the word "good" would suggest that it was trained on its object in a manner commensurate with all that is right and proper in human nature? How could it possibly lapse unless it were already inclined to selfishness and sin? That evil is the privation of the good, a deficiency, does not seem to answer the question of how a perfectly good will, unaffected by any force of attraction beyond the good, could possibly choose evil over good. Despite Augustine's subtle and telling philosophical argument, the question of motivation and inclination remains at the level of human psychology. While it is not at all difficult to understand a lapse of the will in a universe already infected by sin it is very difficult to understand the same lapse in a totally innocent universe in which sin is unknown. In such a universe how could a perfectly good will be tempted? It would seem to be so constituted as to be impervious to temptation. Indeed, the very possibility of temptation would seem to be ruled out by definition, since the will is presumed to be good and hence ordered to that to which it ought to be ordered, without demur. The very possibility of the will departing from its true path seems ruled out, literally ruled out, by the conditions that have to be met for the will to be considered good and prior sin nonexistent.

In summary, it is one thing to provide a definition of *the nature of evil* as "the privation of the good," *privatio boni*. That is a matter of ontology, of the objective reality of evil. It is quite another thing to speak of *a will* that is ordered to the good becoming disordered or re-ordered to that which is bad and wrong. For the will to change there is needed some account of *motivation* or *reasons for changing* and it is here that a defender of Augustine's position must begin to struggle. To describe it simply, as Augustine does, as a lapse or failing of the will is to beg the question, for the question is: How could such a will lapse or fail? What could possibly have caused the will, motivated it, provided it with reason, to change or lapse? Can a perfectly good will change without it being already prone to evil and, if prone to evil, already implicated in sin? That is a matter not of ontology but of psychology.

Augustine is not unaware of the distinction between ontology and psychology but he does not appear to have worked it out clearly in his mind and this leads him, I believe, to an inconsistent position regarding the origin of sin. For one answer Augustine's position tempts one to adopt—and it is one that Augustine, a thinker of considerable subtlety, is well aware of (see, for example, CG14:10)—is that Man sinned because he had already sinned: that he sinned in deed because he had already sinned in his mind or heart. Augustine rightly repudiates the possibility of this happening in paradise, exclaiming, "Heaven forbid, I say, that we should think that before all sin there already existed in paradise such sin..." (Ibid.; 321) Having said this, however, he then proceeds to contradict himself by arguing a few chapters later (CG 14:13; 339-41) that man succumbed to pride in secret before he performed the deed by which he sinned: "This wrong, I repeat, came first in secret and prepared the way for the other wrong that was committed openly." (Ibid, 341) It is hard to see consistency between Augustine's words of repudiation in chapter 10 of Book 14 and his words concerning the corrupting influence of pride in chapter 13 of the same Book. In fact, Augustine is up against the very conditions he has established as prevailing in paradise and cannot satisfactorily answer the question: Can a human being sin in such circumstances? Can a human being sin if the conditions that make sin *psychologically possible* are absent? The negative route of *privatio* might explain evil but lapsation or failure of the will, albeit necessary, is not sufficient to explain sin in a world where sin is not known. Lapsation of the will requires in addition a cause or reason for lapsing, and it is here that Augustine's argument encounters its greatest difficulty.

ENTER THE SNAKE AND PRIDE

While Augustine is well aware of this line of thought, he appears to feel that he has met it by identifying the snake mentioned in Genesis 3 as a tool of the devil, the latter being a fallen angel who seeks to bring about in humankind the fall from divine favour which his own pride had caused him to experience previously (see CG 14:11—13). There is a blending of arguments here that is likely to confuse the reader.

Augustine presents the devil as a creature of superior intellect who deliberately chose as the target for his temptation "the lower member of that human couple in order to arrive gradually at the whole." (CG 14:11; 331) Adam yielded to temptation not because he believed his wife to be telling the truth but because of "the close bond of their alliance." Adam's mistake, he goes on to say, was to believe that his offence would be pardoned—in this way both the man and the woman were "ensnared in the devil's toils." (Ibid; 333) Now this introduction of an agent of seduction and temptation may seem to answer the question about the origin of moral evil along the lines that moral evil came about because there was already on the scene a morally corrupt being who misled the human couple—first the woman and through her the man—into sinning. However, this does not answer the question of how moral evil arose in the first place in a universe in which none had previously existed. It simply puts the origin of evil back, to the fall of the angels in heaven, and the arguments placed against the moral lapse of the human couple can be equally well placed against the moral lapse of the angels. Whether he is dealing with the fall of man or the fall of angels, Augustine is faced with the difficulty of making sin in a sinless universe psychologically possible. Augustine's reference to the devil is also weakened by the fact that it has no scriptural support so long as we stick to the tale we find in Genesis.

Augustine seems to be involved in a contradiction in this part of his argument, since he rightly repudiates the notion that the human couple could have sinned before they sinned but then goes on to say that they committed the sin of pride before they deliberately disobeyed God's prohibition against eating the forbidden fruit.(CG 14:13; 335-6) By turning to pride as the cause of the first sin, Augustine seems to be tacitly admitting the distinction I have made between talk about evil and talk about sin, and admitting that to explain the latter requires some exploration of motivation and reasoning that leads up to the sinful act. He discourses at length on pride which he deems to be the originator of all sin and occurs when man "is too well pleased with himself" and, instead of being grounded in God, is grounded in himself (Ibid., 337). "Accordingly, the evil act, that is, the transgression that involved their eating of forbidden food, was committed only by those who were already evil." (Ibid.) In a nutshell, Augustine's contradiction lies in this: he attempts to argue that what he should designate as a consequence of original sin, namely human pride and the distortion of the human will, is in fact the initiator and cause of the first sin. Augustine seems to be confusing before and after at this juncture: while it makes sense to say that pride was a consequence of sin it cannot with consistency be argued that this same pride was the instigator or cause of the first sin. If there were no evil before man sinned then there could be no sinful pride. Augustine fails to prove his case. Furthermore, if man was guilty of sinful pride before the "original sin" of disobedience, he must have come from the hand of his creator as one already inclined to pride. In other words, Augustine's argument fails to protect God from being implicated in human sin.

In the case of the fall of the angels, Augustine again attempts to explain their sinful action by citing a lapse of the will (CG 12: 9; 39); but once more he feels the need to go further and in this case explain how it was that one group of angels remained faithful to God while another group lapsed and fell. He does so by claiming that the holy angels received "more help" from God than did the bad angels (Ibid; 43). Augustine feels the need to "load the dice" both on behalf of the good angels and against those who lapsed: he does not remain content with his statement that sin is caused by a lapse of the will but feels obliged to explain how it was that some angels adhered to God while others lapsed. He expresses the situation of the angels in such a way that it is hard to see how the holy angels could have done anything other than remain faithful to God (since they "with more help (*amplius adiuti*) achieved such fullness of bliss as brought them the utmost certainty that they would never fall from it." Ibid., 43); nor to see how the bad angels could possibly have remained faithful since they did not receive the "bliss" or "delight" (*beatitudo*) in God that caused the good angels to adhere to the truth. Once more, it is difficult to have any confidence that Augustine has adequately shielded God from implication in the fall of the evil angels, since it appears to be God's provision of sufficient grace or his failure to do so that predestines one group of angels to remain faithful and the other to lapse. All his life Augustine had difficulty in reconciling human freedom with God's grace. As T. Kermit Scott concludes, after examining Augustine's reasoning on this issue, "God predestines the angels and the first humans just as completely and certainly as he does fallen humankind."[4]

Augustine, however, is serenely oblivious of the flaws in his argument and, indeed, is inclined to make the general state of innocence in which Adam and Eve lived before the Fall yet another reason for their condemnation. As he puts it at the end of Book 14, chapter 12, "This command, which forbade the eating of one kind of food where a great abundance of other kinds lay close at hand, was as easy to observe as it was brief to remember, especially since the will was not yet then opposed by desire. Such opposition arose later as punishment for the transgression. Consequently, the crime of violating the command was all the greater in proportion to the ease with which it could have been heeded and upheld." (335) Again, in answer to the objection that the punishment of "eternal death" seems excessive in view of the nature of Adam and Eve's sin, Augustine retorts, "Whoever thinks that condemnation of this sort is either excessive or unjust surely does not know how to gauge the magnitude of wickedness in sinning when the opportunity for not sinning was so ample." (CG 14:15; 347).

THE CONSEQUENCES OF ORIGINAL SIN

Augustine believes his philosophical comments on the nature of evil have satisfactorily answered the questions about the possibility of the origin of human evil and he continues later in Book 12 to explain the *consequences* of sin for Man. "For he (God) created man's nature to be midway, so to speak, between angels and beasts in such a way that, if he should remain in subjection to his creator as his true lord and with dutiful obedience keep his commandment, he was to pass into the company of the angels, obtaining with no intervening death[5] a blissful immortality that has no limit; but if he should make proud and disobedient use of his free will and go counter to the Lord his God, he was to live like a beast, at the mercy of death, enthralled by lust and doomed to eternal punishment after death." (CG 12: 22;111) The notion of man created "midway between angels and beasts" has become something of a common place in western thinking down the centuries—we think of Alexander Pope's lines, "Placed on this isthmus of a middle state/ A being darkly wise and rudely great"—so that it is salutary to recall that this is not part of the biblical account at all but reflects the influence of Platonism on Augustine's thought. One of the problems created by talk of a "Fall" is that it encourages speculation about the human condition before the fall since the significance of such a fall can only be gauged if we know what things were like beforehand. This in turn leads Augustine to construct an elaborate superstructure of suppositions about the privileged life of Adam and Eve before the fall in order to demonstrate what was *lost* in the fall. However, Genesis has very little to say about Man before the incident described in chapter 3.

The Platonic strain in his thought causes Augustine to develop a fondness for angels, pure spirits unencumbered by a body, and in Book

12 of *The City of God* he goes on to say that God foresaw the sin of the first man but at the same time foresaw that "by his grace a company of righteous men would be called to adoption and that, after they were forgiven their sins and made righteous by the Holy Spirit, they would be united with the holy angels in eternal peace, when the last enemy, death, was destroyed." (CG 12:23; 113) In line with the thesis he develops throughout *The City of God*, Augustine argues that even at the point of creating the first man God foresaw "two societies or cities among the human race. For it was from him that mankind was destined to arise, of which one part was to be joined in fellowship with evil angels for punishment and the other with good angels for reward. Such was God's decree, which, though hidden, was yet righteous. For...we know that neither can his grace be unjust nor his justice cruel." (CG 12: 28; 131) He dwells on the statement in Genesis that God made man in his own likeness and from there he speculates on how the sin of Adam is inherited by the entire human race. The act of creating Adam, the first man, took one of two forms: either God implanted in Adam a soul he had already made, or else he created the soul in the act of breathing it into man.[6] A key element of Augustine's thinking is indicated by the heading for Book 12, chapter 28 that "in the first man was the entire plenitude of the human race." Augustine is alert to the significance of this for his account of how we all inherit Adam's sin. He carefully stresses the fact that one man and one alone was directly created by God—even Eve was made from Adam "in order that the human race might derive entirely from one man." (CG 12: 22; 111) Augustine is strictly patriarchal, claiming that sin stems from the male line, but his main reason for stressing that sin derives from Adam is to support his contention that all of humanity is tainted with original sin: all are tainted with sin because all, including Eve, are descended from the very first human created directly by God. Adam is the source of all human sinfulness and no human being is exempt (although Augustine upholds Jesus's freedom from original sin owing to his virginal conception by the power of the Holy Spirit).[7]

While for the sake of strict logic Augustine is at pains to point out that humanity's sinfulness is the result of the sin of Adam, the fount and origin of all human beings, he does provide ammunition, later in *The City of God*, for those who over the centuries have pointed the finger of accusation at the woman. Quoting the verse in 1 Timothy 2:14 (which he attributes to St Paul), "Adam was not deceived, but the woman was deceived," he goes on to say, "He must have meant that Eve had accepted what the serpent said to her as though it were true, while Adam refused to be separated from his sole companion even in a partnership of sin. Yet he was no less guilty if he sinned with knowledge and forethought." (CG14:11; 331)—hence, although humanity is sinful because of Adam since from Adam all other human beings are descended, the instigator of the sin could, on this account, be considered to have been the woman! Augustine did not fail to propagate his view that women were inferior to men and his negative views on women paralleled his negative views on human sexuality. Unfortunately, his views on these matters came to dominate Western Christian thinking.[8]

Much of Book 13 of *The City of God* is a prolonged reflection on death, which Augustine considers to be a punishment for original sin. When man was first created by God obedience to his commandments "was to bring angelic deathlessness and an eternity of bliss with no intervening period of death, whereas disobedience would be very justly punished with death." (CG 13:1; 135) This notion that human beings were created immortal and that mortality only came about as a result of original sin is one that does not sit comfortably with modern scientific thinking which sees death as a natural part of life, or more precisely as the natural conclusion of the biological life cycle. Today we see that all living creatures—plants, animals and human beings—die and this strikes us as perfectly natural. Without death it would be impossible to speak of generations succeeding each other and unless certain things died out to be replaced by others, it would not be possible to speak of the diversity and evolution of species. For the evolutionary principle of Natural Selection to work, three things are needed: random variations, time, and death or elimination. It is hard for us to understand death as some kind of punishment. The scriptural basis of Augustine's thinking is the statement by God in Genesis 2: 17 that "In the day that you eat of it (the fruit of the tree of knowledge of good and evil) you shall die." The notion that man was created immortal is an inference from this statement; it is not something stated explicitly in Genesis but is an inference which Augustine, and following him countless other Christians, have drawn from the divine pronouncement.

It may, however, be quite possible to form another convincing interpretation of these words of the Lord God; as I have just observed, in evolutionary thinking death—or elimination—can be an agent of development and renewal. Augustine's account of death as punishment for the original sin is just part of the general discomfort that any modern person with a reasonable grasp of scientific thought must feel when presented with Augustine's interpretation of Genesis 3.[9] Augustine's thought categories, largely derived from Plato, are so removed from those of modern science that one can well see why some moderns have jumped to the conclusion that Genesis 3 is contradicted by modern science. I shall argue, however, that it is not the third chapter of Genesis that is at variance with modern science but rather the interpretation imposed on Genesis 3 by Augustine. It is time the Christian Church in the West took stock of Augustine's thought and distinguished between that which is enduring and that which can be seen today to be less than convincing.

Another consequence of original sin Augustine reflects on in Book 13 is the shame of being naked expressed by our first parents immediately after they had sinned and the need they felt to cover their "pudenda, that is, shameful members" with fig leaves. (Genesis 3:7-10)[10] Previously they had felt no shame but now they were ashamed. Augustine expands on this reading of the Genesis text with some Platonic reflections of his own but reflections that weigh very strongly with him since he regards the shame experienced by Adam and Eve following their original transgression to be indicative of a more general rebellion of the body against the spirit:

> The soul, in fact, delighting now in its own freedom to do wickedness and scorning to serve God, was stripped of the former subjection of the body, and because it had wilfully deserted its own higher master, no longer kept its lower servant responsive to its will. It did not maintain its own flesh subject to it in all respects, as it could have done for ever if it had itself remained subject to God. Thus it was that the flesh then began to "lust against the spirit." This is our congenital conflict. From the first transgression come the beginning of death in us and the carnal rebellion or even victory that we sustain in our limbs and blighted being. (CG 13:13; 179)

This is an argument Augustine develops in several of his writings, one that he feels strengthens his case since there is strong empirical evidence that man often experiences a conflict between his carnal desires and his rational will. The Platonic strain in his thought caused Augustine to regard the shame of nakedness human beings experience and, in particular, the need they feel of keeping their sexual organs covered, as empirical proof of the conflict between body and spirit generated by the first sin; this was an essential and telling manifestation of the disturbance and corruption of their nature that human beings experienced as a consequence of their sin. If there were nothing to be ashamed of, if we did not share in the primeval guilt of our first parents, then why cover up these parts of our body? It is not only illicit sexual unions that demand that they be carried out in private, Augustine points out, but even that type of legitimate intercourse between a husband and wife that is required for the procreation of children and the survival of the race seeks "a chamber secluded from witnesses." (CG14:18; 363)

This is of a piece with Augustine's reflections elsewhere on the rebellious nature of the male penis. If man were truly integrated and free of the disturbance sin had brought about, the penis would be as subject to his reason and obedient to his will as the foot, hand or tongue (CG 14:23; 14:23; 381 and 384).[11] But, as Augustine is all too aware, with an awareness he presumes also in his readers, the penis is not subject to the will in this way. He notes how at the moment of sexual climax, "There is almost a total eclipse of acumen" and of thought (CG 14:16; 353). In fact, the unruly behaviour of the male sexual organ is, for Augustine, a case—indeed the supreme case—of *concupiscence*, the generic name he gives to the inclination to evil, including the pull of carnal desire, which was both a consequence of man's first sin and a cause of the propagation of the sin throughout the human race.[12] According to Augustine, holy people who are married would prefer it if children could be born without the lust of the body, if the members needed for procreation "would be set in motion when the will urged, not stirred to action when hot lust surged." (CG 14:16; 355)[13] Before their fall, our first parents were unashamed of their nakedness; it was only the disobedience of their sexual organs which they experienced after the fall that caused them to perceive nudity as indecent and hence to experience shame. (CG 14:17; 357) The reason the tree from which they disobediently ate was called the tree of knowledge of good and evil was because after eating from it they were capable of distinguishing between "the good they had lost and the evil into which they had fallen." (Ibid., 359) That is what scripture means when it speaks of their eyes being opened. (Ibid.)

That all human beings inherit the first sin of Adam and indeed are involved not only in all that followed from Adam's sin but also in his guilt as the original sinner, is something Augustine maintains steadfastly in all his writings. Although we were not yet born and had not yet assumed our individual identity, Augustine maintains that each and all of us were implicated in the sin of our first parent:

> We did not yet have individually created and apportioned shapes in which to live as individuals; what already existed was the seminal substance from which we were to be generated. Obviously, when this sub-

stance was debased through sin and shackled with the bond of death in just condemnation, no man could be born of man in any other condition. Thus from the abuse of free will has come the linked sequence of our disaster...as it were from a diseased root, all the way to the catastrophe of the second death that has no end. Only those who are freed through the grace of God are exempt from this fate. (CG 13:14; 181)

Augustine is very strict in his notion of how original sin is inherited and has no time for later notions, popular among some modern theologians, that original sin is mediated by a sinful society—that original sin is something we pick up or acquire from entering into sinful humanity. Augustine wants to know how society became sinful in the first place and he is insistent that all human babies are born with the stain of original sin upon them. (Hence Joseph Ratzinger's broad comment that "sin begets sin"[14] would not be precise enough for Augustine).

TRANSMISSION OF ORIGINAL SIN

Augustine never quite made up his mind concerning the agency by means of which original sin is transmitted.[15] In the passage above it looks as if he considers the male semen—the "seminal substance" (*natura seminalis*)—to be the agent of transmission but elsewhere he veers to the opinion that it is the lust experienced by the male partner when achieving an erection that causes him to sin when engaging in sexual intercourse and that it is this sinful accompaniment to intercourse (which cannot take place unless the penis is erect) that acts as the agent for the transmission of original sin.[16] Elsewhere he speculates that original sin is transmitted to the pre-existent soul as soon as it makes contact with the sinful body it is to inhabit, although he refines this account by speculating further that the soul that consented to being conjoined with a human body may already have been tainted with sin.[17] The failure of Augustine, and of his many successors, to account for the means by which original sin is transmitted to newborn babies must count as a major weakness in his argument.

In all of his accounts of how the first sin is transmitted, Augustine is insistent that original sin is present from the first moment of conception. He does not shrink from the conclusion that babies who have not had the stain of original sin wiped away through the grace of baptism are destined for hell. Indeed, one of his arguments against the Pelagians is that they are unwilling to commit to his belief, which follows logically from his premises, that unbaptised babies are eternally damned in hell.[18] It is true that Augustine at times attempted to temper his position by claiming that unbaptised infants received only the mildest punishment, but he never changed his basic position.[19] For Augustine, the default setting of humanity is damnation; salvation is a bonus, owing everything to God's sovereign mercy, and is reserved for only some human beings, the predestined elect.

Notwithstanding the Platonic influence on his thinking, it is worth noting that there are limits to Augustine's Platonism. For example, he repudiates the notion, which he considers to be Platonic but probably also regarded as Manichean, that "the flesh is the cause of every sort of vice in the case of bad morals," insisting that "the body's decay, which weighs down the soul, is not the cause of the first sin but the punishment for it" (CG 14:3, 271) and that Adam's sinful act was preceded by an evil will (CG 14: 23; 335). He makes it clear that, as regards its character, the first sin was an act of disobedience—man disobeyed God's explicit command. He places little importance on the image of the tree found in the Genesis account other than to see it as a case of the humans' eyes being opened after the event. He sees the sin almost exclusively in terms of Man's disobedience of his Lord's command, even suggesting that what God wished to reinforce was the need in man to obey his master (CG 14:12, 334-5; and 14: 15, 345). God simply wished to show his creature that he was master; to impress on man the need for "wholesome obedience." (Ibid.) Adam's disobedience is contrasted with the obedience of Christ, and a feature of Augustine's reflections on original sin is the contrast he consistently draws between Adam, the bringer of death, and Christ, the bringer of new life, just as he balances his reflections on punishment and condemnation with those on God's mercy and grace. Augustine is known in Church history as the Doctor of Grace and his theology of grace complements his theology of original sin. As Alistair McFadyen has said, "Sin and grace are reciprocally interpreting coordinates in his (Augustine's) theology."[20] While there are aspects of Augustine's thinking that strike a modern sensibility as harsh and even cruel—especially his willingness to see unbaptised babies condemned to hellfire—Augustine's thought is also broad and generous when he turns to the theme of grace. This should not be overlooked.

THE INFLUENCE OF AUGUSTINE

Given the sheer volume of his writings, his speculative reach, his brilliant mastery of Latin and logical turn of mind, it is not surprising that Augustine became the Church Father who most influenced the development of theology in the West. The West has built its theology on Augustine and a central part of this theology has been his doctrine of original sin, which as we have seen is integral to his theology of grace and to the development of his ideas of freedom and predestination. And because he linked original sin with the sexual act, both as the means of its transmission and as something damaged and distorted by the sin's impact, Augustine's profoundly negative views on human sexuality came to pervade Western Christian thought.[21] It is little wonder that it has been extremely difficult for other interpretations of Genesis 3 to win a hearing because there has been no one in the west to rival Augustine in stature or authority.[22] Moreover, the Augustinian understanding of original sin has been such a solid component of a comprehensive theological system of thought that there have been fears that to attempt to dislodge it or to radically alter it is to risk bringing down the whole system of theology in which it stands and to which it gives support.

But Augustine's standing in the East has never matched his standing in the West. The Orthodox Church has never recognized Augustine as a Church "Doctor" partly because they refuse to subscribe to his position on the inheritance of Adam's guilt.[23] Joseph Fizmyer comments on how Augustine claimed that the doctrine of Original Sin was also part of the Greek patristic tradition but that he failed to cite any clear passage from that tradition to uphold the claim.[24] In his masterly survey of the historical genesis of the ideas of the Fall and Original Sin, N.P. Williams draws an important distinction between the traditions of the east and of the west.[25] As well as bringing out the plethora of interpretations that existed in the Christian world before Augustine—so that any attempt to uphold the Augustinian position by appealing to tradition as if it presented a single view of the Fall manifests a profound ignorance of history—Williams identifies the emergence of a Greek understanding of the Fall and Original Sin much milder and more humane than the understanding that came to dominate in the west. Williams traces the historical genesis of each of these two traditions with great care. The Latin or African tradition "condemning human nature as largely or entirely depraved, was riveted on Western Christendom by the genius of Augustine, exaggerated into fantastic and repulsive forms by Luther and Calvin, and until recently was generally believed by Englishmen to be the only traditional Fall-theory."[26] By contrast, the more sober Eastern tradition owes its origins to "the sunny genius of Christian Hellenism, recognizing as it does the good that survives even in fallen man." Williams contends that while Augustine's version of the Fall dominated the West, it "never took captive the mind of the Christian East, and even in the West its millennial domination has now passed away."[27] Williams was speaking in 1924, but I would venture the opinion that Augustine's interpretation of the Fall has proved, in the West, more resistant to "passing away" than he imagined—both in Christian theology and in the popular imagination.

If in recent times Augustine's interpretation of original sin has come under closer scrutiny among Christian theologians and become an object of criticism and attack, this is not unconnected with the new emphasis on scripture as the basis for theological reflection that has grown among Catholic theologians as well as the developing understanding of the Bible that is shared by Catholic and Protestant scholars. It is on the basis of certain key features of the story of Adam and Eve in the Garden of Eden recounted in Genesis 3 that I attempt to offer an alternative interpretation of the events described there and, in this way, to offer an understanding of Christian doctrine that departs in significant ways from that provided by Augustine. My motivation has not been anti-Augustinian but rather Augustine's teaching has been a casualty of the interpretation which attention to all of the data included in the tale told in Genesis 3 gives rise to. And given the pre-eminence of Augustine's interpretation in the West, I have found it valuable for the sake of clarity to contrast my own interpretation with that of Augustine on certain crucial points.

THE ISSUE OF THEOLOGICAL METHOD

It would be too much to expect someone of Augustine's time to distinguish clearly between the different functional specialities of theology since the notion of "functional speciality" only came along much later and could only be developed retrospectively—in the light of the practice of theology over a long period of time.[28] What is true, however, is that Augustine does not distinguish clearly between what today we would call "interpretation" and those other functional specialities we refer to as "systematics" and "communications." What is also very clear is that, although Augustine lived closer in time than do we to the ancient Hebrews, his interpretation of their thinking was inhibited by the relative poverty of the tools at his disposal, especially when we recall that he had very little Greek and next to no Hebrew. Developments in modern methods of research and the labours of countless scholars make it much easier for us than it was for Augustine to enter into the thinking of these ancient peoples. A bold and daring thinker and a pioneer in theology, Augustine was not bashful about using the concepts of Neoplatonism to interpret the mind of the ancient Hebrews and, while this is perhaps understandable, we should not allow ourselves the indulgence of projecting onto the ancient Israelites the worldview of a later time and a quite different place. Hence when reviewing Augustine's interpretation of the biblical narrative it is quite legitimate to see these projections for what they are—and indeed necessary if we are to gain a perspective in tune with the world view of the peoples who actually wrote the stories we are studying.

These reflections should enable us to see that when Augustine is offering us what appears to be an interpretation of the story in Genesis 3 what he is, in fact, doing is much more akin to systematics, to *fides quaerens intellectum*, drawing out what he believes to be the Christian meaning of the story for his contemporaries and later generations, using the thought categories and philosophical concepts of his own time, and in this way, through communications, attempting to build up the faith of the community of believers. This is a perfectly legitimate theological activity but again, with the advantage of hindsight, it behoves us to acknowledge what is going on and not to treat systematics and communications, or what today we would call systematics and communications, as if they were biblical interpretation. As it was, it would have been well nigh impossible for Augustine, ill-equipped as he was, to enter into the mindsets of peoples from cultures[29] totally different from his own, and in truth he made little attempt to do so.

At this point it would be appropriate for me to indicate the kind of approach I wish to take to the sections of the bible I shall examine in some detail and to make it clear that, first and foremost, in developing my interpretation I wish to adopt a *literary approach*. By this I mean that I shall give close attention to the language of the various stories and episodes recounted in the bible and attempt to appreciate the bible stories for the literary artistry they reveal, the way in which the narrative is shaped and the reader engaged. It is important to note that the bible differs from more expository methods of communication in being, first and foremost, narrative, and that narrative tends to work through images and metaphors rather than by simply imparting information. The intention behind narrative is to communicate an experience, indeed to put the reader through an experience, rather than to communicate ideas directly. The truth of literature is primarily its truthfulness to human experience in the world and it is through this kind of truthfulness that the bible works. In the bible the literary impulse to incarnate meaning, *to enact meaning or to present it being acted out*, is dominant.

There is much in the bible, particularly in the first eleven chapters of the Book of Genesis which will form the focus of my attention in the pages to follow, about what is typical or characteristic human behaviour or human reactions; we encounter paradigms of human behaviour and of the human condition. The narrative works more by example than by direct precept, and this places a greater burden of interpretation on the reader than do more expository texts written in more abstract language. Lonergan makes the point by contrasting humanity's understanding of the gospels with its understanding of Euclid: "so, while there have been endless commentators on the clear and simple gospels, there exists little or no exegetical literature on Euclid."[30] We can only hope to interpret the bible correctly if we are sensitive to the kinds of writing it contains, sensitive to the literary genre, the language, the images, the emphases and the tone of each episode, as well as to the general intellectual climate in which the writing took place, and by this means aim to grasp the intention of the authors.[31]

CHARACTERISTICS OF HEBREW NARRATIVE

Robert Alter, who has written extensively on the Hebrew bible as well as translating large sections of it, is one of the strongest modern advocates of approaching and reading the bible as literature. For the sake of brevity, when itemising Alter's comments on the nature of Hebrew narrative and storytelling, I have not attempted to do justice to the many close readings and analyses of actual biblical passages he uses to illustrate the points he makes. It would, however, aid our reading of Genesis 3 to note some of the salient literary characteristics of the bible identified by Alter, such as the following:

The anonymity of the biblical author or authors. There is no quest for fame or even individual recognition among the biblical authors. Rather "the writer disappears into the tradition, makes its voice his, or vice versa."[32] Similarities of style and approach are explained by the literary conventions used, as different authors worked with the same type of conventions.

The intricate process of editing through which the writer's work has come down to us. Many of the stories appear to have been stitched together from a variety of earlier sources and then, "later, probably early in the period of the return from Babylonian exile, a redactor gave final shape to the text, introducing local modifications of wording, adding some editorial framing and bridging, perhaps winnowing out certain materials, perhaps even incorporating bits of old traditions that had not hitherto been part of the text." This accounts for "the surprising degree of artful coherence in the final version of the text."[33] "The biblical narrative...evinces an impressive degree of compositional artistry, even if the composition involved some cutting and pasting either by the writer or by the redactor or by both."[34] Another reason why the Hebrew bible emerges as an integrated work is because the various writers self-consciously built on the tradition, emulating, elaborating or amending previous texts, genres or verbal formulations. [35] In many ways, the bible is a collection of texts in dialogue with each other.

The "laconic quality" of biblical narrative, the total absence of leisurely description for its own sake. The Book of Genesis belongs to the "golden age" of Hebrew narrative and is marked by "the stringent narrative economy of the classical literature."[36] Scene setting, for example, "is accomplished with the barest economy of means" [37]; location is stated simply and nothing is said about dress or appearance unless it has significance in the plot.[38] There is also an absence of moral judgment regarding the actions of the various characters in the stories. These qualities result in disagreements among readers but also force readers to form their own judgments, to engage closely with the text in order to negotiate their own assessment of what it is that has taken place.

The corollary of this: to gain a comprehensive understanding of what is taking place in the narrative, the reader is required to read slowly, paying close attention to whatever details are provided and to the implications underlying certain "leading words" (*leitworter*) or thematic key words.[39] The biblical writers "delighted in an art of indirection, in the possibilities of intimating depths through the merest hint of a surface feature, or through a few words of dialogue fraught with implication."[40] It is not simply that we will fail to "appreciate" the artistry of the writing if we fail to attend to these elements of literary art, but we will fail to gain a true understanding since these are the means by which the writers communicate meaning and value.[41]

Like all literary art, the bible stories seek "to draw me out of myself," to impose on the reader a particular view of reality, to awaken us to spiritual and moral realities we might not otherwise be aware of, to communicate "a troubling, potentially transformative vision of God, man, history and nature."[42]

"The Hebrew writers do, of course, keep in steady focus God and Israel, creation, covenant, and commandments," [43] but in doing so they had to create their own literary medium and to be subservient to its demands, and this required them to be inventive and creative. They were engaged in a literary project that exceeded the powers of literature to accomplish since "we cannot make sense of God in human terms."[44] For "the Hebrew Bible is animated by an untiring, shrewdly perceptive fascination with the theater of human behavior in the textual foreground, seen against a background of forces that can be neither grasped nor controlled by humankind."[45] This throws light on the narrative economy characteristic of Hebrew storytelling, since such economy hints at hidden depths, at a surrounding penumbra of powerful invisible forces that lie in the background, "behind the scenes," so to speak, but ultimately condition, guide or control what is taking place in the foreground. There is the "ever-present potentiality of sudden divine intervention."[46] I have been struck by the fact that Alter's observations on Hebrew narrative economy suggest certain associations with Levy-Bruhl's observations on how the "collective representations" of reality which dominate the thinking of individuals in "primitive" societies are "pre-eminently concerned with...imperceptible forces," that is "forces, influences and actions imperceptible to the senses, though none the less real."[47] I shall have more to say on the "primitive mentality" of the ancient Hebrews in Chapter Three.

Alter is fond of quoting from the opening chapter of the brilliant work of literary commentary, Mimesis[48], in which Eric Auerbach contrasts the lavishly explanatory nature of Greek epic poetry with the non-explanatory quality of Hebrew narrative, drawing attention to the spare, bare representation of reality found in the Hebrew work whereby many of the scenes that take place are "fraught with background." Auerbach's key phrase—"fraught with background"—stands behind many of the insights Alter communicates to his readers on the distinctive and exceptionally reticent nature of the literary artistry found in the Hebrew bible.

To these illuminating comments of Robert Alter I would simply add a few of my own that are well established and no more than commonplace in the literature. Classical Hebrew is a language with a very limited vocabulary and virtually no abstractions. Ideas and situations are communicated by means of highly concrete vocabulary and this tends to favour narrative or story as the means for the communication of complex ideas; in order to get to the meaning of individual nouns and verbs it is often best to find the root meaning of the word in question and to work out the meaning from that. The overall effect is of a world conveyed with powerful immediacy, as the eye, ear or senses receive it, but also, as we have noted, a world under the inscrutable control of YHWH, who is Lord of history. YHWH—which is written as "Yahweh" when vowels are added—is the proper Hebrew name for the God of Israel as distinct from other more generic names, such as "Elohim." In the translation followed in this book, the phrase "the Lord God" is the English translation of the peculiar Hebrew phrase "YHWH Elohim." It is the use of the name YHWH for God in certain stories that caused scholars to attribute them to a distinctive authorial source or tradition known as "Yahwist." The Yahwist writings are generally considered to be the oldest of the writings incorporated in the books of the bible.

My overarching question when attempting to interpret passages of the bible must be: Is this the meaning that was meant? In attempting to answer this question I can only respond by offering hypotheses—that is suggested interpretations—and attempting further to show how the interpretations suggested do justice to the data of the story recounted in the section of the bible under consideration or can be corroborated by reference to similar language or features elsewhere in the bible. In other words, I shall proceed by means of hypothesis and verification.

I should also make it clear at the outset that what I am offering is, in addition to being a work of interpretation, a work of Christian theology. In attempting to make what is basically a work of interpretation into a work of theology I have been assisted by the method of literary interpretation known as typology. Typology works by showing how the full significance of something that happens at the beginning is revealed by reference to how things happen later or at the end. It is a form of Christian interpretation that has had its critics but its justification for a Christian writer is that it was practised by the ancient Hebrews, by Jesus, by the four evangelists and by the Church fathers. Typology differs from allegory by being much more straightforward. Instead of looking for clues that have been hidden or "planted" by a cunning author, the reader is invited to grasp the pattern of events revealed by a particular episode and see these as being typical of other events that come later; in this way the two sets of events—the chronologically earlier and later—are mutually illuminating and this in turn yields a fuller and more satisfying understanding of their significance. For the early Church fathers the significance of many of the events in the history of Israel was understood from the standpoint of events in the life of Christ. I should make it clear that I shall adopt a typological interpretation of the events recounted in Genesis 1-11, though I shall attempt to employ this method of interpretation with some discipline. While it is certainly the case that each book of the bible, and each literary unit within these books, should be understood with reference to the time and circumstances of its composition, typology helps to bring out a certain unity and coherence that can be found in the scriptures through all times, past, present and future.[49] In an address to a gathering of French scholars in Paris, Pope Benedict XVI sought to convey the value of grasping the bible as a whole, as one book:

> This particular structure of the Bible issues a constantly new challenge to every generation. It excludes by its nature everything that today is known as fundamentalism. In effect, the word of God can never simply be equated with the letter of the text. To attain to it involves a transcending and a process of understanding, led by the inner movement of the whole. Only within the dynamic unity of the whole are the many books *one* book. The Word of God and his action in the world are revealed only in the word and history of human beings.[50]

THREE "TRADITIONS" OR "THEMES"

The complexity of the Book of Genesis is well brought out by Carr[51], who argues that Genesis can only be properly understood as a multi-voiced text that developed over centuries. It is this complexity, I believe, the fact that it has probably been drafted and re-drafted over very long stretches of time, which has contributed to the difficulty of offering an interpretation of the story of Adam and Eve in Eden that is convincing in doing justice to the full range of the data contained in the narrative that has come down to us. In my grappling with this story in the context of Genesis 1-11, I have found it helpful to see this section of text as consisting essentially of three layers of meaning; or, to put the point another way, to see the story as being written, and re-written, under the influence of three distinct traditions or ways of thinking. These I have called the Primitive Tradition, the Quest for Immortality theme and the Wisdom Tradition, each being the main focus of Chapters Three, Four and Six respectively. I refer to each of the three as a "tradition" or "theme" in order to convey the idea of mentalities or habits of thought or topics of interest that were prominent in the thinking of the ancient Hebrews at different periods in their history; these are embedded in the Genesis text, and their exploration can help us to discover its meaning in some fullness and depth. I have found different features and facets of the tale told in Genesis 3 to be revealed by examining it from the perspective of each of these three approaches; at the same time, I have found that by blending the three it is possible to reach a reasonably clear, comprehensive and unified understanding of what the tale is telling us.

NOTES

1. Peter Brown, *Augustine of Hippo*, (Revised Edition, London: Faber and Faber, 2000) p. 436.

2. Eugene Portalie SJ, *A Guide to the Thought of St Augustine*, (Chicago: Henry Regnery Company, 1960) p. 184.

3. Henceforth I shall refer to the *City of God* as CG and include references in brackets in the text, giving first the book number, then the number of the chapter, followed by the page reference; page references are from Cambridge: The Harvard University Press/ London: William Heinemann edition of 1988, Vol 4, translated by Philip Levine. Other works by Augustine will be referred to by their Latin title in footnotes.

4. T. Kermit Scott, *Augustine: His Thought in Context*, (New York: Paulist Press, 1995) p. 226-7. It is true that Augustine attempted to reconcile grace and freedom by defining freedom as freedom from coercion; in this way he tried to reconcile freedom with necessity. However, the Western theological tradition has not upheld Augustine's position. Aquinas saw freedom as freedom from necessity and rejected the notion of freedom as the equivalent simply of non-coercion in *De Malo*, q. 6, a. 1. See Bernard Lonergan, *Grace and Freedom: Operative Grace in the Thought of St Thomas Aquinas*, edited by F.E. Crowe and R. M. Doran (Toronto: University of Toronto Press, 2000) p. 317f. It is mistaken to take Augustine as standing in for "the tradition as a whole" in this mat-

ter, as Alistair McFadyen attempts to do in *Bound to Sin*, (Cambridge: Cambridge University Press, 2000) p. 167. In fact, the view attributed by Dr McFadyen to Augustine forms an essential part of an opinion of Jansenius condemned as heretical by Pope Innocent X in 1653.

5. The Pelagians believed that Adam would have died as a consequence of being human but Augustine that Man would have been immortal had Adam not sinned.

6. The first of these views hints at the Neoplatonic belief in the pre-existence of souls which only later become embodied, a position Augustine sets out in *De Genesi Ad Litteram* 7. 24. 35.

7. *De peccato originali*, 47.

8. See Sean Fagan, "The Abuse and our bad Theology" in *Responding to the Ryan Report*, edited by Tony Flannery, (Dublin: Columba Press, 2009). Aquinas reflects the same bias: for example, claiming that the devil chose to tempt the woman because she was weaker than the male. (*Tum quia mulier erat infirmior viro: unde magis seduci potest.*) *Summa Theologiae*, 2-2, q 165 a.2.

9. I am pleased to discover that these misgivings were also expressed by Joseph Ratzinger, the future Pope Benedict XVI, as far back as 1968. See the article "What is Original Sin?" by Gabriel Daly, *The Tablet* (London) for 8 February 1997.

10. With typical precision and pithiness, Augustine's Latin reads: "pudenda texerunt, quae prius eadem membra erant, sed pudenda non erant." CG 13:13; 178.

11. Also *De peccato originali,* 33-4; 36.

12. Ibid., 37.

13. Ibid., 34.

14. Joseph Ratzinger, *In the Beginning: a Catholic Understanding of Creation and Fall*, (Grand Rapids: Eerdmans, 1995) p. 72.

15. Serge Lancel, *Saint Augustine*, (London: SCM Press, 1999) p. 363.

16. *De peccato originali*, 33-34; 39.

17. See the very late work, *Contra Iulianum*, V, 17.

18. *De peccato originali*, 21; *De gestis Pelagii*.

19. Eugene Portalie, op. cit., p. 212.

20. Alistair McFadyen, *Bound to Sin*, op. cit., p. 173.

21. See Sean Fagan, *What Happened to Sin?*, (Dublin: Columba Press, 2008).

22. On the subject of grace, Jansenius attempted to raise Augustine's authority above that of Councils or Pope or any other theologian. See Eugene Portalie, op. cit., p. 322.

23. David L. Edwards, *Christianity: the First Two Thousand Years*, (London: Cassell, 1997) p. 168.

24. Joseph Fitzmyer, *Romans: A New Translation with Introduction and Commentary*, (The Anchor Bible, London: Geoffrey Chapman, 1993) p. 409.

25. N.P. Williams, op. cit., p. 450.

26. Ibid.

27. Ibid.

28. The notion of "functional speciality" in the context of theology is devised and worked out by Bernard Lonergan in *Method in Theology*, (London: Darton, Longman and Todd, 1972); see especially chapter 5. Lonergan divides theology into the eight functional specialities of research, interpretation, history, dialectics, foundations, doctrines, systematics and communications.

29. Plural, since we have to factor in the fact of cultural change over time, something again that Augustine, with his clacissist outlook, would probably have had difficulty in understanding.

30. Bernard Lonergan, op. cit., 154.

31. Although there is agreement among commentators that the story of Adam and Eve in the garden of Eden is from the Yahwist tradition, it is not clear how many hands were involved in creating and writing the story. I shall follow the opinion that the story underwent editing and re-editing over time, and hence shall henceforth refer to authors in the plural.

32. Robert Alter, *The World of Biblical Literature* (London: SPCK, 1992) p. 3.

33. Ibid., p. 4.

34. Ibid., p. 20.

35. Ibid., p. 50-1.

36. Ibid., p. 78.

37. Ibid., p. 65.

38. Ibid., p. 98.

39. Ibid., p. 43, 61.

40. Ibid., p. 65-6.

41. Ibid., p. 63.

42. Ibid., p. 9.

43. Ibid., p. 34.

44. Ibid., p. 23.

45. Ibid., p. 22.

46. Ibid. p. 28 A quotation from Harold Fisch's book, *Poetry with a Purpose: Biblical Poetics and Interpretation* (Bloomington: Indiana University Press, 1988).

47. My understanding of Levy-Bruhl's thinking on this matter is based on the commentary on his work provided by E.E. Evans-Pritchard in *Theories of Primitive Religion* (Oxford: Oxford University Press, 1965) p. 78f.

48. Erich Auerbach, *Mimesis: The Representation of Reality in Western Literature* (Berne, 1946; Princeton: Princeton University Press, paperback edition, 1974).

49. My appreciation of typology has been helped by the comments of Alan Richardson in *The Bible in the Age of Science*, (London: SCM Press, 1961) p. 176-182; also by Frederick E. Crowe SJ, *Theology of the Christian Word*, (New York: Paulist Press, 1978) p. 109, and by the article, "Typology Today", by

Catherine Brown Tkacz, *New Blackfriars*, (Blackwells Oxford) vol 88 no 1017, September 2007.

50. Benedict XVI, *Seeking the God who seeks Us*, The Tablet (London), 20 September 2008, p. 14.

51. David M. Carr, *Reading the Fractures of Genesis: Historical and Literary Approaches*,(Atlanta: John Knox Press, 1996).

Chapter Two
Setting the Context

GENESIS 1-11

It is only possible to understand chapter 3 of the Book of Genesis if we understand it within the context of chapters 1-11. There is widespread agreement among commentators that chapters 1-11 constitute a distinct literary unit within the fifty chapters that make up Genesis. Chapters 1-11 are sometimes referred to as the mythological chapters since, unlike chapters 12-50, they do not pretend to be about events or characters in history, except in the very broad sense that what they portray is true or typical of what actual historical people did and do. They are not history but myth, albeit the myth of the Hebrews is quite different in style and character from the myth, say, of the Greeks or of most other peoples. Hebrew myth is free of the fantastical tales spun by the Greek imagination, and there is evidence that it had already undergone a degree of "demythologisation" by the time it was written down, so that instead of the myriad gods, goddesses and fabulous creatures of the Greeks we find only a strict monotheism[1]; the incidents recorded in Hebrew myth are more prosaic, more akin to what we find in human history than are many of the deeds and events recorded in Greek myth. Hence the temptation of some Christian fundamentalists to treat the first eleven chapters of Genesis as if they were an accurate historical record of what took place at the beginning of time—but the overwhelming view of scholars repudiates such an idea.

However, the mythological chapters of Genesis are organically linked to the historical sections of the bible that follow; they belong to the same literary composition because they act as a prelude to these later sections. By this I mean that they are analogous to the musical overture to an opera or a symphony. They introduce, briefly but tellingly, the themes and motifs we shall encounter in the longer and more detailed work that is to come; they provide a taster for what follows; they depict patterns and schemes and disclose moral and spiritual insights that we come to recognise as typical in the bible narrative. At the same time they contain messages of their own that transcend time and place because they exemplify forms of human behaviour that are universal. That is why it is difficult to avoid typological interpretation when dealing with Genesis 1-11, since the messages contained in these chapters can stand on their own but also gain enormously in significance and impact when we recognise how they are linked to events that come later. What John Romer says about the stories of Joseph and the Patriarchs is even more true of the tales told in the first eleven chapters of Genesis: they are stories "that hold in them all the seeds of the later history of ancient Israel."[2]

Genesis 3 stands within chapters 1-11 and draws much of its meaning and power from the role it plays within this larger literary unit. Alan Richardson has aptly described these chapters as comprising five parables: the two Creation stories; the Fall of man; Cain and Abel; the Flood; and the tower of Babel.[3] Richardson prefers the word "parable" to "myth" since the latter might suggest that they have no historical basis, whereas Christians and those who wrote the stories believe that God created the world. Parables are stories that seek to convey a moral or spiritual message. They have a distinctive style in that all details that might distract from the message are omitted; everything included is subordinate to the communication of the message. Parables may be colourful but their colour is there to assist the effective communication of the message. For the most part, parables are homely and straightforward in construction and language.

To describe the story of Adam and Eve as parable (or myth, for that matter) suggests that it should not be understood as an account of an historical event. To make this point would appear to be unnecessary except that in the *Catechism of the Catholic Church*, published under the auspices of Pope John Paul II, we read: "The account of the fall in Genesis 3 uses figurative language, but affirms a primeval event, a deed that took place *at the beginning of the history of man." *[4] This would seem to say that the deed described in Genesis 3 belongs literally to history and thereby to imply that the story of Adam and Eve in the Garden of Eden is historical. It is hard to believe that the authors of the *Catechism* could have had this intention since one would immediately wish to ask who could have witnessed this deed, how might it have been recorded (in an oral tradition or in writing? in what language? etc.) and how transmitted to the authors of the Genesis tale? Just to ask the questions is enough to demonstrate the absurdity of holding to the historicity of the Genesis story, to the belief that the tale is an account of a deed that took place in history. For something to be designated as "historical" certain basic criteria have to be met, and these criteria simply cannot be met in the case of the Adam and Eve story.

Now the authors of the *Catechism* were not stupid and they made the point they made for a reason, namely to ensure that the reality of original sin was upheld. From the surrounding text it is clear that the *Catechism's* authors were afraid that if the reality of original sin were to be lost then a great deal of the Christian "history of salvation" would begin to unravel. However, I do not believe that it is necessary to insist on the historicity of the tale in Genesis 3 in order to uphold the reality of sin in human history. One can perfectly well insist on the reality of sin *even from the outset of human history* without feeling obliged to insist on the historicity of the story of Adam and Eve in the garden. I shall attempt to explain why later. The reason for the aptness of Richardson's description of the Adam and Eve story in Genesis 3 as "parable" is because the word clearly indicates that the story is not intended to be taken as a record of a deed that actually took place but rather as a fictional tale designed to exemplify or illustrate human behaviour. Whereas Augustine clearly believed that the deed of eating from the forbidden fruit in the garden was historical and *causative*—causing a distortion and corruption of human nature and the onset of concupiscence—the word "parable" conveys the idea that the story is not literally historical and is not causative but *illustrative*.

However, to describe Genesis 1-11 as consisting of five parables might give the impression that this section of Genesis consists of five isolated incidents, and I do not believe that this is the case. There is in fact a strong narrative flow from the first chapter right through to the end of chapter 11 and we can begin to bring this out by referring to the major protagonists in each sub-section of chapters 1-11. In chapters 1 and 2, where we find the two different accounts of creation, God is the main, indeed the sole, protagonist. We read in the first account told in chapter

1, commonly known as the Priestly account or as coming from the Priestly—or P—tradition, that God created everything out of nothing. That simple statement is immensely important and reverberates right through the bible. Everything we are and know on earth depends for its existence on God; nothing exists independently of God. All the products of human genius and ingenuity that enrich our lives are, in the final analysis, simply the result of God's initial free gift of creation. It also follows that while we humans are totally dependent on God, God is not dependent on us in any way whatsoever.

In the second creation account told in chapter 2, written in a quite different style and believed to come from the Yahwist—or J—tradition[5], we read that God created man from the dust of the ground, breathed into his nostrils the spirit of life and planted a garden for him in Eden, in the east. Out of the ground God made to grow every kind of tree that is pleasant to the sight and good for food, and in the middle of the garden, the tree of life and the tree of knowledge of good and evil. God assigned to man the task of tilling and looking after the garden and told him that he could eat freely of every tree in the garden but not from the tree of knowledge of good and evil, adding that "in the day you eat of it you shall die." (Genesis 2: 17) Next the Lord God said it was not good for man to be alone and for this reason he created every beast of the ground and bird of the air and brought them to the man so that he could name them. Yet for man "there was not found a helper fit for him." So the Lord God formed woman from one of the man's ribs while he was in a deep sleep and took the woman to the man, who proclaimed that the woman was bone of his bone and flesh of his flesh. The authors then add words that convey divine approval of marriage: "Therefore a man leaves his father and his mother and cleaves to his wife, and they become one flesh." (Genesis 2: 24) The chapter ends with the words, "And the man and his wife were both naked, and were not ashamed."

In both creation accounts God is the main protagonist and Man is the object of his affection and blessing. By "blessing" OT authors had in mind the bestowal of the good things in human life, the things that humans tend to prize more than anything else: health, fertility, children, love, fidelity, long life, wealth, food, wine and peace. Clearly in both stories Man is placed in a very special relationship with God and is presented as the pinnacle or centre of creation. In the first account by the Priestly author, where Man is created last, Man's creation is presented as God's masterpiece, the crowning glory of creation, and Man is said to be created in "the image and likeness" of God himself and is given dominion over all other creatures. In the second, Yahwist account, where Man is created first, everything else that is created is created for his sake; Man stands at the centre of creation and, uniquely among all the earth's creatures, God breathes the spirit of life into his nostrils, an image that conveys the sense of a deep bond of intimacy between Man and God.

GENESIS 3

If God is the main actor in chapters 1 and 2, then the main actor in chapter 3 is, in the first half, the snake and, in the second half, God once more. The woman has an important but fairly brief talking role towards the middle of the chapter and the man, who has nothing to say during the temptation scene, is assigned a crucial walk-on part. What Robert Alter has described as the "laconic quality of biblical narrative," its "extreme reticence in telling us what we should think"[6] is very much in evidence in this chapter: the reader is not helped by the use of value-laden nouns or adjectives. There are no references to "sin" or "wrongdoing" or "transgression" or a "fall" or "disobedience" or "rebellion"; all of these terms, widely circulated in the traditional Augustinian interpretation of this chapter, are conspicuous by their absence.

Chapter 3 almost has the characteristics of a self-contained short story with its own beginning, middle and end. It begins by introducing the snake as the most cunning of all wild creatures and ends with the dramatic image of the revolving flaming sword that bars the way to the tree of life. In between there is a sense of heightened tension, a conflict between the divine and the human wills, followed by a painful denouement. It is a gripping, fascinating tale despite the fact that, for the most part, the language in which it is told is simple, muted and undramatic. At the traditional climax of the story we read simply that the woman took and ate the fruit of the tree of knowledge; "and she also gave some to her husband, and he ate." (Genesis 3: 6) I shall discuss this chapter at some length in later sections since this book is at heart a search for a convincing interpretation of the events recorded in chapter 3, but here I shall confine myself to saying that chapter 3 is broadly about a change wrought in Man that causes him to be seen as profoundly different from the other animals created by God.

In chapter 4, the style of writing changes yet again. The man and the woman, only recently named Adam and Eve, have children and most of the story concerns the slaying by their son Cain of Cain's brother Abel.

The tone of the language is far less muted than in chapter 3 as we read of how "sin is couching at the door," of how Cain "rose up against his brother Abel, and killed him," of how God chastised Cain telling him "your brother's blood is crying to me from the ground," and of how Cain cried to God "Am I my brother's keeper?" From chapter 4 onwards, Man is centre stage and human beings are the main actors, the agents who do things and get things done. With chapter 4 we enter human history. The history is still in the form of mythological narrative; we are not dealing with actual historical events; but we are dealing with Man as a self-determining agent of change and with the passage of time, as one generation follows another. Chronology takes on a much sharper focus than was the case in the first three chapters of Genesis. As far as human beings are concerned, there is little or no sense of the passing of time in chapters 1-3 of Genesis; these chapters seem to stand outside of time.[7] Not so from chapter 4 onwards. From the beginning of chapter 4, we find ourselves in a rapidly changing world. We read of the downward moral spiralling of the human characters, of the evil things that they do and, alongside that, we read of the emergence of what we would call civilisation: the invention and manufacture of musical instruments, the husbanding of livestock and the building of the first cities. Human violence and civilisation both come to the fore in chapter 4. In the remaining chapters of this section of Genesis, Man shares centre stage with God and what is recorded is a working out of a new relationship—or covenant—that is established between God and Man. In keeping with the traditional interpretation, I wish to maintain that what occurs from chapter 4 onwards is presented as following, as effect from cause, from the events that are recounted in chapter 3. Chapter 3 plays a pivotal role in the switch from God as the major protagonist in the bible to the situation in which the main protagonists are Man and God as related beings.

So what is it exactly that occurs in Genesis 3? That is the central question I wish to address. To find the answer, let us begin with the statement that follows the central incident, the eating from the forbidden tree: "Then the eyes of both were opened, and they knew that they were naked; and they sewed fig leaves together and made themselves aprons." (Gen 3: 7) We have seen how Augustine interprets this as evidence of a conflict between the rational faculties of our first parents and their bodies; the shame that caused them to cover their nakedness was a product of their inability, resulting from the first sin, to control their bodily urges by means of reason. Augustine felt that this shame was empirical proof of sin, a concrete fact he could point to as evidence that Man had sinned.

By contrast, I wish to propose the view that the sense of shame experienced by Adam and Eve was a result of their becoming human. For ancient people only animals went about naked; humans were distinguished from animals in so far as they alone wore clothes; for the ancient Hebrews, clothes were appropriate, nakedness was inappropriate, for human beings.[8] Wearing clothes was a human characteristic, one that marked out the difference between Man and the beasts. James Barr tells us that the Hebrew word used for "shame" at this point in the story is not associated with guilt or wrong-doing or loss of innocence but simply means "shy" or "embarrassed"[9]—for these ancient people it was undignified for human beings to be seen naked; and we are not so very far removed from them in our attitudes to human nakedness today, as a moment's reflection should confirm. The fact that Adam and Eve experienced shame so suddenly—at the end of chapter 2 we were told that the man and his wife were naked and unashamed—was because they had suddenly become human. Before they ate from the forbidden fruit they were not human, at least not fully human. Now they were human. In recognition of this fact, the Lord God, once he had meted out to them the punishment due to them for their transgression, made garments from skins "and clothed them." Augustine cites this as evidence of God's solicitude for our first parents shortly after they had offended him by sinning.[10] It takes on an altogether deeper significance if it is seen to be an acknowledgement and acceptance by God of the pair's new human status and as his fatherly preparation for them to go forth into the world as self-determining historical agents. The social and psychological importance of clothes for humans could hardly be more touchingly revealed.

Max Muller, a contemporary of Darwin's and Professor of Comparative Philology at Oxford who held anti-Darwinian views on the evolution of human cultures, maintained that language constituted an impassable barrier, a Rubicon, separating man from the beasts; in the interpretation of Genesis being put forward here, that Rubicon is the wearing of clothes: clothes mark out more than language or any other accomplishment the fundamental difference between Man and the rest of the animal kingdom. What is more, the human status of the couple is reinforced by the fact that it is at this point in the story (the end of chapter 3 and the beginning of chapter 4) that for the first time we are told their names, Adam and Eve. They are now named persons.

The punishments the Lord God administered to the first humans are another way of indicating their difference from the other animals. The woman is condemned to bear children in pain and to be subject to her husband; the man is condemned to earn his bread with the sweat of his brow; the ground is cursed because of him and we are told that it will yield him "thorns and thistles," symbols of pain and hardship. The pain of childbirth was something that must have struck the ancient authors as a distinctively human characteristic since, although other animals can suffer "difficult births," as a rule they do not suffer the intense pains of human labour.[11] Likewise, the other animals do not work on their environment in order to make it support them; rather they interact with their environment and appear to enjoy its fruits without the intervention of hard work. So it is that the mythical tale of Genesis 3 portrays what the authors perceived to be distinctively human characteristics, and ones humans complain of as unpleasant, as punishments meted out to them by the Lord God for their action in eating from the forbidden tree. This is an aetiological myth, a tale that explains how things are by explaining how they came to be that way. In this it resembles the *Just So* stories of Rudyard Kipling, a form of story extremely popular in the culture and folklore of the Indian sub-continent, which frequently involves talking animals and the like, and which attempts to explain by means of a fanciful tale how some factual but distinctive feature—such as the camel's hump or the leopard's spots—came to be. As we find them in Genesis 3, the punishments support the claim that Genesis 3 is about the origins or birth of Man as fully and recognisably human. What the tale clearly does not say is that the image of God in Man was defaced or diminished on account of the human action described in Genesis 3.[12]

HOMINISATION

How then did Man, God's creative masterpiece, become human? The answer is that he ate from the tree of knowledge of good and evil. The ability to discriminate between good and evil, moral discernment, was— once more—a characteristic that Man did not share with the other animals. The ancient Hebrews saw knowledge as belonging in the first place to God, as a divine attribute.[13] Chapter 3 of Genesis depicts Man's eating from the fruit of the tree of knowledge as a "breakthrough" moment, as a decisive and irrevocable step taken by Man, causing him to become distanced from the other animals created by God and closer in his make-up to God himself. It is true that the second creation story, which like the story of Adam and Eve belongs to the Yahwist tradition, relates that at the moment of creation God breathed his spirit into Man, indicating how he differed from the other animals. But that was only the first step in the "humanising" of Man. What I am suggesting is that the "humanising" of Man is reported in Genesis as coming about in two stages: first, God creates Man by breathing his spirit into the dust of the earth. In this way, hominid Man is created. This is a crucial stage since it creates a basic kinship between God and Man, a God-given ontological link that, setting Man apart from the other animals, will form the basis for the God-Man relationship that is to develop and mature throughout history. But at this first stage what is created merely has the potentiality of becoming the human being known to the authors. A second stage was needed to bring about a fully recognisable human being, the creature whose puzzling nature and make up the Yahwist authors are seeking to explain. This second stage occurred when Man ate from the tree of knowledge. Man suddenly came to enjoy one of the supreme attributes of God himself, namely knowledge. This second stage in the humanising of Man makes history possible: possessed of knowledge and the freedom of action that goes with it, Man was now equipped to become a self-determining agent of change and discovery. Man was about to embark on the great journey known as human history. It is this new form of consciousness, the consciousness making human knowledge and with it human history possible, that differentiates Man from other animals and causes the human couple, in the tale, to become aware that they are naked. Previously, like the other animals, they had not been ashamed of being naked, and now they were. This marks a profound change in their make up.

HUMAN CONSCIOUSNESS

For human consciousness is, first and foremost, self-presence. Unless I am present to myself nothing else can be present to me. If I am in a coma or a dreamless sleep I am not present to myself and so cannot be conscious of anything else. But once I am present to myself, other things can become present to me. Conversely, whenever I am aware of something I am also aware, with an awareness that is not explicit or the result of reflection or introspection, of myself as the subject of that awareness. When I know something, for example, I also know that I know it. Human consciousness is always self-consciousness, even if the "self" is not an explicit object of awareness but only implicit—the reader reading these words is aware of the words but also of self as reading the words, without necessarily adverting to this latter fact. Self-presence is simply something that quietly runs alongside the presence to me of anything else.

Human consciousness is consciousness to the power of two, and it is this "doubling up" of consciousness that frees Man from being fixed in the "here and now" particularity and transience of sensory contact and makes him uniquely capable of abstract thought, generalisation and moral judgement. It is also the basis of what philosophers term "free will," an essential element of an action being deemed moral since actions that are not free are not considered to be within man's control and hence the language of morality cannot be applied to them. But because human consciousness is doubled up, is raised to the power of two, it is possible for me to stand back from my immediate concrete experience and to think of a range of possible actions that are open to me in order to achieve a particular goal. I have no need to act in a way set down or determined by instinct or by custom; I am freed from the constraints of this time and place and so can store or park some ideas while I think of others. And it is the possibility of my choosing from a range of options and selecting one and acting on that that constitutes human freedom of action. In the same way, it is possible for me to know myself and to reflect on who and what I am; a cow does not know it is a cow and a dog does not know that it is a dog or what "dogginess" is; but we humans do inquire into our own nature and are also aware, in a more immediate way, of ourselves as moral agents. So self-knowledge, freedom, imagination and the power of decision are human attributes and the tale in Genesis 3 once more portrays them as characteristics that set Man apart from the other animals. They are also the characteristics that make Man a moral and spiritual being, akin to God himself, and form the basis for the history that is to follow—both the mythological history of Genesis 4-11 and the more literal "history" that constitutes the bulk of the biblical narrative.

THE IMPLICATIONS OF GENESIS 1-3

Genesis 1-3 sets out the basic condition of humanity; as Pope John Paul II said, the first three chapters of Genesis form the "immutable basis of all Christian anthropology." [14] These chapters reveal the basic human situation and determine the fundamental parameters of human action. Human history can only take place within and on the basis of these parameters. So it is that, following the eating from the tree of knowledge of good and evil, Man becomes a morally responsible being. Cain's question to God—*Am I my brother's keeper?*—reflects the anguish and novel sense of responsibility experienced by Man once he is endowed with knowledge of good and evil. Man is now fully human and capable of entering human history as a self-determining, intellectual and moral being. He is no longer tied to God's apron strings nor can he expect any more to play a merely passive role protected by divine guidance and control; he has achieved a maturity and level of intelligence that enable him to become creative in his own right. The story of the Fall of Man, as it has traditionally been called, that follows on the story of God's creation is, in fact, the story of Man's passage or ascent to the very knowledge that will enable him to become a co-creator of the planet under God. The sudden shame experienced by the man and the woman once they have eaten from the tree of knowledge is evidence of the dawning of human intelligence and freedom. For it is the same human self-consciousness that makes men and women aware of, and embarrassed by, their nakedness and wear clothes that also causes them to be capable of moral discernment. *Pace* St Augustine, it is not that the human couple have suddenly become ashamed of involuntary sexual arousal but rather they are now self-present, self-aware, and possessed of a sense of their dignity in a way that is not possible for non-human animals.[15]

The question then arises of why the authors of Genesis present Man's acquisition of freedom, knowledge and powers of decision as an action forbidden by God. To get a reasonably satisfactory answer to this teasing question will be the burden of much of this book and such an answer will have to wait until we have had time to explore further the mindsets or ways of thinking of the ancient Hebrews in the next chapter. Here I would confine myself to saying that the Israelite authors who redacted the materials that make up Genesis 1-11, probably during the exilic or post-exilic period (approximately the sixth, fifth or fourth centuries BC), besides feeling themselves constrained by what had been passed down to them, were determined that God could not be held responsible for the forms of behaviour manifested by these free and intelligent human beings. By this stage there was clear acceptance that freedom and intelligence made sin possible and the authors wished to dissociate God completely from sin, which was solely Man's responsibility. They could not allow Man any excuse for blaming his own sinful conduct on God. Hence they told the tale as one of Man's "illicit" acquisition of gifts that are first and foremost attributes of God himself. But the tale is more complicated than that. It is also possible that these ancient peoples could imagine a time when men and women were much closer in nature to the other animals. There is evidence of this in the folktales and mythology of many peoples, and the Hebrew author of Ecclesiastes considers that Man has much in common with beasts even if he is divinely created (Eclessiastes 3: 18f).[16] How Man, of all the animals on earth, came to be so singularly different from the other animals was something requiring explanation. The explanation devised by the ancient Hebrews was that Man somehow acquired an attribute of God himself, a particular kind of knowledge that the other animals manifestly did not have—knowledge of good and evil.

GENESIS 4-9

In narrating the story told in Genesis 3, the Yahwist authors were confronted by the need to explain the origin of Man's nature, including the fact that he showed intelligence which was regarded as being primarily an attribute of God, without implicating God in Man's misuse of his intelligence through sin. The solution was to present the human acquisition of intelligence as an act of disobedience of God's explicit command. In this way Man's possession of intelligence was explained in a way that did justice to the authors' artistic purposes, while God was kept apart from any implication in Man's sinning.

As I have already said, the mythological history that follows chapter 3 of Genesis would not have been possible unless Man had taken centre stage equipped with human intelligence. His use of his intelligence from chapter 4 onwards is somewhat ambiguous. It is true that there are references to the emergence of such evidence of culture and civilisation as musical instruments, artefacts and cities—interestingly through the line of Cain who, unlike his brother Abel, was a settler and, as such, fulfilled a necessary condition for the emergence of city life and hence of civilisation—but the main focus of Genesis chapters 4, 5 and 6 is on human sinfulness. That which made Man human also made him a sinner—once more, uniquely in all of the animal kingdom. Following Cain's slaying of his brother and the unnatural union of the "sons of God" with the "daughters of men," we read,

> The Lord saw that the wickedness of man was great in the earth, and that every imagination of the thoughts of his heart was only evil con-

tinually. And the Lord was sorry that he had made man on the earth, and it grieved him to his heart. So the Lord said, "I will blot out man whom I have created from the face of the ground, man and beast and creeping things and birds of the air, for I am sorry that I have made them."[17]

We read further that "the earth was corrupt in God's sight, and the earth was filled with violence." Things look bleak for humankind at this point. But then we read that "Noah found favour in the eyes of the Lord." There occurs what is to become a recognisable pattern in the bible narrative as God takes pity on Man because he has found a remnant that is good, in this case Noah and his family. The idea of the Ark that will enable Noah to survive the coming Flood is also God's idea, and that is another feature of the history of salvation: it is not through human agency that Man is saved but through God's favour and intervention.[18] So it is that Noah and his family are saved and from this saved remnant the rest of humanity is born.

Coinciding with this act of salvation, in order to maintain it into the future, God determines to form a covenant between himself and humankind. With great literary skill and not a little irony the authors show God changing his mind on the basis of the very considerations that had almost led him to blot Man out. We read how God said in his heart,

"I will never again curse the ground because of man, for the imagination of man's heart is evil from his youth."[19]

The repetition of nearly the same words that were used earlier by God to justify his decision to wipe Man out calls attention to the significance of this new decision[20]. The repetition of the words that "the imagination of man's heart is evil," echoing God's earlier and seemingly damning verdict on humankind, suggests the interim nature of most of Genesis 4-8, since the words, mirroring each other, act like brackets to enclose a certain section of the text and of the actions recounted there. The repetition of these words is a subtle stylistic device, pointing up the complete u-turn in God's thinking, with the interlude of time between Man's fateful transgression and the conclusion of the Flood being consigned to the past, left behind, forgotten, as God charts a bold new way forward for humanity. This radical change or reversal is quite touching since it shows God using Man's inclination to evil as grounds for initiating the means for his salvation, namely the covenant he proceeds to establish between Man and himself. This is an early instance of what is to become almost a law in the bible narrative: namely, the context of whatever it is that causes the God-Man relationship to go wrong is used by God as a means for the establishment of a new and higher source of blessing for Man. So instead of wiping Man out, God enters into an alliance with him and comforts him by telling him that never again will he destroy all living creatures. And as he does so he takes Man's sinful nature into account laying down new rules designed to keep Man's wayward nature in check, telling him, for example, that "Whoever sheds the blood of man, by man shall his blood be shed; for God made man in his own image."[21] And once more he commands Man to "be fruitful and multiply." So it is that Man is saved through God's merciful intervention once he has found a remnant of humanity that is good, and a pattern of salvation is established that will be repeated many times in the biblical narrative. The survival of Noah and his family represents a second chance for humanity and a new creation by God. According to the bible, it is from this new post-Noachic generation that humankind as we know it is descended. The notion of a new creation is one that will come to prominence with the coming of Christ.

The covenant made by God with Noah and his family is represented in the narrative as an accommodation God in his mercy is willing to make in order to retain his union with sinful, wayward humanity. Man's mutation from hominid creature to a recognisable human being had presented God with a problem and the solution he devises to meet this is the covenant. Man's mutation has meant that the perfect world created by God has gone and what we are left with is a new morally imperfect world. The covenant is to be God's method of bringing this new imperfect world to a higher level of perfection. It indicates that God is willing to accept human beings as they now are with the proviso that he now wishes to transform them in and through history. A covenant of this kind requires freedom and intelligence on both sides; it would not have been possible, for example, between God and any other animal. The fact that it is made with all of creation—God says, "Behold, I establish my covenant with you and your descendants after you, and with every living creature that is with you, the birds, the cattle, and every beast of the earth with you, as many as came out of the ark."[22]—is only possible because Man stands at the head of all created things. Man is the medium through whom God establishes a covenant with all living creatures: hence the repeated references to "you" in the passage just quoted. God's relationship with the rest of his creation has not changed; what has changed is his relationship with Man. That has now been placed on a new footing, one that acknowledges Man's new independence and freedom of action and reinforces his status as the head of the animal kingdom, albeit he is one whom the other animals now fear and dread.[23]

THE TOWER OF BABEL: GENESIS 11

The final parable of Genesis 1-11 is the myth of the Tower of Babel. Babel is not very difficult code for Babylon, a centre of a civilisation adjacent to Israel that stood for a good deal to which Israel was opposed. But the myth is not directed against Babylon in any specific sense but is one with universal human significance. Once more it is a tale concerning what it is that differentiates humanity from the other animals, this time focusing on the ability of humans to converse and communicate with each other through language. Language is one of the great distinguishing features of humanity, something that elevates human beings above the rest of nature. Coming hard on the heals of the story of the covenant established between God and humanity, the Babel myth is a reminder that God will not tolerate human pride, that he remains the Lord of history, something that the Hebrew authors believed very strongly. The story builds on the references that have already been made to the emergence of civilisation and the city states of Mesopotamia. The people in the tale decide to build a city with a tower that will have its "top in the heavens" in order "to make a name for ourselves."[24] The tower the authors have in mind is probably in the style of the ziggurats or temple-towers of the Babylonians by means of which the Babylonians wished to make contact with the divine. To the Hebrew mind such attempts by Man are illicit encroachments on the divine. Man cannot hope to achieve union with God through his own artifice or contrivance; any union with the divine will be determined by God and God alone and will be in terms laid down by God. Technological advancement will not bring Man any closer to God and any merely human constructs devised for this purpose will be destroyed just as surely as God destroys the tower of Babel by creating linguistic confusion among the people of the city. This is, of course, an aetiological myth that is used to explain the immense diversity of tongues and languages among human beings, to show that language can divide as well as unite. It contains a warning to human beings of the mess they get into when they make their own wills and their own status—"let us make a name for ourselves"—the centre of their endeavours. While the covenant established by God is a recognition of Man's status, the story of the tower of Babel is a reminder that the covenant requires Man to operate within the limitations laid down by God. And it shows God as once more jealously protective of his prerogatives.

By the end of chapter 11 of the Book of Genesis, the divine plan of salvation has been sketched fairly clearly and many basic facts about Man and about Man's relationship both with God and his fellow creatures (including the relationship between husband and wife) have also been established. The stage has been set for the drama of salvation history to unfold. The drama is one that involves all human beings without exception. All of us are in this story together; it is *the* human story because it concerns that most basic relationship, the relationship between God and Man. It is humanity's story, one that provides us with guidelines and suggestions for the roles we should play. That is one of the functions of myth: Mircea Eliade considers myth to deal in ontology, with the way things really are, to "reveal the structure of reality, and the multiple modalities of being in the world..."[25] Myths, according to Eliade, are probably true because they are validated by present experience. Karen Armstrong provides an insight into the difference between our modern way of thinking and the mythological imagination when she writes:

> Since the eighteenth century, we have developed a scientific view of history; we are concerned above all with what actually happened. But in the pre-modern world, when people wrote about the past they were more concerned with what an event had meant. A myth was an event which, in some sense, had happened once, but which also happened all the time. Because of our strictly chronological view of history, we have no word for such an occurrence, but mythology is an art form that points beyond history to what is timeless in human existence, helping us to get beyond the chaotic flux of random events, and glimpse the core of reality.[26]

Genesis 1-11, the strictly mythological section of the first book of the bible, provides an insight into the fundamental human way of being in the world, the basic structure of the plan of salvation and the basic concepts and spiritual insights that will be "enfleshed" in the stuff of human history that follows, beginning with the "patriarchal history" of Abraham and his successors.[27] And because it is a timeless story, a mythic tale that is outside of time, it applies to all times and in this way provides a metanarrative within which each of us can place the events of our own life stories.

CONCLUSION

In this chapter I have attempted to set out the innovative and controversial element of my interpretation of Genesis 1-11—that Genesis 3 is about Adam and Eve's mutation from proto-human into fully recognisable human beings—in a fairly rudimentary way and have sought to verify it by appeal to a changed form of consciousness for which Man's shame at his nakedness provides some evidence. This entails the notion that Man was not complete when he first came from the hand of God, that there was room for development and mutation, an understanding of the actual history of Man that the modern theory of evolution has made highly probable. While the theory of evolution provides some comfort for someone wishing to interpret Genesis 3 in this way, it should perhaps be pointed out that the interpretation has in no way been prompted by the wish to make the bible conform with evolution; rather evolution has provided some *a priori* encouragement for believing that such an interpretation would not appear absurd. But the interpretation itself is not dependent on any scientific theory but is largely a literary task, a task of using linguistic features and the stories we encounter in the bible as a means of entering into the mindset of the ancient Hebrews. If the interpretation also succeeds in making the Genesis story a good deal more compatible with the outlook of modern science than the traditional Augustinian interpretation, so much the better; it will indeed be paradoxical if exploration of the thinking of the ancient Hebrews at different stages of their history has such a happy outcome. The justification of the interpretation, however, will be dependent on how far it fits with the data discovered in the literary text; and on how far it yields an enriched theological interpretation of Genesis 1-11 and a clearer and more satisfying grasp of the meaning of Genesis 3.

NOTES

1. There was a development among the Hebrews of the notion of the one God and there are traces in the bible of there having been previous polytheistic beliefs; but in the bible the Hebrews always exalted the God of Israel, Yahweh, above all other supposed gods, and they came in time to the conclusion that there could only be one God. (Isa 43: 10, 15) See James O'Connell, *The Mystery of Being: the Presence and Absence of God* (Dublin: Veritas, 2009) p. 41-42.

2. John Romer, *Testament: the Bible and History*, (London: Michael O'Mara Books Ltd, 1996) p. 45.

3. Alan Richardson, *Genesis 1-11*, (London: SCM Press, 1953) p. 27-8.

4. *Catechism of the Catholic Church*, (London: Geoffrey Chapman, 1994) p. 390. My italics.

5. The distinction made between the different literary traditions in the Old Testament is apparently less secure than it was once thought to be, but I have decided to continue to refer to the stories running from the second creation account (Gen 2: 4b) to the end of Genesis 4, in keeping with a well established practice, as being written by the Yahwist authors; my argument is not, however, dependent on this choice.

6. Robert Alter, op. cit., p. 65.

7. Of course, the first creation account in the first chapter of Genesis is reported as taking place over seven days, but this account from the Priestly tradition hardly concerns the human race; the days belong to God, to a different order of being; they do not reflect the passing of time for humans but rather the ordered rationality of God's approach to the task of creation. In the Priestly tradition, the seven days taken for creating the world are based on the seven-day organisation of worship in the Temple.

8. James Barr, op. cit., p. 62. Anthropologist Victor Turner indicates an association between animals and nakedness, human beings and wearing clothes in *The Ritual Process* (New Brunswick: Aldine Transaction, 2008) p. 39.

9. Ibid., p. 63.

10. Augustine, *Confessions*, Book Thirteen, XV.

11. Commenting on the thinking of one primitive tribe, the anthropologist Mary Douglas says they believe "It is the nature of humans to reproduce with pain and danger...By contrast, it is thought that animals...reproduce without pain or danger." See *Purity and Danger*, (London: Routledge, 1966) p. 169.

12. James Barr, op. cit., p. 71.

13. Ibid., p. 60.

14. Quoted in Fergus Kerr, *Twentieth Century Catholic Theologians*, (Oxford: Blackwell Publishing, 2007) p. 194.

15. The author who has provided the most penetrating and illuminating account of human consciousness, in my opinion, is Bernard Lonergan. See, for

example, the references to consciousness in his *Method in Theology*, op. cit. See also Joseph Fitzpatrick, *Philosophical Encounters: Lonergan and the Analytical Tradition*, (Toronto: University of Toronto Press, 2005) pp. 211 and 215.

16. Joseph Blenkinsopp speaks of the intimate link between Man and the animal world being felt intuitively in the Old Testament, since like Man the animals breathe and bleed and "the blood is the life" (Lev 17: 11). See Joseph Blenkinsopp, *A Sketchbook of Biblical Theology*, (London: Burns and Oates, 1968) p. 98.

17. Genesis 6:5-8.

18. Later we read how it is God who approaches the Patriarchs to discuss how his plan of salvation will take shape in history; likewise, when the Israelites are slaves in Egypt, it is God who takes the initiative to achieve their deliverance and freedom.

19. Genesis 8: 21.

20. The frequent use of near verbatim repetition in Hebrew narrative is discussed by Robert Alter, op. cit., pp. 35-40, and by Mary Phil Korsak, *At the Start... Genesis Made New* (Louvain: Louvain Cahiers, 1992) p. 199.

21. Genesis 9: 6.

22. Genesis 9: 9-10.

23. Genesis 9:2-3.

24. Genesis 11: 4.

25. Mircea Eliade, *Myths, Dreams and Mysteries*, (London: Fontana Collins, 1968) p. 17.

26. Karen Armstrong, *A Short History of Myth*, (London: Canongate, 2005) p. 7.

27. When referring to biblical "history" here and elsewhere I use the word in a fairly broad sense, meaning that which is presented in the bible as history, as a record of events that took place. I am quite willing to concede that what is presented in the bible as history may not always meet the standards modern scholarship demands for something to qualify as "history." By these standards, for example, the biblical figures of Abraham and Moses conform more to legend than to history.

Chapter Three
The Primitive Tradition

If we are to gain an insight into the meaning of the story told in Genesis 3 by entering into the mindset of the ancient Hebrews at different periods of their history, then a good starting place would be to attempt to understand the story as it would have been understood by the Hebrews during what anthropologists term the "primitive period" of their existence. Fortunately for us, we have an excellent guide to the modes of thinking of primitive people, and in particular of primitive Hebrew people, in the work of the distinguished anthropologist, Mary Douglas, in her by now classic text, *Purity and Danger.*[1] Although Douglas illustrates the theoretical position she sets out in that book by reference to the Book of Leviticus and, in particular, the "abominations" and prohibitions we find in Leviticus 11-15, it is my belief that her thinking has broader application and throws a very sharp light on the narrative we find in Chapters 1-11 of the Book of Genesis and, in particular, on the story of Adam and Eve in the Garden of Eden recounted in Genesis 3. For the sake of clarity, it will be necessary for me first to set out Douglas's theoretical thinking at some length, a task made less onerous by the brisk directness of her writing style, before attempting to show in some detail how it might be thought to apply to Genesis 1-11.

THE HOLINESS OF YAHWEH

We should be better able to understand what Mary Douglas is saying in *Purity and Danger* if we develop an appreciation of the concept she considers to be central to the designations of "clean" and "unclean" as applied to animals, food and other things by the ancient Hebrews. This is the concept of divine Holiness. For the ancient Hebrews, at least by the time the various sections of the Book of Leviticus came to be written, God was totally "other," an exalted being far beyond humanity and human understanding. This is a motif that is repeated throughout the OT, one that forms a constant backdrop to everything that is recounted there. As it is expressed by the prophet Isaiah:

> For my thoughts are not your thoughts, neither are your ways my ways, says the Lord. For as the heavens are higher than the earth, so are my ways higher than your ways and my thoughts than your thoughts. (Isaiah 55: 8-9)

It is a theme of many of the psalms:

> The Lord is high above all nations, and his glory above the heavens! Who is like the Lord our God, who is seated on high, who looks far down upon the heavens and the earth? (Ps. 113: 4-6)

To express this divine exaltation, the Hebrews employed the word "Holy." This is the quintessential attribute of Yahweh. It means more than we normally think of when we use the word "holy." For the Hebrews the word "holy" could only be employed of people or places metaphorically since it was, strictly speaking, a word reserved for God himself. It was a word suggesting how God was set apart, different from all else:

> I am God, and not man, the Holy One in your midst. (Hosea, 11:9)

Isaiah frequently refers to "The Holy One of Israel," suggesting how God is inscrutable, incomprehensible, awesome, and the same phrase is found in other books of the OT. Holiness as used of God is not a moral category; it would be absurd to say that God lived a holy life.[2] Rather the word suggests that God is not a thing alongside other things, that God stands apart from everything else, that no mere human can bear to stand in his presence:

Who is able to stand before the Lord, this holy God? (1 Samuel 6: 20)

At the very centre of the temple in Jerusalem lay the "Holy of Holies," the place where Yahweh was present among his people, where no one might enter, save the high priest, and that only once a year.[3] The temple's architecture was designed so that proximity and access to this Holy place, the place of God's presence on earth, was determined by the holiness of the office bearer in the eyes of the community.[4] Commenting on the conditions required for approaching the sanctuary where God dwells, the psalmist says, "Who shall ascend the hill of the Lord? / Who shall stand in his holy place?/ He who has clean hands and a pure heart..." (Ps 23) The animals offered as sacrifice in the temple had to be unblemished and perfect of their kind.

The Holiness of Yahweh is strange, frightening and awe-inspiring. After seeing Yahweh in a vision, the prophet Isaiah proclaims: "Woe is me! For I am lost; I am a man of unclean lips, and I dwell in the midst of a people of unclean lips; for my eyes have seen the King, the Lord of hosts!" (Isaiah 6:5) Uncleanness is the opposite of holiness; things that were unclean or defiled were things that were somehow opposed to the holiness of Yahweh.[5]

Perhaps the awe-inspiring quality of Yahweh's presence is best brought out in the contacts Moses has with God. When Moses discovers that it is God who is speaking to him in the desert, we read: "Moses hid his face, for he was afraid to look at God." (Exodus 3:6) Later, when he has recovered his confidence, he asks God:

"I pray thee, show me thy glory." And (God) said, "I will make all my goodness pass before you, and will proclaim before you my name 'The Lord'; and I will be gracious to whom I will be gracious, and will show mercy on whom I will show mercy. But," he said, "you cannot see my face; for man shall not see me and live." And the Lord said, "Behold, there is a place by me where you shall stand upon the rock; and while my glory passes by I will put you in a cleft of the rock, and I will cover you with my hand until I have passed by; then I will take away my hand, and you shall see my back; but my face shall not be seen." (Exodus 33: 18-23)

Purity and Danger

This almost humorous account and the others we have touched on should suffice to show just how central to the thinking of the ancient Hebrews was the concept of Yahweh's holiness. It is from this central concept of God's Holiness, according to Mary Douglas, that there follows or flows the classification of some animals and other creatures as "clean" and "unclean" in chapters 11-15 of Leviticus and, hence, as fit or unfit to eat. In Leviticus 10: 10, we read of how the Lord commanded Aaron, "You are to distinguish between the holy and the common, and between the clean and the unclean." Commenting on the Hebrew meaning of the word "holy," Douglas says that apart from its root meaning of being "set apart" holiness connotes "wholeness" and "completeness":

> To be holy is to be whole, to be one; holiness is unity, integrity, perfection of the individual and of the kind. The dietary rules (of the Book of Leviticus) merely develop the metaphor of holiness on the same lines... But in general the underlying principle of cleanness in animals is that they shall conform fully to their class. Those species are unclean which are imperfect members of their class; or whose class itself confounds the general scheme of the world.[6]

The holiness of Yahweh was for the ancient Hebrews the central principle or fact by means of which they organised their universe and distinguished between what was dangerous and what was propitious:

> Fertility of women, livestock and fields is promised as a result of blessing and this is obtained by keeping covenant with God and observing all his precepts and ceremonies (Deut. XXVIII, 15-24)...positive and negative precepts are held to be efficacious and not just expressive: observing them draws down prosperity, infringing them brings danger. We are thus entitled to treat them in the same way as we treat primitive ritual avoidances whose breach unleashes danger to men. The precepts and ceremonies alike are focused on the holiness of God which men must create in their own lives. So this is a universe in which men prosper by conforming to holiness and perish when they deviate from it...[7]

Holiness requires that members of the tribe or race should not confuse the different classes of things; it involves discrimination, definition and order; "morality does not conflict with holiness, but holiness is more a matter of separating that which should be separated than of protecting...rights."[8] Order is the opposite of chaos: it was by a series of acts of separation—of the earth from the firmament, of the waters from dry land, of night from day etc.—that, in the first creation account from the Priestly tradition, God brought order out of the primeval chaos. The primitive Hebrews brought order into their lives by a similar series of separations and distinctions; the alternative to such classification was a breakdown of order and a return to chaos, and that risked conflict with divinely sanctioned order, resulting in ruin and misery. It is because holiness is associated with completeness, wholeness and oneness that hybrids and the confusion of classes are regarded as abominations.

It is from this general category of holiness that the ancient Hebrews derived their classification of what could and could not be eaten and the taboos attached to this classification. So for example, cloven-footed animals that chew the cud could be eaten, but those that were only cloven footed but did not chew the cud, such as the camel, or which chewed the cud but were not cloven-footed, like the badger, were taboo and could not be eaten. Likewise the hare, "because it chews the cud but does not part the hoof, is unclean to you." Pigs were also outlawed because they failed fully to conform to what was perceived to be the perfection and wholeness of the class of animals deemed fit to eat; for this reason they were judged to be unclean. (Leviticus 11: 3-8)

The abominations and prohibitions of Leviticus are not irrational, as some have claimed[9], nor were they imposed simply for reasons of hygiene, as others have maintained[10], but derive from the requirement to observe holiness in one's life in conformity with "the oneness, purity and completeness of God."[11] "The abominations of Leviticus are the obscure unclassifiable elements which do not fit the pattern of the cosmos. They are incompatible with holiness and blessing."[12] As Douglas puts it in a slightly later work, "In *Purity and Danger* I argued that the dietary rules in Leviticus XI afford a shorthand summary of the categories of Israelite culture...The dietary rules, I suggested, should be taken as a whole and related to the totality of symbolic structures organising the universe. In this way the abominations are seen as anomalies within a particular logical scheme."[13]

To breach these basic classifications by, for example, eating or even touching animals deemed unclean, was to make oneself unclean, to become polluted. And to be unclean was to be a danger to oneself and to others.

A polluting person is always in the wrong. He has developed some wrong condition or simply crossed some line which should not have been crossed and this displacement unleashes danger for someone...Pollution can be committed intentionally, but intention is irrelevant to its effect—it is more likely to happen inadvertently.[14]

On the peculiar nature of the dangers pollution unleashes, Douglas comments,

This is as near as I can get to defining a particular class of dangers which are not powers invested in humans, but which can be released by human action. The power which presents a danger for careless humans is very evidently a power inhering in the structure of ideas, a power by which the structure is expected to protect itself.[15]

The breakdown of the strict system of classification by which the cosmos is ordered creates a dangerous situation, and that is why hybrids and other anomalies are regarded as dangerous and why "transitional states" are dangerous.

Danger lies in transitional states, simply because transition is neither one state nor the next, it is undefinable. The person who must pass from one to another is himself in danger and emanates danger to others.[16]

Douglas refers approvingly to Van Gennep, an anthropologist who

saw society as a house with rooms and corridors in which passage from one to another is dangerous...The danger is controlled by ritual which precisely separates him (the initiate) from his old status, segregates him for a time and then publicly declares his entry to his new status... To say that the boys (novices) risk their lives says precisely that to go out of the formal structure and to enter the margins is to be exposed to power that is enough to kill them or make their manhood. The theme of death and rebirth, of course, has other symbolic functions: the initiates die to their old life and are reborn to the new. The whole repertoire of ideas concerning pollution and purification are used to mark the gravity of the event and the power of ritual to remake a man.[17]

APPLICATION TO GENESIS 1-11

It strikes me that this array of thinking from a distinguished anthropologist on how primitive people made sense of their universe by means of distinctions and classifications grounded in their most profound religious concept[18] helps us to see the basic pattern of the events recounted in Genesis 1-11. With their profound understanding of the oneness, wholeness and completeness of God, the ancient Hebrews must have regarded whatever came from the hand of God as sharing the same oneness, wholeness and completeness. Above all, the creature who stood at the summit of creation, the one regarded as God's masterpiece, who was made in the image and likeness of God himself, must have been considered to be endowed with these qualities of integrity and completeness. For man then to breach that integrity, to shatter that state of completeness, by trespassing on what was strictly speaking the divine attribute of knowledge of good and evil represented a breakdown of order and definition of immense proportions. We have seen how even to breach basic classifications in the matter of dealing with animals considered as potential foodstuffs was to incur pollution, to become defiled; how much more must it have struck the ancient Hebrews that to cross the threshold separating the created realm from the divine was to incur pollution and defilement and unleash danger on a cosmic scale. The basic order of the cosmos was shattered by Man's acquisition of the divine attribute of knowledge. Man was now a strange anomaly, a hybrid of animality and divinity. The danger unleashed in the world on account of this violation of the boundaries, as described in chapter 3 of Genesis, is seen in what follows—Cain's fratricide and the violence that fills the earth. It is little wonder that God begins to take stock and wonder about wiping Man out and starting all over again.

ANOMOLIES

Commenting on anomalies, Mary Douglas says:

> Any given system of classification must give rise to anomalies, and any given culture must confront events which seem to defy its assumptions. It cannot ignore the anomalies which its scheme produces...This is why, I suggest, we find in any culture worthy of the name various provisions for dealing with ambiguous or anomalous events.[19]

How to deal with the anomaly of the newly emerged human, the hybrid of animality and divinity, was the problem confronting the Lord God from chapter 4 of Genesis onwards. The strange hybrid of animal impulses and "divine" rationality had unleashed great evil upon the world, resulting in Cain's violent slaying of his own brother. Mary Douglas considers how primitive societies react to such anomalies:

> There are several ways of treating anomalies. Negatively, we can ignore, just not perceive them, or perceiving we can condemn. Positively, we can deliberately confront the anomaly and try to create a new pattern of reality in which it has a place.[20]

It is, I would suggest, this second, positive course of action that we come across in Genesis 1-11. The dangerous "transitional period" that follows on Genesis 3, during which Cain becomes an outcast and violence fills the earth, culminates in the Flood and the new creation. The evil unleashed by Man's fateful crossing of the line separating the divine from the created realm should not be thought of as typical of human life or history, but rather as characteristic of a specific "transitional period" leading up to the Flood and a new beginning.

Douglas quotes Eliade on the aptness of the imagery of water to suggest death and rebirth:

> In water everything is "dissolved," every "form" is broken up, everything that has happened ceases to exist; nothing that was before remains after immersion in water, not an outline, not a "sign," not an event. Immersion is the equivalent, at the human level, of death at the cosmic level, of the cataclysm (the Flood) which periodically dissolves the world into the primeval ocean. Breaking up all forms, doing away with the past, water possesses this power of purifying, of regenerating, of giving new birth...Water purifies and regenerates because it nullifies the past, and restores—even if only for a moment—the integrity of the dawn of things.[21]

In the last chapter we saw in Genesis how God made use of the Flood to create the world anew so that the new post-Flood order of reality "fits" with the new condition of Man. The anomaly represented by the "New Man" that comes about after eating from the fruit is overcome by God's act of re-creation as he designs a universe in which this "New Man" can fit. This clears up the meaning of the much disputed words of Yahweh to

Adam indicating that he would die on the day he ate of the fruit of the tree of knowledge of good and evil (from which Augustine infers that Man was created immortal, the "launching pad" for his argument in support of original sin), since these words refer to the fact that when this happened Man would die to his old self. In fact, the story of Man at this point is a *narrative dramatisation* of the ritual death and re-birth that is undergone by the novices referred to by Mary Douglas, a ritual death and re-birth brought about by the dissolution of the old world by flooding and the creation of the new. The Great Flood of Genesis marks a radical point of transition: a profound shift in Man's relationship with the rest of the world, including the other animals, and in his relationship with God.

A RITE OF PASSAGE

In an age that is weak on ritual, it is easy to underestimate the importance for primitive societies of rites of passage leading from childhood or adolescence to adulthood.[22] Anthropologists see rites of passage as consisting of three phases or stages: first there is separation, when a rupture occurs within the normal routines of society and family life and the novices are isolated from the rest of society; second, there is a period of transition which is often associated with liminality or marginality, when the novices are segregated, placed outside the limits and controls of society, a period often associated with danger, role reversal, disorder, disorientation and licence; and finally there is re-incorporation when the novices are initiated back into society but as changed, transformed, capable of assuming adult status and the freedoms and responsibilities that go with it. This transformation is the point of the rite and so abrupt and complete is the shift from the novices' previous state that it is commonplace to consider the novices as having died and been re-born. Rites of passage are as much about leaving things behind, consigning them to the past, as they are about getting on with the new.

The pattern associated with rites of passage would appear to be the pattern underlying the stories told in Genesis 1-9: first, there is an age or stage of innocence and total dependency on God, as found in Genesis 1-2, which is ruptured by the events described in chapter 3; this is followed by a transitional period of disorder, danger and liminality, brought about by these events, as described in Genesis 4-8: a "betwixt and between" period when Man appears cut off from God, and God begins to think of wiping Man out; and finally there is a stage of reincorporation or readjustment as, following the Flood[23], Man comes of age and is now accepted by God as a self-determining agent of change, capable of assuming an adult role involving the exercise of his newly acquired freedom and responsibility. The terms governing this new adult role can be found in God's establishment of the covenant with Man in Genesis 9: 8-17.

What is distinctive about the rite of passage begun in chapter 3 of Genesis is its scale. Genesis 3-9 is the account of a rite of passage affecting the whole human race; it is a cosmic rite of passage concerning the birth, or rather the death and rebirth, of the race. The mythical tale does not concern the passage to adulthood of particular individuals or of a particular social class or group, but of the species. In terms of Man's constitution, it is the passage or ascent of the species from a hominid or proto-human state to a fully human state on the basis of the acquisition by the hominid creature of intellectual and rational consciousness.[24] This, I believe, accounts for the prominence of the woman in the story, something that has intrigued commentators over the centuries. For if the story concerns some original sin committed by the first creature created by God, the man Adam, from whom all of humanity, and with it all sin, is descended, it is surprising that in the episode dealing with how this first sin was committed it is the woman and not the man who commands centre stage. It is the woman and not the man who dialogues with the snake, who admires the fruit as good for food, pleasing to the eye and to be desired to make one wise, who takes and eats and, only then, gives to her husband who also eats. If it is from Adam that all human beings, including Eve, inherit original sin (*peccatum originale originatum*), then the prominence of Eve in this story is puzzling.

Augustine, of course, accounted for the central role allotted to the woman on the basis of the devil's—the snake's—cunning, since the devil, Augustine claimed, deliberately selected the weaker member of the pair as the object of his wily plan, knowing that on account of the bond between them the stronger member of the pair would then be more likely to yield to temptation himself. Contrary to this Augustinian interpretation, however, I would suggest that in trying to grasp the meaning of the story we should take the advice of Robert Alter and look for some detail, *leitworter* or thematic key phrase that throws light on the story's hidden depth. We should, I would suggest, pick up the reference towards the end of the story to the fact that the man "called his wife's name Eve, because she was the mother of all living." (Gen 3: 20) There is an etymological association between the Hebrew name "Eve" and the word for "living" and this hints at the true meaning of this story: for if, as I maintain, it is with the birth or re-birth of the race that this story is concerned, it is quite fitting that the focus should be on the woman, on the mother of this new race that is about to come into being—chapter 4 of Genesis is precisely about the generation of children that succeeds Adam and Eve and this is also the central theme of chapter 5. Eve is the source, the gateway of the human race.

The humanity of all of Eve's offspring is suggested by the fact that each of them is named. The strongly patriarchal nature of Hebrew society is suggested by the fact that it is Adam who names his wife (3:20), just as he had named all the animals God had brought to him (2: 19), and by the fact that succeeding generations are referred to as "the generations of Adam" (Gen 5: 1); and although "daughters" are mentioned as well as "sons," among the many names listed all are male. Notwithstanding the patriarchal nature of Hebrew society, however, the authors of Genesis 3 saw fit to give the central human role to the woman, and the reason is that the story told there is mainly concerned with the birth of humankind. That is why Eve is called "the mother of all living" just prior to the naming of "the generations of Adam," and Eve's role as child bearer is also stressed in the "sentence" on her pronounced by God towards the end of the chapter. In these early chapters of Genesis we find the first humans obeying the divine injunction to "be fruitful and multiply, and fill the earth." (Gen 1: 28) These chapters are concerned with the emergence of the human race upon the face of the earth, first in nature, then in history. That is their overarching theme.

In social and religious terms, the re-birth or passage described in Genesis 3 can be expressed as the race's transition from infancy to adulthood, where both infancy and adulthood are defined by humanity's relationship with God, the Creator. Man passes from a stage of complete dependence on God to a new, precarious adult stage in which he begins to enjoy a degree of independence from God and newfound freedom and powers of self-determination. This is the new situation that the bible from now on is concerned with. Once totally dependent on God, Man's relationship with God has now become problematic; his acquisition of autonomy includes the freedom and capacity to sin, to react against the values of God. God, on this reckoning, is prepared to "let go," to entrust Man with the risks, responsibilities and opportunities for good or ill that come with adulthood. What comes after chapter 3, both in the context of Genesis 1-11 and in the later historical sections of the bible, concerns the various ways in which Man uses and abuses his newly acquired knowledge, freedom and powers of decision.

With reference to Hebrew religion and culture, this same passage can be seen to mark a shift from nature to history. From this point on God will no longer be revealed simply through nature—as the divine will continue to be for peoples such as the Babylonians with their fertility cults—but will be revealed through his dealings with his chosen people in history. God will be the Lord of history and the Hebrews will become the people moulded by this history, the people who escaped from slavery in Egypt, and spent forty years wandering in the desert before conquering and settling in the land of Canaan, and so forth. Hebrew-Jewish identity will be shaped and defined by the narrative of their historical dealings with God. (See, for example, Exodus 20: 1 or Isaiah 49: 6-8). History is a *human* preserve: generally speaking, history books make few references to the deeds of non-human animals; and individuals, tribes and races acquire their identity from the narrative of their history.

Like all myth, the Adam and Eve story is an expression of the tribe's or the people's self-understanding at a particular period of their history. What it denotes is a self-conscious recognition by the Hebrews that they have moved beyond the stage of nature worship, consisting of the veneration of the deities believed to be in control of such natural functions as fertility and sexuality; they have cast off any previous fixation with the periodicity of the seasons and a corresponding cyclical understanding of time and come to an understanding of change and development through the events of history, developing in this way a more linear conception of time. In place of a multitude of deities believed to oversee the processes of nature, they have embraced the idea that there is only one God and this one God is the Lord of history, characterised not by his power over the processes of growth and fertility but by the wisdom and knowledge required if progress and prosperity are to be achieved over time. With reference to history, power lies in the wisdom and acumen to adopt the right course of action and to make the right choices at the right time; it lies in the ability to pass on one's knowledge and understanding to one's descendants who can build on the knowledge and the cultural treasures their predecessors have accumulated. The thought categories of the ancient Hebrews were now finely attuned to the notion that they were an *historical people* and their God was involved in their history.

These thought categories are very different from the scientific outlook of men and women of today. When they told a story about Man ascending into full rational consciousness the ancient Israelites were not attempting, like Darwin, to formulate a theory that made sense of a range of detailed observations of natural phenomena; rather they were coming to terms with a change they had detected in their own national or tribal consciousness and articulating this change in the form of story. Deeply conscious of how their own religious and ethnic identity had been moulded by the event of the exodus from Egypt, they were acknowledging that they were historical animals, shaped by historical developments in a way that the other animals were not, and they were speculating on the primeval event that had made this possible.

The rite of passage described in Genesis 3 is a single passage with three dimensions: at the most basic level, it is a passage from the hominid or proto-human state to the human state. But it is also a passage from childhood to adulthood and a passage from nature to history and culture. The earliest stirrings of human history are recounted in mythological fashion in chapter 4 of Genesis, hard on the heals of Man's acquisition of the status of being human and being adult. Man is no longer simply a product of nature but an intelligent and self-determining agent of change and development, someone who can fashion instruments from bronze and iron, play musical instruments and build cities (Gen 4: 17f). In Genesis 4 we find Man transformed into a historical being. The moment of hominisation is also the moment when Man shifts from nature to history and culture, and from innocence to adulthood. The traditional Augustinian interpretation of Genesis 3 is right in finding in Genesis 3 a profound shift in the human-God relationship. But it mistakes the nature of this shift, placing all the emphasis on human rebellion and sin. The more literary and anthropological approach adopted here reveals that Genesis 3 does concern a shift in the God-Man relationship because it repositions Man by placing him in a totally new relationship with God and with the rest of the animal kingdom. That is one of the functions of myth: it "helps human beings to locate themselves, to know where they belong vis-à-vis God, the universe, and their fellow human beings."[25]

Gabriel Daly quotes Goethe, "Man is the first conversation which nature holds with God."[26] The arrival of Man marks an epochal change in world process, to some extent setting Man apart from nature and opening up the possibility of one group of animals taking control of their own lives. It also makes possible new forms of relationship and this has deep religious significance as far as Man's relationship with God is concerned. As Daly comments, "In men and women creation arrives at a point where God can offer it an invitation to intimacy. Hominisation, however, means freedom to refuse as well as to accept. Sin is refusal of, or apathy towards, the offer."[27] The ambiguities and complexities of the new relationship between God and Man are well brought out in the mythological chapters of Genesis that follow chapter 3 as well as in the more historical narratives of the Old Testament that follow, from chapter 12 onwards.

Chapters 4-8 of the Book of Genesis—from Cain's fratricide to the Flood—should be seen as concerning *the dangerous middle period of the rite of passage*, a period when humankind was outcast upon the earth and hence out of control, when "violence filled the earth" and God wondered if he should destroy humanity and start anew. It was during this dangerous interim period that there occurred yet another violation of the human-divine boundary, yet another indicator of the breakdown of the proper order of things, with the unnatural sexual union between some divine beings ("sons of God") and earthly women ("daughters of men").

THE NEPHILIM

Genesis 6 opens with this passage: "When men began to multiply on the face of the ground, and daughters were born to them, the sons of God saw that the daughters of men were fair; and they took to wife such of them as they chose." (Gen 6: 1-2) Verse 4 continues, "The Nephilim were on the earth in those days, and also afterward, when the sons of God came in to the daughters of men, and they bore children to them. These were the mighty men that were of old, the men of renown." Commentators are agreed that "the sons of God" is a reference to angelic or divine beings, to beings linked or connected to God himself. Further biblical references to the Nephilim, the mighty men or giants of old who are presented in Genesis 6 as the unnatural products of sexual union between divine beings and earthly women, are rare. However, there are several in the Wisdom tradition suggesting that by the time they are mentioned the Nephilim are known to have disappeared, to have been wiped out and become extinct. The Book of Wisdom says, "For even at the beginning, when arrogant giants were perishing, the hope of the world took refuge on a raft, and guided by thy hand left to the world the seed of a new generation." (Wis 14: 6) This would suggest that the Nephilim were wiped out by the flood which Man had survived by virtue of God's advice to Noah that he build an Ark. It would appear that the Nephilim did not enjoy God's favour in the way that humankind did. This is reinforced by another passage, in the Book of Baruch, which occurs in the context of a poem in praise of Wisdom. The Baruch poem declares that no one can achieve wisdom by their own efforts; God alone can bestow it and he has chosen to bestow it on the Israelites to whom he has given the Law; Wisdom is observance of the Mosaic Law, something the giants did not possess. The Lord did not give this group "the way to knowledge"—that is, wisdom—and, although they were skilled in war, "they perished through their folly." (Bar 3: 26-28)

There is, however, a basic discrepancy in the biblical references to these giants of old which suggests that the historical basis for their actual existence is very doubtful. For in the Book of Numbers there is a reported sighting of them that speaks of them as giants occupying the land of Canaan, at that point being targeted by Moses as the land he wished his followers to occupy, and compared with whom Moses's spies report that "they felt like grasshoppers" (Num 13: 33). It hardly needs to be pointed out that it would not have been possible for these giants to occupy the land of Canaan at the time of Moses if they had been wiped out much earlier at the time of the flood.

This causes one to wonder as to the reasons why the biblical redactors chose to include stories of the Nephilim, and such wonderment is increased by the fact that talk of divine beings fraternising or mingling with human beings is very rare in the bible. Sexual liaisons between the "gods" and human creatures is commonplace in the mythological tales of the Greeks and the Babylonians, but the Hebrew exaltation of God did not favour tales of this kind of union. For the Hebrews, God was totally "other," not part of this world, and beyond human ken. The question arises: how did the "risky" tale of the Nephilim survive the various editing processes scholars claim the Old Testament went through? What is the literary or narrative function served by this story? James Barr observes that the story of the Nephilim in Genesis 6 was not taken up by any of the Christian denominations because it explained nothing in their experience and, indeed, "strained belief."[28]

There are, I believe, at least two reasons why this fanciful tale about giants was retained by the redactors. The first is that this story reinforces the message of Genesis 3 in a more heavy handed and obvious manner. As one respected commentary observes, "The Bible is reticent about stories of the 'gods'; here it alludes to such a story only to show that the mixing of heaven and earth, which had been forbidden to the first man and the woman in the garden by the prohibition against eating of the tree of knowledge of good and bad, and of the tree of life, is taboo."[29] In this way the Nephilim story mirrors or repeats the theme of the transgression of the boundary separating the divine from the created realm that is found in Genesis 3, emphasizing the scale of the breakdown of order unleashed by this transgression that is narrated in Genesis 4-8. The second reason for the retention of this story is that it reinforces the point that for the ancient Hebrews the possession of intelligence could only be explained if the possessor was, in some way, a divine being. The Nephilim may not have been favoured by God with divine wisdom, but they were the products of the sexual union of divine beings with earthly women; they were different from the Israelites and had not been blessed with the wisdom the Lord had bestowed on his chosen people, but like the Israelites they were set apart from the beasts in possessing intelligence. They were an example of how intelligence on its own was not sufficient to lead a good life, a life of union with God, and that in addition to intelligence there was needed the guidance and education the Israelites enjoyed by means of the covenant and the Mosaic Law—and that is a third reason why this untypical tale was retained by the redactors.

THE COVENANT

As I have said, the story of the Nephilim illustrates the sheer scale of the breakdown of order characteristic of the dangerous middle period of a rite of passage: "this Near Eastern myth is cited to illustrate the increase of sin and violence that led up to the great flood."[30] At this point, as we have seen, things are so bad that the Lord God thinks of wiping out his creation and starting all over again. On reflection, however, because of the worthiness of Noah and his family, God decides to form a covenant with Man and to bring about a new creation. Within the terms of the covenant Man will be enabled to mature and grow in the exercise of his newfound freedom, to refine his ethical and spiritual understanding and so come to terms with his newly acquired divinity.

The great historical covenant known to all Israelites was, of course, that established between God and Moses in the wilderness of Sinai. The religious covenant was based on the contractual agreements that men of different tribes drew up with each other. Among ancient nomadic peoples, the established customs and laws were peculiar to each tribe or ethnic grouping; they did not cover or guarantee justice for strangers or outsiders. For this reason different tribes would draw up covenants which would give the stranger a measure of recognition as a blood relation or fellow tribesman in return for the stranger's commitment to uphold the conditions of the covenant. The covenant would be sealed with an oath and solemn declaration and would frequently be confirmed or ratified by some rite involving a communal meal or a mingling of the blood of the tribal chief and the covenanter.[31] Covenants between Israel and other peoples are mentioned frequently in the OT, usually marking some practical agreement to do with the mutual recognition of land boundaries or water rights, and the like.

In the religious context, the covenant between God and the Israelites in Sinai occurs not long after the exodus from Egypt and indicates that God has chosen the Israelites as his people, his chosen possession out of all the peoples of the earth, a kingdom of priests, a holy nation (Exodus 19: 5f). The covenant means that from now on Israel is part of God's tribe. It is initiated by Yahweh and its terms are laid down by him; it is not dependent on the merits of the Israelites themselves. In the covenant in Sinai, God imposes his law or commandments on the people—the Ten Commandments—and in return the people commit themselves to obey what God commands; the central condition laid down by Yahweh is that the people should not worship idols or any man-made god. Two covenant rituals are mentioned in Exodus 24. In one, the blood of sacrificial animals is sprinkled on the altar, representing Yahweh, and then on the people, indicating that Yahweh and the Israelites now belong to one blood, one family. In the other, Moses, Aaron and his sons and 70 elders, representing all of the Israelite people, share a meal with Yahweh, symbolising the union between the two parties, rather like the union that occurs at a wedding. And as in a marriage, the conditions of the covenant are dependent upon the two parties having exclusive rights and obligations, the one to the other. The covenant is much more than a list of conditions and obligations that each side has to commit to; these are simply the external manifestations of a profound new reality which is a bonding, a state of intimacy and friendship, of kinship even, between God and Man.

It is probable that this historical covenant in Sinai was retrojected back into more ancient Hebrew tradition[32] and we read in Genesis 17 of the covenant made between God and Abraham, the original divine promise and the responding leap of faith, on which the special relationship between God and Israel was founded, and in Genesis 6 of the universal covenant Yahweh makes with Noah. Circumcision is the sign of the tribal covenant with Abraham while the rainbow is the symbol of the universal covenant made with Noah. The rainbow forms an arch in the heavens: on one side it rests on God; on the other it rests on the remnant of humanity with whom God has found it possible to enter into an alliance. In the course of Israelite history, the terms of the Sinai covenant were renewed and solemnly ratified on more than one occasion; for instance, Joshua, Moses's immediate successor and the military conqueror of Canaan, made the people renew their choice after they arrived in Canaan, the land God had first promised to Abraham (Joshua 8: 30-35; 24: 19-28). Likewise, King Josiah re-commits to the covenant before all the elders and the people of Judah and Jerusalem, after finding the book of the covenant, and as part of this commitment has all the apparatus of idol worship destroyed (2 Kings, 23: 1-25). Later we read of the covenant being renewed under Nehemiah, the governor of Judah, and Ezra, a priest and scribe (Nehemiah 8 and 9). These acts of renewal appear to have been occasioned and motivated by the tendency of the Israelites to adopt the practices and mores of their idolatrous neighbours and their failure to observe the Mosaic Law: these idolatrous practices were renounced and the people's commitment to the Law and the covenant was renewed.

We can see, therefore, how the divine initiative of the covenant that we find mentioned in Genesis 9 is a forerunner and prototype of the Mosaic covenant that stood at the heart of Israel's self-understanding and of its liturgical and religious practice throughout its history. It would not be too much to say that the covenant made Israel—that it was through the discipline and order imposed by the covenant, and the Law that emerged as the conditions the covenant laid down, that Israel was schooled in divine wisdom and drew closer to Yahweh. This was part of the divinisation of Israel that Yahweh undertook in order to overcome the anomaly incurred by humanity when Adam ate from the forbidden fruit of the tree of knowledge of good and evil. During the dangerous transitional period that followed this fateful deed, God not only decided not to wipe man out; he also decided to make Man whole in accordance with his own wholeness and holiness, and his instrument for achieving this was the covenant. Humankind was summoned to conform its acquired powers of understanding and freedom of action to the will of Yahweh, and in this way to acquire divine wisdom; humankind was being summoned to become divine, to become worthy of fellowship with God. For much of its history the covenant was equated with the Law of Moses, and fidelity to the covenant meant fidelity to the Mosaic Law. And, as we have seen, prolonged infidelity to the Mosaic Law occasioned acts of repentance and renewal of the covenant.

The covenant is the instrument of re-adjustment through which God educates humankind and helps Man to live at peace with his newly acquired "divine" powers, to take possession of them and begin to use them properly—as God wishes him to use them. God chooses not to destroy Man but rather to re-cast the whole of creation around this new "anomalous" creature. The "historical" sections of the bible that follow on Genesis 1-11 are the story of God's education of Man through his election of the Hebrews for his special covenantal tuition, leading up to the coming of Christ.[33] To interpret the mythological story told in Genesis 1-11 in the thought categories of "Primitive Religion" is to see it as it was probably first narrated, as a story attempting to make sense of humankind by explaining Man as an anomaly of nature, as a strange hybrid with characteristics in common with the other animals but also as possessing attributes that set him apart from the other animals, just as surely as Yahweh is set apart from all of creation. The story was told in the form of a rite of passage, describing how the human race passed from childhood to adulthood by eating from the tree of knowledge of good and evil, thereby acquiring the kind of knowledge that at once placed Man above the other animals and made him more akin to God, a vision of Man that is conveyed in Psalm 8: 5-8: "(T)hou hast made him little less than God,/..thou hast put all things under his feet,/ all sheep and oxen,/ and also the beasts of the field, the birds of the air, and the fish of the sea..."

To view Genesis 1-11 through the lens of the primitive tradition has the value of enabling us to grasp the basic outline of the story shorn of the various interpretations that were to become attached to it later. It is to see it in the most basic terms of creation, "transgression," anomaly, pollution, danger and divine accommodation; it is to see it as a rite of passage from infancy and dependence, on the one side, to adulthood and a potentially dangerous form of autonomy or independence from God, on the other; it is to see it as a shift from nature to history and culture. Like all myth, such as the tale of Oedipus in Greek mythology, it possesses elemental human significance—except that the Hebrew story is told as a prelude or overture to the history of a people and the "divine accommodation," as I have termed the covenant, is something that will be played out and developed in the course of the history of this people.

But the covenant was not to be the end of the story but only the means to a more glorious end. It was the prophet Jeremiah who eventually opened up the prospect of a day when the covenant would be renewed in a more permanent fashion because the Law would be seen to be engraved in the hearts of the people and the precise strictures of the Mosaic Law would become redundant:

Behold, the days are coming, says the Lord, when I will make a new covenant with the house of Israel and the house of Judah, not like the covenant which I made with their fathers when I took them by the hand to bring them out of the land of Egypt, my covenant which they broke, though I was their husband, says the Lord. But this is the covenant which I will make with the house of Israel after those days, says the Lord: I will put my law within them, and I will write it upon their hearts; and I will be their God, and they shall be my people. And no longer shall each man teach his neighbour and each his brother, saying, "Know the Lord," for they shall all know me, from the least of them to the greatest, says the Lord; for I will forgive their iniquity, and I will remember their sin no more. (Jeremiah 31: 31-34)

THE CHRISTIAN ERA

For the Christian, the era prophesied by Jeremiah arrived with the coming of Jesus, the Christ, a point recognised and acclaimed by the author of the epistle to the Hebrews who quotes the Jeremiah passage at length (Hb 8: 8-13). Now, a central dimension of Jesus's earthly mission was restoring people to their full humanity, making people whole. This is most obvious in the many cases of his curing of people suffering from physical ailments: the blind, the lame, the infirm, the paralytic, the seriously ill. We see it also in his healing of those with more mysterious illnesses, such as on the many occasions when he is reported as casting out demons; and, of course, in his forgiveness of sins, an action that scandalised his Pharisee critics more than his miracles of physical healing. (Luke 5: 21) On all of these occasions, Jesus can be seen to be the one who makes people whole, the repairer of human brokenness; and a feature of his dealings with the recipients of his healing powers is his attention to them as individuals, his caring for them as people, his ability to restore to them their dignity as human beings. This is particularly seen in the episodes where he reaches out to those condemned or outcast by respectable Jewish society, such as in his refusal to condemn the woman caught in adultery (Jn 8:1ff) or in his healing of a leper (Mt 8: 1-4) and in his consorting with lepers (Mk 14:3) who, in accordance with the legal requirements set down in the Book of Leviticus, should have removed themselves from society because they were "unclean." (Leviticus 13: 46)

Jewish society at the time of Jesus was regulated to a large extent by two codes of conduct, the purity code and the property code, and Jesus was willing to defy both if it meant it would break down the barriers creating human isolation and exclusion, the barriers preventing or inhibiting the rule of love that should govern human affairs.[34] This was seen, for example, in the apparently harmless curing (Mt 9:18-26; Lk 8: 43-48) of a woman who had suffered for 12 years from haemorrhaging since, in keeping with strict Jewish law, such a woman was deemed "unclean" (Lev 15:25) and should have been avoided; it was also seen in the willingness of Jesus to practise what is termed "table fellowship," sitting down at table with public sinners like prostitutes and tax collectors, a fact that provoked criticism from the scribes and Pharisees. (Mt 9:11; Lk 7: 39; 19:7-10) When the Pharisees condemned his followers for eating with unclean hands, Jesus retorted that it is not what goes into the mouth that defiles a man but what comes out of the mouth. (Mt 15: 1ff; Mk 7:1ff) He challenged the law whenever it was in danger of sacrificing human beings to some norm or regulation, recognising that the law was made for Man and not Man for the law: "And why do you transgress the commandment of God for the sake of your tradition?" (Mt 15: 3; Mk 7:8) He was adept at defying and undermining the patriarchal laws and customs that ensured that women were maintained in an inferior position in society.[35] His wish to restore people to their full humanity, to their full worth as human beings, took precedence over the customs of his own people even when these were sanctioned by ancient religious law. He showed himself willing, for example, to challenge even the paramountcy of the family in Jewish life (Mt 10: 35-37; 12: 48-50; Mk 3: 31-35) because he sought a wider unity of human beings by "subordinating all human goods to the reign of God."[36] This was nothing less than a revaluation of the central Hebrew value, since membership of the chosen people was through familial descent.[37]

While Jesus was totally confident of his own unique relationship with the Father, he emphatically did not present himself as a member of some elite or privileged group in Jewish society but rather prized common humanity above tradition and the law. There is an egalitarian quality about Jesus, as we find him in the gospels, in his encounters with people from a wide variety of social backgrounds—men and women, Jews and Gentiles—that has not always received the attention it deserves.

On reflection, it would appear that Jesus saw it as part of his mission to undermine the barriers and divisions between people and classes that arose from observance of the rituals and practices demanded by the Law, and which were rooted ultimately in the ancient Hebrew concept of Holiness. This was not some mere act of social rebellion; we are not talking here about "Jesus the socialist." It goes much deeper than that. By dispensing with so many of the external rituals of his own society and tradition and focussing attention on what lay within, on "purity of heart,"[38] Jesus, in line with many of the prophets before him, was *redefining the meaning of wholeness and holiness*, the epicentral religious concept by reference to which the ancient Hebrews, his ancestors, had organised their society. And in so doing, he was also undermining the forces that made God into a distant, remote being, someone unapproachable except by members of a priestly caste or by the High Priest in the "Holy of Holies" of the Temple. Hence the powerful significance of the tearing of the curtain of the temple reported in all three synoptic gospels at the precise moment of Jesus's death (Mt 27:51; Mk 15:38; Lk 23:45): from now on, through Jesus people could have free and ready access to the Father. It would no longer be necessary to exalt the sacred by distancing the people from the divine. God dwelt in Jesus, who replaced the temple,[39] and through the same Spirit that was in Jesus he would dwell in the hearts of his people. By the very same token, Man need no longer be regarded as a hybrid, an anomaly of nature, since by means of the Spirit he would now have the resources and opportunity to become whole and complete by being at one with God.

CHRISTOLOGY

The Christian claim that Jesus was fully human and fully divine has often been presented as an absurdity and to orthodox Jews, in particular, the Christian worship of Jesus can appear to be no better than idolatry, a practice totally at odds with the terms of the covenant. However, in the light of the preceding interpretation of Genesis 1-11, the notion of Christ as the God-Man, as perfectly human and perfectly divine, begins to seem less of an anomaly and more of a fulfilment of what we might expect in the divine plan of salvation. For the action taken by God to overcome the anomalous situation of humankind following the incident described in Genesis 3 consists precisely in the divinisation of Man; and I have attempted briefly to suggest the lines along which this divinisation progressed in the course of Jewish history. Now the divinisation of Man might be thought of as diminishing Man's humanity by expanding and enhancing his divine attributes. On the other hand, divinisation might be thought of as making Man more fully complete as Man. This is the paradox of salvation: the more complete we become as divine, the more complete we become as human. The reason is that it is our divine attribute that defines us as human and sets us apart from the beasts.[40] Therefore, the more closely we are united to God, the more our human nature and our human stature are enhanced and ennobled. That is why the Christian teaching about Jesus being both God and man need no longer be seen as an oddity, as the presentation of some kind of freak or "impossible being" as the model that human beings should strive to emulate and follow; rather Jesus can now truly be seen as no oddity but as the perfect human being, the kind of human being we should indeed be aiming to model ourselves on. Jesus is perfect as human because as God he is perfect, and Man grows in human perfection in so far as his "godlike" spiritual attributes (those he acquired in Eden) of thinking, knowing, deliberating, evaluating, deciding, choosing, controlling, loving and acting are refined and developed.[41]

The realization of this profound truth is important to Christology, the study of the nature of Christ. Despite the fact that early Church Councils, such as the Council of Nicea in 325 AD and the Council of Chalcedon in 451 AD, solemnly defined that Christ was a single person with both a divine and a human nature, and notwithstanding the fact that the contrary (Monophysite) view, that Christ had only one—divine—nature, was condemned at Chalcedon, in practice there has been a tendency over time for Christians to view Christ almost exclusively as divine or almost exclusively as human. The issue of Christ's two natures—two natures in one person—has been a particularly difficult one for Christianity to interpret in a way that makes sense to the ordinary man or woman in the street. The temptation has always been in effect to annul or mentally wipe out one of the two natures and to focus exclusively on the other. Indeed, for some nineteen centuries the *de facto* situation was that most Christians were monophysite in their belief, considering Jesus to be God with some kind of human nature bolted on. This was to deny the true humanity of Jesus who, on this interpretation, was made to look like God posing as a human being; it presents a picture that completely undermines the recognisable human being we encounter in all four gospels.

In the twentieth century the pendulum swung the other way as the improved sophistication of scriptural studies threw ever sharper light on Jesus the Jew—on Jesus in his social, historical and cultural milieu. This tended to encourage the view of Jesus the man—and quite commonly as merely a man—and the corollary that his redemption was merely exemplarist: Jesus was a good man who set a good example but did, and indeed could do, nothing else.[42] So in the Christian era there has tended to be a kind of "see-saw quality" about Christology: when Christ's divinity was up, his humanity was down; when his humanity was up, his divinity was down; it would appear that one could only be appreciated at the expense of the other. But once we grasp the fact that Man has a divine attribute, the attribute acquired from the tree of knowledge of good and evil, and that it is this attribute that precisely distinguishes and defines him as human, then it is quite possible to see that there is no conflict between divinity and humanity, but rather that perfection in humanity, the enhancement and ennobling of Man's divine attribute, is equivalent to the divinisation of Man. The appreciation that we are divinised by the completion and perfecting of our "Godlike" attributes of knowledge, freedom and understanding should help us to grasp how it was possible for one person to combine the human and the divine, to be at once fully God while remaining fully human.

These reflections gain in depth and relevance when we think of the words of one of the greatest theologians of the twentieth century, the Belgian Dominican Edward Schillebeeckx. For time and again Schillebeeckx emphasizes that Christ's humanity reveals divinity. In an interview given in 1982, he said, "We cannot approach God himself, except in Jesus, in all his humanity. We only need to look at him to know who God is. That is the meaning of what people call the incarnation of God in Jesus of Nazareth. We may have no conception of what God is, of what 'he' could be, but we do have some conception of who Jesus is. Therefore Jesus is God's countenance. By stressing the man Jesus you can have some conception of what God is and how he regards human beings. Without Jesus you cannot do that."[43] What is memorable about Schillebeeckx's statement here and elsewhere is his insistence that God is revealed in and through the *humanity* of "the man Jesus." Elsewhere he writes, "what is called in Christian faith the *divinity of Jesus* is located inside Jesus' humanity and not next to it or on the other side of it."[44] This insight of a great theologian—which is really saying little more than was said by Jesus as reported in Matthew 11: 26: "no one knows the Father except the Son and anyone to whom the Son chooses to reveal him" or in John 14: 10 "I am in the Father and the Father in me"—is clearly supported by the position being advocated here: that Jesus was divine and revealed who and what God is by virtue of being, in moral and spiritual terms, a perfect human being. I certainly cannot claim that Schillebeeckx supports the position I am putting forward, but I can say that someone who challenged him with the question, "How can we learn about God by attending to Jesus's humanity?" could find an answer in these pages.

The language of perfection, which we saw to be the language used in the OT about God, is also the language used in the NT about Christ. The Hebrew word for "perfect"—*tom*—refers to one who has kept his integrity and is in this way like God. So at the start of the Book of Job, Job is described as a "perfect and upright man"; here "perfect" indicates blamelessness, being without blemish, and refers to someone who is lacking in duplicity or deceit. In the NT, the Greek word for "perfect"—*teleios*—also means complete, finished and when used of a person means "adult" or "mature." So in 1 Corinthians (14:20), Paul urges his listeners, "Do not be children in your thinking; be babes in evil, but in thinking mature (*teleioi*)." And the model for maturity is Christ, as Paul indicates when he tells the Ephesians that the gifts of Christ are "for building up the Body of Christ, until we all attain to the unity of the faith and of the knowledge of the Son of God, to mature manhood, to the measure of the stature of the fullness of Christ; so that we may no longer be children, tossed to and fro and carried about with every wind of doctrine..." (Eph. 4: 11-14).

In Hebrews 5: 14 there is a striking image of maturity that links directly to a central theme of this book. The author complains that his Jewish audience have become "dull of hearing" and are not ready to understand his explanation of what he means when he describes Jesus as "being made perfect" so that "he became the source of salvation," adding that "though by this time you ought to be teachers, you need someone to teach you again the first principles of God's word. You need milk, not solid food; for everyone who lives on milk is unskilled in the word of righteousness, for he is a child. But solid food is for the mature (*teleion*), for those who have their faculties trained by practice to distinguish good from evil." This reference back to knowledge of good and evil suggests that this is knowledge that needs to be acquired, developed and refined over time, not a once and for all gift or acquisition; its proper use requires regular practice, resulting in growth and maturation. The author of Hebrews is suggesting here that maturation, growing in perfection, is the work of history, of time, taking forward what the OT reveals about the covenant and its purpose. This notion of maturation and spiritual growth is pervasive in the thinking of St Paul, who tells the Philippians: "And it is my prayer that your love may abound more and more, with knowledge and all discernment, so that you may approve what is excellent, and may be pure and blameless for the day of Christ, filled with the fruits of righteousness which come through Jesus Christ, to the glory and praise of God." (Philippians 1: 9-11) The ability to discern between good and evil links back to the central event of Genesis 3 and, when cultivated and developed over time, is seen to be a mark of maturity and spiritual perfection.

One might also ask if the development of this ability would be so lauded as an indicator of spiritual maturity if, as Augustine believed, Man's acquisition of the power to exercise it was a heinous crime against God! Time and again Man's acquisition of the *knowledge of good and evil* is held up by followers of Augustine as an excuse for accusing Man of pride, of attempting to "play God" by determining for himself what is good and bad. Thomas Aquinas, for example, acknowledging his debt to Augustine on this question, claimed that the principal element in Man's "original sin" was in seeking to be like God precisely by determining for himself which actions were good and which bad (*ut scilicet per virtutem propriae naturae determinaret sibi quid esset bonum et quid malum ad agendum.*)[45] Aquinas's judgment here has been regulative for Catholic commentary on this phrase down through the centuries and has also carried weight beyond the boundaries of traditional Catholicism. However, in this book that interpretation of the meaning of the phrase will be shown to be a complete travesty. What is clear from the other scriptural references to "knowing good and evil"—to be explored in Chapter Six— is that such knowledge is a positive acquisition, the indicator of wisdom, the mark of mature adulthood; it is not something that distances Man from God but, on the contrary, something that, under God, can draw Man closer to him. "Behold, the man has become like one of us, knowing good and evil..."—this statement by the Lord God is not said in any spirit of condemnation or even irony, but is part of a sober, calculated judgment delivered with solemnity at the end of chapter 3 of Genesis, a statement of the literal truth. Man is now divine in a way that was not the case before he ate from the fruit of the tree of knowledge. He is also human for exactly the same reason, and human because he is divine.

The vocabulary of the Christian era harks back to the vocabulary and conceptual scheme of more primitive Hebrew thought, conveying the message of Christ as complete, mature, holy, through whom the Christian reaches up to the holiness of God himself. (As Paul says in Romans 8:26-27, the Spirit of Christ intercedes for us according to the will of God even if we do not know how we ought to pray!) The references to "perfect" and "perfection" in the Christian scriptures take forward the notion of perfection found in ancient Israelite thought, suggesting Christ as the means by which the Christian will achieve completeness and thus make up for what has been missing in his human nature up till that point.

In the NT, we find three notions that come together: God as perfect; Jesus as the perfect man; the Christian who is urged to "put on Christ Jesus" (Romans 13:14), to be perfect in and through Jesus. In the NT, the word "perfect" (*teleios*) appears to have a greater developmental element, to include the idea of becoming or growing to perfection; one becomes more like Christ over time and in this way more like God. In the Christian era Christ emerges as the one through and in whom, by the power of his Spirit, we are purified of our human imperfections, divinised, reconciled with the Father, and drawn into the Trinitarian life of God.

The modern Christian thinker who has perhaps best expressed these ideas is Dietrich Bonhoeffer through his notion of *Gestaltung* (restructuring, metamorphosis, conversion). Commenting on this idea, Vivienne Blackburn writes:

> If we respond to Christ and allow *Gestaltung* to take place within us, we find our true humanity. We become the creatures of God we really are...The metamorphosis of grace allows the Christian to act in the service of others. It brings freedom: "Not chained by principles, but bound by love for God, he is freed from the problems and conflicts of ethical decision-making." It brings the capacity to see people as they really are, not as members of sects or races, to avoid the temptation either to denigrate or to hero-worship others.[46]

Bernard Lonergan also comments on the notion of conversion in a way that is pertinent to a developing topic of this book, by linking conversion to consciousness, and precisely to what he calls the fourth level of consciousness, the "existential level" that goes beyond thinking and reasoning (though it does not leave these behind) and is concerned with the more self-conscious activities of deliberating, evaluating, controlling, choosing, deciding and acting: the level of consciousness at which the self is most sharply at stake; in short, consciousness as conscience. He then adds,

> But it is this type of consciousness at its root, as brought to fulfilment, as having undergone conversion, as possessing a basis that may be broadened and deepened and heightened and enriched but not superseded, as ever more ready to deliberate and evaluate and decide and act with the easy freedom of those that do all good because they are in love. The gift of God's love takes over the ground and root of the fourth level

of man's waking consciousness. It takes over the peak of the soul, the *apex animae.*[47]

The doctrine of the two natures of Christ—the traditional, orthodox Christian understanding of who Christ was—reaches back to Genesis 3 and the human acquisition of the divine attribute of knowledge. The interpretation of this doctrine put forward here has the merit of bringing the Christ revealed in the gospels into contact with the Adam who features in some of the earliest writings in the bible. The division between God and Man is overcome in Christ, who is both God and Man. In the gospel of John, Jesus self-consciously claims to be the replacement of the temple in Jerusalem and the inner sanctum of the temple, the Holy of Holies, where God was present among his people: he presents himself, his body and person, as the new locus in which God now dwells on earth, as the new meeting place of God and Man. (Jn 2: 18-22)[48] What is more, by means of the notion of "perfection" or "being made perfect" we can begin to see how Christ's relationship to the rest of humanity is one of bringing it to perfection and in this way of divinising humanity and overcoming the anomalous "transitional" situation humanity found itself in at the end of Genesis 3. There is surely here the basis for the development of an accessible and orthodox doctrine of redemption and atonement, as well as of much besides. And we are not talking at the level of doctrine merely; if we look to history, on this interpretation Christ can be seen as the completion of the great mythical covenant with Noah and of the great historical covenant between Yahweh and Moses. In and through him, God and humanity meet and division is overcome.

DIVINISATION AND THE SPIRIT

One of the principal ways in which the divinity of Jesus is conveyed in the NT is by revealing him as one filled with the Spirit of God who, in turn, after the resurrection dispenses the Spirit or sends the Spirit to guide the Church and lead his followers to the truth (Jn 14: 26; 16: 13; 20: 22). In the infancy narrative in Matthew's gospel and in Luke, the conception of Jesus is attributed to the Holy Spirit, indicating that Jesus's mission on earth will be a highly significant part of God's mysterious plan of salvation; that Jesus's birth is a gift to humanity from God (Mt 1:18, 20; Luke 1: 34-35).[49] In all four gospels, but more particularly in Luke and John, the actions and words of Jesus are seen to be inspired or moved by the Spirit (see, for example, Luke 4:1), which is seen to be a power or force made manifest in Jesus's dominion over nature and his miraculous acts of healing and the like. In Acts the Spirit is a power inspiring the apostles and others to courageous, selfless action in proclaiming Jesus as the long-awaited saviour and in this way building up the early Church. (Acts 2:22; 3: 11ff) In Paul, in particular, the Spirit of God is affirmed as being uniquely present in Jesus, and specifically in the risen Jesus (Romans 1:3), and through the risen Lord the Spirit becomes a gift conferred on Christian believers (Romans 5:2 f), confirming them as "heirs of God and fellow heirs with Christ, provided we suffer with him in order that we may also be glorified with him." (Romans 8: 16f) So it is that the divinity of "the man Jesus" is manifested by the fact that the Spirit of God reigns in him; and the role of the Spirit in the divinisation of human beings, as presented in Paul's writings, is something that will be developed at greater length in Chapter Six.

NOTES

1. Mary Douglas, *Purity and Danger: An Analysis of the Concepts of Pollution and Taboo*, (London: Routledge, 1966).

2. B. Van Iersel, *The Bible on the Living God*, (London: Sheed and Ward, 1965); original Dutch publication 1962. Much of this section is indebted to this book, notably chapter 6.

3. On the Day of Atonement, *Yom Kippur.*

4. B. Van Iersel, op. cit., p. 50.

5. Ibid., p. 51: "Uncleanness here is the exact opposite of holiness; and this makes it easier for us to understand why ancient Israel put so much store by her purity laws. We often do not know the exact reason for holding certain objects and actions unclean; what is certain is that contact with them placed man in a sphere which was the very opposite of Yahweh's."

6. Mary Douglas, op. cit., pp. 55-56.

7. Ibid., p. 51-2.

8. Ibid., p. 54-5.

9. Ibid., p. 46-7.

10. Ibid., p. 46.

11. Ibid., p. 58.

12. Ibid., p. 96.

13. Mary Douglas, *Natural Symbols: explorations in cosmology*, (London: Cresset Press, 1970) p. 38.

14. Ibid., p. 114.

15. Ibid.

16. Ibid., p. 97.

17. Ibid.

18. Mary Douglas was a student and associate of E.E. Evans-Pritchard who in *Theories of Primitive Religion* (Oxford: Oxford University Press, 1965) is critical of various modern psychological and sociological theories put forward by anthropologists that attempt to explain how primitive people came by their irrational beliefs by attributing to them the steps by which they themselves might have come to entertain such beliefs. By contrast, Evans-Pritchard claims that primitive people reason intelligently from premises we consider absurd; but we can follow their reasoning and it is wrong to treat them as unintelligent. He approves of Levy-Bruhl's position of seeing religious beliefs as "meaningful when seen as parts of patterns of ideas and behaviour, each part having an intelligible relationship to the others" (86).

19. Ibid., p. 40.

20. Ibid., p. 39.

21. Ibid., p. 162; Mircea Eliade, *Patterns in Comparative Religion*, (London: Sheed & Ward, 1958).

22. It is, I trust, clear that the application of the adjective "primitive" to the ancient Hebrews implies no condescension; Robert Alter tends to suggest that the word carries such associations when applied to Hebrew literature (see, for example, his comments in *The World of Biblical Literature*, op. cit., pp. 21, 57, and elsewhere), but I think what he is objecting to is the categorisation as "primitive" of certain Hebrew literary forms such as genealogies, aetiological tales, laws and itineraries. He would surely not deny that in common with other tribes and peoples, at some point in their history the ancient Hebrews most probably employed "primitive" categories of thought, or that there is evidence of a primitive mentality or outlook in the prohibitions and abominations found in the Book of Leviticus, as analysed by Mary Douglas.

23. Robert Alter refers to the "rite of passage through water" to be found in the OT in op. cit., p. 79.

24. As Lonergan observes, consciousness is not only cognitive but is also constitutive. See Bernard Lonergan SJ, *Collection*, (London: Darton, Longman & Todd, 1967), edited by F.E. Crowe SJ, p. 176. Human beings are constituted by intellectual and rational consciousness.

25. John Ashton, *Studying John: Approaches to the Fourth Gospel*, (Oxford: Clarendon Paperbacks, 1998) p. 33.

26. Gabriel Daly O.S.A., *Creation and Redemption*, (Dublin: Gill and Macmillan, 1988) p. 116.

27. Gabriel Daly O.S.A., Ibid.

28. James Barr, op. cit., p. 84.

29. *The New Jerome Biblical Commentary*, edited by Raymond E. Brown, Joseph A. Fitzmyer and Roland E. Murphy (Englewood Cliffs: Prentice Hall, 1990) p. 14.

30. Gerald O'Collins S.J., "The Virginal Conception and Its Meanings," *New Blackfriars*, Vol 89 No 1022, July 2008, p. 432.

31. B. Van Iersel, op. cit., chapter 10.

32. John L. McKenzie, *Dictionary of the Bible*, (London: Geoffrey Chapman, 1965) p. 154; also, B. Van Iersel, op. cit., p. 96.

33. For the caution to be exercised whenever I talk of "history" in the context of the bible, see note 27 at end of previous chapter.

34. For an extended authoritative commentary on this, see L. William Countryman, *Dirt, Greed and Sex: Sexual Ethics in the New Testament and their Implications for Today* (London: SCM Press, 1988).

35. Ibid., p. 150ff, p. 176.

36. Ibid., p. 167.

37. Ibid., p. 168.

38. Ibid., p. 141.

39. See, for example, the passage in John 2: 14-22.

40. This is in complete accord with Aquinas who, in *Summa Theologiae* 1, 93.6, considers the image of God in Man to reside in his possession of mind: "In sola creatura rationali invenitur similitudo Dei per modum imaginis..."

41. Once more, Lonergan is probably the thinker who has contributed most to our understanding of Man's conscious operations of thinking, knowing, deciding and acting etc. : see his work *Insight: a Study of Human Understanding* (London: Longman, Green and Co, 1957), and Vol 3 of *Collected Works of Bernard Lonergan*, (Toronto: University of Toronto Press, 1992). Lonergan beautifully relates these activities to different levels of human consciousness: see Chapter One of Lonergan's *Method in Theology* (op. cit.) as well as my book, *Philosophical Encounters: Lonergan and the Analytical Tradition*, op. cit., p. 215.

42. Charles C. Hefling Jr, "Lonergan on Christ's Satisfaction," *Method: Journal of Lonergan Studies*, Vol. 10, No 1, Spring 1992, p. 54.

43. Quoted in *Edward Schillebeeckx: Portrait of a Theologian* by John Bowden (London: SCM 1983) p. 96. In a footnote, the author says that Schillebeeckx has made the same point many times.

44. Edward Schillebeeckx, "God the Living One," *New Blackfriars*, Vol 62 No 735, September 1981, p. 364. What the Belgian theologian is contesting here is the idea that "religious" salvation history runs parallel to or alongside the "secular" history of human liberation and emancipation; rather, he holds for them being one and the same.

45. *Summa Theologiae* 2-2. 163, 2.

46. Vivienne Blackburn, *Dietrich Bonhoeffer and Simone Weil: A Study in Christian Responsiveness*, (Bern: Peter Lang, 2004) p. 98. The quotation from Bonhoeffer is from *Ethik als Gestaltung*.

47. Bernard Lonergan SJ, *A Second Collection*, (London: Darton, Longman and Todd, 1974) p. 173.

48. The scene where Jesus does this gains in force and significance from being placed by the gospel writer at the outset of Jesus's public ministry.

49. Gerald O'Collins SJ, op. cit., p. 439.

Chapter Four
The Quest for Immortality

The literature of the ancient Near East together with the Egyptian pyramids, the custom of mummification and the elaborate tombs of the pharaohs in the "Valley of the Kings" on the west bank of the Nile testify to early Near Eastern Man's preoccupation with the possibility of escaping death and so living for ever. This aspiration was not peculiar to the people of the Near East but occurred all over the ancient world, as modern archaeological findings have revealed, most notably perhaps in the form of the vast terra cotta army, comprising about 7,000 soldiers, created to mark the death of the first Emperor of China, Shi Huang Di. But it was the Egyptian experience that would have been best known to the ancient Hebrews, whose forefathers were most probably involved in the construction of the vast pyramids. The Hebrew conception of God, which we dwelt on in the last two chapters, would have made such efforts by humans to guarantee safe passage to a prosperous and pleasurable afterlife appear blasphemous, an intrusion on the prerogative of Yahweh, the Holy one, who alone was immortal. It is possible to see the story in Genesis 3 as a Hebrew response to the ridiculously proud (in the eyes of the Israelites) aspirations entertained by the powerful and prosperous Egyptian kings.

Northrop Frye is one of several authors who have interpreted Genesis 3 as a story about the human quest for immortality: "The story of the fall of man in Genesis seems originally to have been one of the sardonic folktales of the Near East that explain how man once had immortality nearly within his grasp, but was cheated out of it by frightened or malicious deities."[1] Frye here seems to be assimilating the Genesis tale to others found in ancient literature, which portray humanity's loss at the dawn of time of the gift of immortality brought about by malice, negligence or inept fumbling, and in so doing taking his lead from the interpretation of Genesis 3 put forward by Sir James Frazer in his *Folklore in the Old Testament*.[2]

Frazer, who adopted the "comparative method" in Old Testament studies, regarded the tale told in Genesis 3 as one among many such mythological tales about Man's quest for immortality. In his treatment of the Genesis account, he feels himself free to take great liberties with the text that has come down to us. First, he expresses surprise that the tree of knowledge stands at the centre of the tale and the tree of life appears to be ignored.[3] He puts forward the view that there were previously two stories of the fall, one featuring the tree of knowledge and one the tree of life, which were put together unskilfully.[4] He speculates further that in the earlier version, the tree of life (and hence immortality) was open to Man but Man chose to disobey God and to eat from the forbidden tree of knowledge, and so he died—Man lost immortality through his own carelessness, by making the wrong choice. Instead immortality was achieved by the snake which, Frazer suggests, did eat from the tree of life. He attempts to bolster this rather free interpretation of the text by reporting many stories from other cultures of Man almost attaining immortality but losing it through a perversion of the message or some other disaster.[5] Frazer is not interested in the way that Genesis 3 fits or fails to fit with the rest of the bible or even with the rest of Genesis 1-11; he seems smitten with his own comparative approach and treats the Genesis tale as but one specimen of a whole genre of "immortality tales" to be found in various cultures—hence the freedom he takes in imposing on Genesis the features of the immortality tales he has found elsewhere. The possibility that the Genesis story might be *interestingly different* from these other stories is not a hypothesis he is willing to entertain.

Apart from his slur on the literary skills of the Yahwist authors of Genesis 3, Frazer's most daring and glaring comment is his suggestion that the snake ate from the tree of life. He is aware that this amounts to a re-writing of the text as we have it, commenting a little later on "the silence of the narrator as to the eating of the fruit of the tree of life by the serpent and the consequent attainment of immortality by the reptile."[6] However, he remains undaunted and concludes triumphantly with the observation that commentators have looked "in vain for the part that should have been played in the narrative by the tree of life" and expresses the hope that through "the comparative method" he has supplied "the blank in the canvas."[7]

No biblical commentator today takes seriously Frazer's interpretation—or rather his radical reconstruction of the Genesis text. But the theme of immortality is nevertheless a central component of the Genesis tale and the tree of life is an important image, one that Augustine tends to overlook; indeed, Augustine's interpretation is amazing for the scant attention it gives to the speech put into the mouth of the Lord God at the end of chapter 3 of Genesis, which must be considered the most authoritative *biblical* commentary we have on the meaning of the events described earlier in that chapter. Augustine's stance on immortality is that it would have been Man's if he had not sinned and lost it. But in the tale immortality is not presented as something that Man *loses*, either through some supposed sin or some kind of Frazerian bad judgement or carelessness. Rather immortality is something that the Lord God very deliberately *prevents* him from acquiring: "'Behold, the man has become like one of us, knowing good and evil; and now lest he put forth his hand and take also of the tree of life, and eat, and live for ever'—therefore the Lord God sent him forth from the garden of Eden...."

THE EPIC OF GILGAMESH

Frazer appears to want to impose on Genesis 3 the imagery and story pattern that we encounter in ancient literature, such as in the great Babylonian poem, *The Epic of Gilgamesh*. The oldest epic poem in existence, written in cuneiform script on clay tablets and ante-dating the Book of Genesis, *Gilgamesh* recounts the exploits of the eponymous hero and his friend and fellow warrior Enkidu and is widely considered to have been a major influence on the Genesis tale, referring as it does to a flood, a saving ark, a snake and the tree of life. One can see why Frazer was tempted to assimilate the Genesis tale to *Gilgamesh* for these and other features of the *Gilgamesh* poem bear a truly remarkable resemblance to the Genesis story.

For example, the account of the great flood in *Gilgamesh* shows many similarities to the account of the flood in Genesis.[8] In *Gilgamesh*, the flood is willed by a god, Enlil, the god of the earth and air. But Ea, god of water and wisdom, tells the human male character, Utnapishtim, to build a boat or ark, complete with a roof so that it will let in no water, and fill it with provisions and seeds in order to survive the flood. He promises to confer great gifts on him and his people once the flood has subsided. Utnapishtim, the only mortal to discover the secret of eternal life, tells King Gilgamesh how he fashioned the ark from wood, covering the hull with pitch, and gives precise details of the ark's design. The savagery of the storm while it rages and Utnapishtim's relief and joy when it appears to be ending are vividly described. When the storm abates, the ark comes to rest on Mount Nimush and Utnapishtim sends out a bird to see if it might find dry land, but the bird returns exhausted; this is repeated before Utnapishtim sends out a raven that flies off, finds food and has no need to return to the ark. The similarities between the *Gilgamesh* account of a great flood and that to be found in Genesis 6-9 are too close and too detailed to be coincidental. Without any doubt, the *Gilgamesh* flood story shares many of the features of the story of "Noah's Flood" in Genesis.

The resemblance of the story of the flood in *Gilgamesh* to that of the flood in Genesis has often been remarked upon. Less remarked upon but of much greater importance for my argument in this book is the story of the *humanising* of King Gilgamesh's warrior companion, Enkidu, and its similarities with the story of Adam and Eve in Genesis 3. Before he is civilised, Enkidu lives at one with the wild beasts, eats grass and drinks "from the watery holes of herds."[9] Then, after making love to the temple priestess, Shamhat, who deliberately sets out to seduce him, he becomes human and the other animals flee from him. Shamhat, a sacred prostitute and priestess of Ishtar, the goddess of love and sexuality, tells Enkidu, "Now you are as if a god, with no more need of dumb beasts, however fair." She clothes him and he begins to "learn new human ways."[10] In the poem, the seduction of Enkidu by Shamhat is carefully plotted and planned. The method by which Enkidu will be sexually seduced, humanised and distanced from the other animals is spelt out in virtually the same words, first, to the "hunter" by his father, and then again by King Gilgamesh himself.[11] The reason for the creation and humanising of Enkidu is also made clear by the chief of the gods, Anu, who gives strict instructions to Aruru, goddess of creation, concerning the kind of human being Enkidu must be if he is to become a fit companion for King Gilgamesh.[12] Gilgamesh himself is notified of Enkidu's imminent arrival in dreams that his mother, the wise goddess Ninsun, interprets for him, reassuring him that Enkidu will be powerful and strong like himself and will be his intimate friend and companion.[13] There is nothing accidental in the creation and humanising of Enkidu—both are the result of careful deliberation and planning, and the information communicated by the narrative means that the reader's expectations have been formed before Enkidu encounters Shamhat. It is this quality of explicitness, the fact that so much surrounding the creation and humanising of Enkidu is openly articulated, that enables the *Gilgamesh* poem to help us gain a handle on the typically more cryptic tale told in Genesis 3.[14] Provided there are enough similarities of a striking kind—similarities that could not be mere coincidence but are the result of copying or of using a common source—between the Babylonian epic and the story in Genesis 3, then we might look to the epic poem for a clue as to the *precise literary genre* of the Genesis story, and this in turn should show us how we ought to read this story.

Many of the features of Genesis 3, as interpreted in this book, are here: the hominid "animal" Enkidu becomes fully human following an unexpected seduction and a symbolic initiation and in doing so is differentiated from the other animals, who now fear him; upon being made human, he is told that he has become godlike; he begins to wear clothes and to become civilised. The close similarities between this episode in *Gilgamesh* and the story of Adam and Eve recounted in Genesis 3 provide further evidence, if any were needed, that the Genesis story is a work of the human imagination and cannot possibly be taken as an account of an historical event.

What is more, the *primitive mindset* that can be found to underly the story of Enkidu's ascent or elevation from the animal state to the human state appears to be similar to the mindset found in Genesis. For Babylonian religion consisted largely of nature worship, especially of the forces of fertility and sexuality.[15] The sexual seduction of Enkidu by Shamhat, the priestess of Ishtar, goddess of sexuality, represented Enkidu's crossing of a line separating the earthly realm from the world of the gods, a contact by this proto-human animal with the divine powers controlling fertility in nature, a kind of communion with or participation in the divine. In the translation used here, Shamhat is referred to as "The dispenser of Ishtar's sacrament."[16] It is this sacramental act of communion, the crossing of the line separating the gods from the created realm by Enkidu, that leads to his transformation. He becomes human by coming to share in divinity and it is in this way that he is made the equal of King Gilgamesh,[17] a human figure whose mother is a goddess. As in the Genesis tale, the result is a somewhat intermediate creature, neither mere animal nor god. The animals have their contentment, this episode seems to be suggesting, and the gods have their immortality; Man alone is an intermediate hybrid whose angst and suffering stem from the fact that he is neither quite one thing nor the other. So while Enkidu has been human-ised and civilised, something is still lacking. According to the *Gilgamesh* epic, that something is immortality. Enkidu has been humanised by be-coming like a god, but the gods have withheld from him the gift of im-mortality. Following Enkidu's death, King Gilgamesh is determined to put right what he perceives to be an affront to his friend and himself and to acquire immortality for himself, and the overriding theme of the rest of the poem is the king's quest for eternal life.

The death of Enkidu plunges Gilgamesh into profound, uncontrolla-ble grief. Addressing his dying friend, he asks:

> Why should you be so condemned and why should
> I go on living?
> Will my own sad eyes soon never look on you again?

Tablets IX-XI describe the long and hazardous journey Gilgamesh un-dertakes to find the secret of eternal life. Resolute and undeterred by the dangers he encounters, the distraught Gilgamesh seeks to locate Utnap-ishtim, who along with his wife is the only human to survive the Great Flood. Throughout the journey he is obsessed with the death of his boon companion and *alter ego*, Enkidu:

> I roam the lonely path with death upon my mind
> And think of nothing but my dear friend.
> Over many seas and across many mountains I roam.
> I can't stop pacing. I can't stop crying.
> My friend has died and half my heart is torn from me.[18]

In an "Appreciation" of *Gilgamesh*, the literary scholar, James G. Keenan, considers the episode following the death of Enkidu to be like a rite of passage: "On his harrowing journey, itself a dreamlike 'liminal experience,' Gilgamesh experiences the kinds of disorientation and suf-fering that typify rites of passage described years ago by Arnold van Gennep (*The Rites of Passage*) and more recently by Victor Turner (*The Ritual Process*). He no longer looks kinglike; he becomes worn and hag-gard, even frightening to behold."[19] This gives support to the view ar-gued for in this work that the period following Genesis 3, the interlude comprising chapters 4-8 of Genesis, is in fact the dangerous middle pe-riod typical of rites of passage. During this interim period Man is out of control, disorientated and dangerous; it is a period of time when "violence fills the earth" and God considers wiping out human beings and all of his creation, a situation that is brought to a close by the Flood and the restoration of a new order by means of the covenant.

The following table, consisting of numbered incidents drawn respectively from *Gilgamesh* and Genesis, illustrates some of the *similarities* between the two works; I refer first to similarities in the creation stories in order to provide a broad context before moving on to similarities in the accounts of the humanising of Enkidu in *Gilgamesh* and the humanising of the man and the woman in Genesis, which is my main interest:

Epic of Gilgamesh	**Genesis**
1. Enkidu is created from the clay of the earth; he is created in the image of Ninurta, god of war and agriculture. He is created to become the boon companion of Gilgamesh, and like Gilgamesh he is in part divine.	1. Man is created in the image of God; he is fashioned from the dust of the ground and God breathes his spirit into him. The purpose of his creation is not made clear but both of the creation stories in Genesis suggest a strong bond of intimacy between God and humanity.
2. Enkidu is tempted by the temple love-priestess Shamhat who, in accordance with the previously announced plan, displays her physical charms before him.	2. The woman is tempted by the snake which promises her knowledge like that of God.
3. Enkidu makes love (for a whole week!) to Shamhat, "the dispenser of Ishtar's sacrament."	3. The man follows the woman in eating from the tree of knowledge of good and evil (knowledge being primarily an attribute of God).
4. Following their love-making, Enkidu is covered with some of Shamhat's clothes.	4. After eating from the tree, the couple cover themselves with aprons made from figleaves because they are suddenly ashamed of being naked.

5. Enkidu is described by Shamhat as being "like a god."	5. The Lord God says that the human couple have become "like one of us."
6. Enkidu begins to learn "new human ways"; he has "turned into a man"; "he became like a human being./ He put on a garment,/And now he is like a man."[20]	6. Nothing quite as explicit, but God makes clothes for the couple, shortly to be named Adam and Eve.
7. Enkidu's former companions, the other animals, now fear him and flee from him.	7. The other animals now fear and dread humans (Genesis 9: 2).
8. Despite being godlike, Enkidu dies—the gods withhold immortality from him, keeping it for themselves.	8. God prevents Adam and Eve gaining access to the second tree in case "they take also from the tree of life, and eat, and live forever"; he banishes them from Eden.
9. Gilgamesh is plunged into mourning and embarks on his dangerous journey to find eternal life, an episode that resembles the dangerous interim period typical of a rite of passage.	9. The chapters that follow—Genesis 4-8—resemble the dangerous middle period described by van Gennep as typical of rites of passage. The earth is filled with violence and God thinks of wiping out humanity.
10. Gilgamesh sets out on his quest to acquire immortality for himself; the quest for immortality becomes the unifying theme of the poem.[21] He finally becomes reconciled to his mortality, acquires wisdom, and his rite of passage is complete.	10. The Flood does away with the old order and inaugurates a new creation; the rite of passage is complete. God forms a covenant with human beings, through which they can learn how to live wisely in their new state. The tree of life remains at the centre of the garden.

Although there are obvious differences between these episodes in *Gilgamesh* and the story in Genesis 3, which I shall shortly explore, there are clear similarities in respect of thematic content and narrative structure. The similarities in thematic content are those mentioned in the numbered boxes (temptation, the wearing of clothes, becoming godlike etc.), while the similarities in narrative structure refer to the order of events and the causal connections between them. In terms of narrative structure, both episodes *begin* with temptation scenes and *end* with some kind of resolution of their characters' quest for eternal life; and both episodes *turn on* a central event which has a transforming effect on the main protagonists—a transformation effected by something akin to a deeply symbolic or sacramental act whereby a hominid creature partakes of the godhead and becomes fully human. This is very explicitly stated in *Gilgamesh*, more obliquely implied by the Yahwist authors of Genesis 3, where the clue to the change that has come about is suggested by the couple's wearing of clothes immediately after the act of eating, since the wearing of clothes was something that clearly demarcated humans from the other animals. In view of these various resemblances, there is strong evidence that the episode of Enkidu and Shamhat in Gilgamesh is the model for the story of Adam and Eve in Genesis 3 (although Enkidu and Shamhat are never treated as a "couple"), while the episode of Gilgamesh's nightmarish journey resembles Genesis 4-8 in being typical of the second of the three stages that make up a rite of passage.

RITES OF PASSAGE: *GILGAMESH* AND GENESIS

It is this last point that suggests the most important lesson we can learn from a comparison of *Gilgamesh* with the Genesis 3 story. For, as James Keenan observes, *Gilgamesh* is, at least in part, about a rite of passage. If we examine the structure of the *Gilgmesh* poem, we can see how it resembles the three stages that van Gennep considers to be typical of rites of passage: there is, first, the disruption caused by some personal or social trauma—in this case, the terrible pain and loss suffered by King Gilgamesh upon the death of his close friend, Enkidu. This is followed by Gilgamesh's brutal confrontation with the horror of death, his prolonged lamentations for his friend and his frantic, perilous journey to meet Utnapishtim, from whom he wishes to learn the secret of eternal life—as we have seen, this episode corresponds to the second, dangerous period, a period of disorientation and flux, the state of being "betwixt and between" typical of rites of passage. The third stage in the rite of passage is Gilgamesh's resignation and wise acceptance that only the gods are immortal and that humans, even great kings like himself, must reconcile themselves to living a good and enjoyable life here on earth.

In a previous section, I indicated how the early chapters of Genesis also conform to the pattern of a rite of passage, as the proto-human couple move from an original state of innocence and dependence to one, following their fateful crossing of the line separating the created order from the divine symbolised by their eating from the tree of knowledge, where they achieve a measure of autonomy and independence by becoming human; chapters 4-8 of Genesis correspond to the dangerous middle period of such a passage, as Man abuses his new-found autonomy and relative independence from God, a period we are told when "violence fills the earth" and God is inclined to wipe out humankind; then the episode of the Flood, representing the third and final stage, does away with the old order and gives birth to a new creation, and the covenant introduced by God initiates a wholly new relationship between God and Man. The lesson to be learned from this comparison of *Gilgamesh* with the early chapters of Genesis is that it suggests and supports the view that Genesis 3 ought to be read not as some kind of morality tale but as the story of a rite of passage. To apply the calculus of moral reasoning—a form of reasoning that developed relatively late among the Hebrews[22]—to the story of Adam and Eve in Eden is seriously to miss the point. The Hebrew authors of Genesis in this primitive period of their history[23] were not moralists or moralisers but storytellers[24] with a keen sense of the boundary separating the divine from the created realm. The prohibition against eating from the tree of knowledge (Gen 2:17) should be seen as part of the mechanics of the plot: it indicates and marks out what was part of the natural order—the trees providing the couple with food (Gen 2:16)—and what was strictly God's and, therefore, out of bounds—the two trees, of knowledge and of life respectively, in the middle of the garden. For the ancient Hebrews, knowledge and life were primarily attributes of God. The divine prohibition serves to demarcate the natural and the supernatural.

The Genesis text demands to be read as the tale of a rite of passage and the point of interest in such a tale is not the rightness or wrongness of certain deeds but the *transformation* that takes place in the character or characters involved. Rites of passage are about change, transformation, metamorphosis and it is this central feature of the Adam and Eve story—the radical change brought about through the symbolic act of crossing the divide between the created and the divine realm by eating from the tree of knowledge—that should capture and retain our interest—not the notions of wrongdoing, sin and the so-called Fall of Man. The story of Adam and Eve is the beginning of the story of Man's transformation and divinisation: as the Lord God says, "Behold the man has become like one of us, knowing good and evil." (Gen 3:22) To view the story in Genesis 3 through the lens of the *Gilgamesh* epic is to see it aright and to correct our modern tendency to read the story as a moral tale, a tale of sinful disobedience. The striking fact that both *Gilgamesh* and Genesis 3 are, at heart, about the humanisation, or hominisation, of proto-human creatures should teach us that, like *Gilgamesh*, Genesis 3 is not a morality tale but the story of a rite of passage. Once we have grasped that fact it becomes much easier to see how the third chapter of Genesis is an organic part of the literary unit of Genesis 1-9; for we can see how Genesis 3 relates back to Genesis 1-2 (the stage of innocence) and forward to Genesis 4-8 (the dangerous interlude) and then to Genesis 9 (the third stage of resolution or denouement).

THE NEGLECT OF THE *GILGAMESH* CONNECTION WITH GENESIS 3

A question that arises naturally at this point is why the influence of *Gilgamesh* on the Adam and Eve story in Genesis 3 has not received more recognition in the past, especially when compared with the shock and publicity in England that greeted the revelation in 1872 of the striking similarity between the flood episode in *Gilgamesh* Tablet XI and "Noah's flood" in Genesis 6-8.[25] When the brilliant young scholar, George Smith, who worked at the British Museum in London, announced that year that he had deciphered a fragment of a clay tablet unearthed in the ancient Mesopotamian site of Nineveh that told of a great flood containing many of the features of the great biblical flood known to every English schoolboy, there was a such a hullabaloo that he was invited to set out his findings at a public lecture attended by the Prime Minister, William Gladstone, and other notables. Coming just over a decade after the publication of Darwin's great work, *On the Origin of Species*, Smith's findings raised yet more questions in the minds of nineteenth century English men and women concerning the authority and historicity of the bible, so much so that the *Daily Telegraph* provided the funds for Smith to return to Nineveh to find other parts of the tablet. When Smith announced that he had found another fragment about the flood, the newspaper decided that his mission had been successfully completed and he was asked to return to England. In fact, we now know that the fragment Smith had come across was not from *Gilgamesh* but related to a flood story in an earlier Mesopotamian text known as the poem of *Atrahasis*, which was found to be a major influence on Genesis 1-11. Since those days, scholars have established that wholesale copying or borrowing from previously existing texts was commonplace among ancient Near Eastern storytellers.[26] This last point indicates part of the answer that can be given to the question: why have the parallels between *Gilgamesh* and Genesis 3 not received anything like the attention surrounding those between the flood story in *Gilgamesh* and the flood story in Genesis 6-8?

My answer to this question consists of three parts. The first part of the answer is to point to the fact that the similarities between the two flood stories are much more obvious; they lie on the surface of both accounts, we might say, since both are patently about a flood. By contrast, the similarities between the *Gilgamesh* episode involving Enkidu and Shamhat and the event described in Genesis 3 are much less obvious, since one episode is about a prolonged session of love-making and the other apparently concerns a couple eating forbidden fruit. Likewise, the similarities between the episode of Gilgamesh's journey in search of the tree of life and Genesis 4-8 are not immediately apparent. It is only when we go below the surface of the two tales and (a), see that the actions of Shamhat and Enkidu in the one and of the man and the woman in the other have deep symbolic significance and, in addition, that each is tied to a range of common features such as temptation, becoming godlike, wearing clothes etc.; and (b), note that the episode of Gilgamesh's journey in search of Utnapishtim and eternal life has the same quality of "liminality" and disorientation as the events described in Genesis 4-8—it is only when we grasp these narrative and structural features that lie below the surface that the similarities between these events in the two tales begin to emerge. A second part of my answer would be to point to the custom, just noted, among ancient Near Eastern storytellers of using older texts as models or templates for other later stories. This is most vividly seen in the use made by *Gilgamesh* of an older text, the Old Babylonian poem of *Atrahasis*, in its account of the flood; this same text then provided the model for the account of "Noah's Flood" in Genesis 6-8. Given this Near Eastern tradition of imitation or copying, it is not difficult to see how so many of the features of the Enkidu-Shamhat encounter in *Gilgamesh* caught the attention of the biblical story tellers, who followed precedent by incorporating them in their tale *while making allowances for fundamental differences in outlook between the religious culture of the Babylonians and that of the Israelites.* In doing this, the biblical authors were simply following the example of the Babylonian authors of *Gilgamesh* themselves, who took various stories stemming from earlier Sumerian sources and wove them into one continuous story while adapting them to their own views and beliefs.[27]

The third part of my answer to the question that has been raised (Why has the connection between *Gilgamesh* and Genesis 3 not been clearly identified before?) would be to point out that the description in *Gilgamesh* of Enkidu and Shamhat making love is very explicit, protracted and highly erotic, and this has probably been sufficient to blind some Christian commentators to a possible parallel with anything in the bible. For example, Alexander Heidel in his well known book, *The Gilgamesh Epic and Old Testament Parallels*, draws many parallels between the Babylonian work and the Old Testament in respect of beliefs about the afterlife and the episode of the Flood, but fails completely to mention any resemblance between the huminisation of Enkidu and the episode described in Genesis 3; indeed, Heidel subscribes completely to the traditional, Augustinian interpretation of Genesis 3.[28] However, although his work is admirable in many ways, Heidel was a relatively early commentator who found the erotic scenes in *Gilgamesh* so distasteful that in his own English translation, published in 1946, he switched to Latin for what he referred to as "the more objectionable passages"[29] (presumably on the principle that this would prevent schoolboys being corrupted by the descriptions of the couple's love-making unless they were willing to work assiduously on their Latin and improve it in the process!) It is not surprising that he failed to see any parallel between the Enkidu-Shamhat encounter and the story in Genesis 3.[30]

THE DISTINCTIVENESS OF GENESIS

The use of source material in creative art is one thing and plagiarism is another, and the story in Genesis 3 has not been plagiarised. Indeed, plagiarism would have been unlikely because the ancient Hebrews held radically different religious views from the Babylonians and were deeply opposed to the values and beliefs of their polytheistic neighbours. While the Babylonians were in many respects—certainly militarily and technologically—superior to the Hebrews, in the field of religion the Hebrews looked down on them as inferior idol-worshippers. This explains the differences between the two stories: if *Gilgamesh* is a major influence on

Genesis, it would appear that the Yahwist story tellers wished to adapt their materials to their own quite different ends. As Alexander Heidel remarks of the similarities between the Babylonian and the Hebrew accounts of the flood: "The skeleton is the same in both cases, but the flesh and blood and, above all, the animating spirit are different. It is here that we meet the most far-reaching divergencies between the Hebrew and the Mesopotamian stories."[31] For example, it is significant that in the Hebrew myth Man is not initiated into full and recognisable humanity by becoming godlike through some sexual encounter with a sacred prostitute, but by eating from the tree of knowledge: knowledge, or wisdom, rather than control of fertility in nature, was one of the outstanding characteristics of the Hebrew God, who was the Lord of history. In addition, the snake in *Gilgamesh* is not the cunning tempter of Genesis (that role is played by Shamhat, the temple love-priestess); rather the snake, attracted by its pleasant odour to the tree of life while a relaxed Gilgamesh is bathing, swallows the magic plant and in this way deprives humanity of immortality and, by good fortune, gains for itself the power of eternal youth, shedding its skin each year and acquiring a new one.

Genesis proposes a totally different solution to the quest for eternal life that King Gilgamesh is relentlessly engaged in—a quest presented in the poem as at once heroic but tragically doomed to failure. In the Genesis tale, Man does not *lose* eternal life but is *deliberately prevented by God* from achieving access to the tree of life. There is no tragic accident in Genesis; no snake comes along to swallow a magic plant. God is the Lord of history and firmly in control of events. Following the dissolution of the old and the inauguration of the new world order by means of the Flood, Man's hope of achieving eternal life in time is opened up through the covenant God proposes to Noah, which is to be exemplified historically in the covenants with Abraham, Moses and, Christians believe, definitively and finally with Jesus. The divine plan is not about undoing what Adam did but about bringing what Adam started to fruition by enabling the incomplete species to achieve completion through union with God. For the Israelites, union with God brought with it the gift of eternal life.

Another obvious difference between Genesis and *Gilgamesh* is that Enkidu is single, whereas Adam and Eve are a couple; this is significant, since it points to the fact that Adam and Eve, though not yet named, are presented as the very first human beings in existence, the progenitors of the human race, whereas Enkidu is not presented as the first human being nor as the first of many; indeed, by means of his encounter with

Shamhat Enkidu is initiated into a stable and established civilisation. The significance of the Genesis couple being the first humans is that the transformation they undergo is even more radical than the transformation experienced by the Babylonian hero. Enkidu moves from the life of a beast to that of a human being; what occurs is a transition or ascent from nature to civilisation through the agency of "a female representative of extreme urban Culture."[32] In the case of the Genesis story, the transition, which involves the first human couple and all of their descendants, is from nature to history rather than from nature to civilisation, and while history brings with it the notions of culture and civilisation, it presumes an even more radical transformation, namely the acquisition of the knowledge and freedom and powers of reasoning required for the human couple and their descendants to be self-determining agents of change. The metamorphosis of the hominid couple in Genesis is much more radical than the transformation experienced by Enkidu. That is why the most basic transformation of the man and the woman in Genesis is from animal to human being, from innocent, obedient creatures to ones that are intelligent and free, who are beginning to enjoy a dangerous measure of autonomy. The authors of Genesis were careful to adapt the materials drawn from Babylonian sources to Israel's distinctive theological vision.

What is most distinctively different about the Genesis tale is its response to the question of death and immortality, a question that appears to have haunted the imagination of ancient peoples. The *Gilgamesh* poem, which was well known throughout the Near East, might be seen, like the immense pyramids and the opulent tombs of the pharaohs, as posing the question to which Genesis sets out to provide an answer. Following the death of Enkidu, the hero Gilgamesh spends his days searching for immortality, hoping and believing that it might be gained, rather like glory in battle, through acts of great heroism or through a combination of human endeavour and deep cunning. It is the gentle Siduri, the divine barmaid—"She whose drinks refresh the soul"—who tells him why his quest is in vain:

> Remember always, mighty king,
> that gods decreed the fates of all
> many years ago. *They alone are let*
> *to be eternal, while we frail humans die*
> as you yourself must someday do.[33]

The values of the *Giglamesh* epic are completely different from those of Genesis. Where the values celebrated in *Gilgamesh* are the martial values of the epic warrior-hero, Genesis is religious, spiritual and visionary. The emphasis throughout *Gilgamesh* is on physical prowess, the superb physiques of Gilgamesh and Enkidu, their amazing height and magnificent physical strength, the bravery and excitement of battle, male bonding, the physical charms of Shamhat, the joy and pleasure of heterosexual encounter, the mighty walls of the city of Uruk, the enjoyment of eating bread and drinking ale, the fearless confrontation of danger etc. Although Enkidu is humanised and civilized and there is an acknowledgement and celebration of the superiority of civilized life to life in a state of nature, that is just about as far as the *Gilgamesh* vision goes. The wisdom King Gilgamesh gains towards the end of his quest is in line with the advice given him by Siduri, who tells him to abandon his foolish dreams of immortality and settle for an enjoyable life on this side of the grave.[34] This advice represents the poem's resolution or denouement, the conclusion of the rite of passage undergone by King Gilgamesh[35]. The values of *Gilgamesh* remain firmly anchored in this earth, earthbound.

In *Gilgamesh* the gods and goddesses squabble and scheme against each other; such divine behaviour is completely foreign to the majestic, if intimate, God of Genesis. What is particularly absent in *Gilgamesh* is the sweep of the rite of passage we find in Genesis, the transition of the whole species from nature to history and culture, and the opening up of a new future for all of humankind. The flood in *Gilgamesh* results in the deification of the sole survivors, Utnapishtim and his wife, who thereby acquire immortality and join the ranks of the gods[36] but, unlike the flood in Genesis, the flood in *Gilgamesh* does not inaugurate a new creation for the race, nor does it open up a new chapter in the relationship between the human and the divine. Utnapishtim is the exception, a one-off; the common fate of humanity is that of Gilgamesh who has to face up to the inevitability and finality of death.[37] Genesis 3, on the other hand, tells the story of a rite of passage involving the whole human race that is at once the mutation from proto-human to fully human consciousness and the graduation to a new level of maturity and adulthood; it is about Man's coming of age as a self-determining historical agent capable of entering into a new, covenantal relationship with God. We might say that *Gilgamesh* is right—immortality is the prerogative of the divine. But the solution presented in Genesis is that Man *can* become divine, with the permission and agency of God, and in that way "gain" immortality.

Genesis 3 is not a tragedy for humanity; it is not about human ambition tragically thwarted but rather about God's bounty in bringing immortality—life with Yahweh—within human reach. And because God is the Lord of history, Man's action in acquiring knowledge of good and evil should not be seen as some feat of Promethean pride, a wresting from God of something that God does not wish to part with, for which Man will in turn be punished. For the ancient Hebrews—and here they differ sharply from the Greeks as well as the Babylonians—there could be no question of God being "caught out" or misled in that fashion or of Man outwitting God even to the slightest degree.

It is for these reasons that Sir James Frazer's attempt to assimilate the story in Genesis 3 to the pattern of the tale told in *Gilgamesh* can be seen to be mistaken. As always when dealing with the myths of the ancient Israelites, simple assimilation to the mythical tales of other civilisations, such as the Greek or the Babylonian, ought to be avoided. What can be said is that the authors of Genesis 3 appear to have found in the Enkidu-Shamhat episode in *Gilgamesh* a story which in terms of thematic content and narrative structure enabled them to indicate important shifts and changes that took place in the course of world process in the relationship between God and his creatures. The transformation that took place in Enkidu and his ascent from a feral to a civilised form of existence, which enabled him to become a recognisable member of the human family, presented a model of story telling that suited the purposes of the Yahwist authors. However, the Yahwist authors, with the advantage of building on what they took from the Babylonian literary canon, loaded the story with greater symbolic meaning than the simple ascent to civilised humanity of one feral creature that is found in *Gilgamesh*. Like the Babylonians before them, they saw the story as an ascent from a lower order to a higher order of existence, and for them this necessarily involved a change in the human-divine relationship. So they presented the transformation that took place in the hominid couple as a story about the differentiation of humans from the rest of the animal kingdom by means of their divinisation—in a word, hominisation. In addition, they presented this ascent as a fateful occurrence that symbolised Man's coming of age, a shift from innocence to adulthood that saw Man becoming a self-determining rational being, making possible both sin and human creativity, and alongside that, equipping Man to assume the responsibility of entering into a new covenantal relationship with God. All of these shifts were built into the story in Genesis 3.

This was a truly remarkable piece of artistic compression which the Yahwist storytellers were able to accomplish by borrowing the format of a rite of passage and exploiting it with great sophistication, so that the story spilling out from the fateful act of transgression in Genesis 3 moves into a second, interim stage recounted in Genesis 4-8, and culminates in a third and final stage, namely the end of the flood scene in Genesis 9, at which point the old creation is left behind and a new creation is born and, together with this, a new kind of creature, the human beings whose strange nature and relationship with God the mythological chapters of Genesis 1-11 were designed to illustrate and explain.[38]. It is with these new, transformed creatures and their descendants that God enters into the covenantal relationship that will stand at the centre of his dealings with the Hebrews in history.

The Yahwist mythographers made wonderfully creative use of the materials they borrowed from Babylonia. The *Gilgamesh* story reinforces the view that Genesis 3 is above all about the beginning of a process of *transformation* that will climax in the Noachic covenant. In this way it introduces the theme—that of transformation, elevation and divinisation—that will span the whole of the Old Testament and play an even more powerful role in the New.[39] By coming to understand how a story like *Gilgamesh* influenced a tale in the Book of Genesis we begin to enter the thought categories of this ancient world and in this way learn how to read both the Old and the New Testaments. Before Man could be elevated by God to the divine level that would make union with God possible he had, first, to be elevated from the animal to the human state. It is the story of this first ascent or elevation that is told in chapters 3 to 9 of Genesis; the story of the second elevation begins with the inauguration of the covenant (Gen 9: 8-17). From an authorial point of view, what is happening in these early chapters of Genesis is a fairly broad brush description of Man's emergence in nature followed swiftly by a similar description of his entry into history—specifically, salvation history.

FOUNDATIONAL IMAGE

The foundation of the two elevations I have referred to was laid, in the Yahwist account, at the earlier stage when the Lord God breathed his spirit into the nostrils of the man he had formed from the dust of the ground (Gen 2: 7). There are two strands or themes in this image of God's creation of Man that point the way forward. The first is this: the man (in Hebrew, *adam*) is formed from the dust of the ground (*adamah*); we should never forget this association of man with the earth—one translation renders *adam* as "the groundling," corresponding with *adamah*, meaning "ground."[40] Man is continuous with the basic stuff of the earth, he is thoroughly material. But within the material that is Man there is a creative spiritual element that continues to shape and mould him. Man does not come from the hand of God ready-made and finished; rather he is both naturally and supernaturally an emergent being, a being in transit. The story told in Genesis 3 of the hominisation of Man is not another creation narrative any more than the story told in *Gilgamesh* of the humanisation of Enkidu amounts to a second creation of this noble warrior. Rather, hominisation/humanisation is the realisation of a potentiality that has been there since creation, the blossoming into a power in Man of the spirit of God breathed into him at the point of creation: Genesis 3 portrays the first major actualisation of the spirit of God that has been in Man since creation. This is what I term the *first elevation*, the ascent of Man to full human consciousness, and it is a purely natural phenomenon—it is described in the story as the result of the man, or rather of the woman, taking the fruit from the tree and eating it. In modern scientific terms, it is the evolution of Man from a lower form of animal life.

The *second elevation*, however, is not a development within nature but occurs when God decides to intervene in human history. The fundamental point or principle to be grasped with reference to this second elevation is that only that which is of God can become one with God. That is a fundamental law of what might be called "theological physics." In the Hebrew understanding of God, which has been inherited by Christianity, God so transcends his creation that he is completely other, completely different. God is quite removed from everything in creation. He is not a thing alongside other things, a cause alongside other causes, in the universe. He explains nothing that happens in the universe for the simple reason that he is not part of the universe's scheme of things. God is not the explanation of anything in the universe and for this reason it is quite wrong to speak of "the God hypothesis," as some modern atheists are fond of doing, since this is to treat God as if he had some causative function within the universe, like gravity or oxygen.

All of this stems from the Hebrew insistence that God created the universe from nothing. Creation from nothing has as a necessary consequence that God is not part of his creation, is not contained within his creation. God simply makes the difference between the universe's existing and not existing. He is not the explanation of anything in the universe but he is the explanation of explanation, the explanation of things in the universe having an explanation at all: to do that he must stand outside the universe's own intra-universe explanatory system, outside the universe's own processes. It is for these reasons that we speak of God being totally other, as absolutely transcending the universe. One of the great benefits of this understanding of God's transcendence is that it clears the way for the scientific investigation of the material universe, since the material universe cannot be considered, as it is and has been within certain pagan philosophies, to be either itself divine or populated by divine beings. In exploring the universe we are not interfering with divinity, we do not incur any religious taboos. Neither can the material universe be considered, as it is in the *Gilgamesh* epic, to be at the bidding of capricious deities who act out of spite or anger against humanity, and so forth.

It is for the same reason that we say that only that which is of God can become one with God. For if God is totally other, quite different from anything in creation, if he is unique and totally *sui generis*, then it follows that nothing in creation is like him—nothing, that is, except Man. For God made Man in his own image and he breathed his spirit into him. So in the whole of the universe Man is unique in possessing from the time of his creation that which is of God. And, as I have already said, the story in Genesis 3 is about the actualisation of this potentiality that had been there since creation. By eating from the tree of knowledge, the hominid couple became even more like God, grew in their kinship with God and, as we have argued, by this same act they became human since it is the possession of the godlike attributes of intelligence and freedom that constitutes Man as Man. The purpose of the covenant and of God's dealings with Man in Hebrew and Christian revelation is to assist Man to become ever more like him, to share ever more fully in the holiness and wholeness that is God's essential characteristic. Such is the purpose of the second elevation and it is the reason why this elevation is not the work of nature but a supernatural occurrence, requiring the direct intervention of God. The second elevation addresses the human need for fulfilment through union with God. Man is a natural being, a product of nature, who "desires by nature a fulfilment, which can only come 'supernaturally,' as a gift by sheer divine grace."[41] This teaching of Aquinas and some of the early Fathers of the Church is prefigured in the Genesis narrative by the twin elevations, one natural and the other supernatural, which are the focus of attention at this point.[42] The first elevation is symbolised by the tree of knowledge of good and evil, the second by the tree of life.

In the narrative told in Genesis 3, God deliberately prevents Man from gaining access to the tree of life. Augustine saw this as a punishment for Man's offending God by his sin of disobedience. In the interpretation proposed here, however, God's action is neither punitive nor conclusive but rather serves to draw attention to the fact that what is about to happen is God's work and is not something that humans can arrogate to themselves or simply presume; in fact the divine intervention, this premeditated act of prevention, turns out to be the prelude to a plan of human salvation, initiated by God, which will enable Man to grow in likeness to him, to grow in holiness and wholeness, by living his life in line with the covenant and the commandments which God will decree in his revelation to the Israelites. These commandments regard not only Man's relationship with God but, as integral with this, Man's relationship with his fellow human beings. So after the transformation of proto-human creatures into fully recognisable human beings, recounted in Genesis 3, there follows the long and difficult transformation over time of these new human creatures into beings capable of living in friendship with God *because they have become like him.* This is the process known as salvation history: the work of God's transforming of humanity over time—humanity being possessed of intelligence and free will, and therefore capable of responding positively or negatively to God's invitation to friendship with him.

As Robert Alter comments, entering into a covenant with God is a "potentially ambiguous act fraught with peril as well as with promise."[43] On the negative side, Man is free to turn down God's invitation to intimacy, friendship and personal fulfilment; he is even more likely to ignore it or overlook it because he is too distracted by his own plans, cares and ambitions. On the positive side, God's covenant with Man inaugurates a phase of human transformation that will culminate in the final transformation God will bring about at the *eschaton*, the end of time. This final transformation, the gifting to some human beings of the eternal life of friendship with God, will both set the seal on and glorify what these humans have done and achieved in respect of becoming God-like in history, in the lives they have led. And this final transformation is the ground of the hope that shapes the perspective of Christian living on this earth: the ground of our love for God, who has shown such love for us, as well as of our love for our fellow human beings and for God's created universe. "Transformation" is, or ought to be, a key term in Christian theology because the Judaeo-Christian religious tradition is not primarily concerned with human behaviour or conduct, it is not a system of morality, but is primarily about our relationship with God. And for Man to enjoy friendship with God he stands in need of transformation, of becoming more and more a creature full of love for God and all of his creation and, in this way, of becoming more like God, who is love (1 Jn 4: 8, 16).

JAMES BARR

A more recent attempt to interpret the story in Genesis 3 along the lines of a quest for immortality was undertaken by the eminent Professor of Hebrew Studies and Old Testament scholar, the late James Barr. Barr sets out his thesis and his intentions in the opening page of the Preface to *The Garden of Eden and the Hope of Immortality:*[44]

> Central to the presentation offered here is a reading of the story of the Garden of Eden, not as a tale of the origins of sin and death, but as a tale of a chance of immortality, briefly accessible to humanity but quickly lost. Old Testament scholars have long known that the reading of the story of the "Fall of Man" in the traditional sense, though hallowed by St Paul's use of it, cannot stand up to examination through a close reading of the Genesis text. But though this has long been evident, scholars have not, on the whole, succeeded in formulating a general picture of the purpose and impact of the story which could rival the traditional one and could carry an equal force or similar relevance over so wide a range of biblical materials and theological considerations. My suggestion is that the perception of the place of immortality in the narrative can do much to fulfil that need.[45]

Barr's book started out as the annual contribution to a series of lectures dedicated to the theme of immortality. Focusing closely on the story of Adam and Eve in the Garden of Eden, he says that this has traditionally been seen as being about original sin. However, he puts this traditional view down to St Paul and observes that there is nothing about original sin in the gospels.[46] Even in Paul what he calls "the Adam-Christ typology" is not widespread but is confined to Romans 5, 1 Corinthians 15 and 1 Timothy. Barr does not see the story in Genesis 3 as being about an immortal creature that became mortal, but rather the opposite—the cultural assumption in the Old Testament was that death was natural for human beings. Noting the absence of any reference to "sin," "evil" or "rebellion" in Genesis 3, Barr goes on to say that "within the Hebrew Bible itself the story of Adam and Eve is nowhere cited as the explanation for sin and evil in the world."[47] The Old Testament is deeply conscious of the evil in the world but nowhere does it account for this by reference to Adam's original sin or original disobedience. It is taken for granted that everyone has sinned but in the Old Testament as a whole there is as much reference to the righteous as there is to sinners.[48] He refuses to see the matter of nakedness and clothing in the story as requiring interpretation in terms of guilt and goes on to rubbish the claim upheld by many commentators that the motivation of the couple was to be like God.[49] Referring to the style of the writing, he quotes with approval Sean McEvenue who observes of the story in Genesis 3:

> Distance between the author and the reader is maintained by a witty style. The reader is never invited to identify, or sympathize, with anyone in the story....The treatment of sin or evil is not marked by theological or philosophical depth; rather its most memorable passages, the treatment of temptation in 3: 1-6 and of guilt in 3: 7-13, are characterized by a dramatic subtlety which one associates more easily with comedy than with tragedy.[50]

To sum up, Barr argues that so long as one concentrates on the story as told in Genesis 3 there is little or no support for the traditional interpretation. He attributes the traditional interpretation, with its emphasis on disobedience, sin and the origin of moral evil in the world, to St Paul's reading of the story under the influence of what he calls "later strata of the Old Testament" and in particular the "Hellenistic" Wisdom tradition. The two texts he quotes as being regulative for Paul's thinking are Wisdom 2.23 and IV Ezra 7. 116-118 (as well as 3.21). The first of these reads, "God created man for incorruption and made him in the image of his own eternity; but through the devil's envy death entered the world, and those who belong to his party experience it." This supports the idea that man was destined to be immortal but lost his chance through sin. The second text quoted goes on to say, "O Adam, what have you done! For though it was you that sinned, the fall was not yours alone, but ours also who are your descendants!" This supports the notion of original sin as something all humanity inherits. The passage from IV Ezra 3.21 says something very similar.[51] It would be possible to add to the texts quoted by Barr. For example, Sirach says, "From a woman sin had its beginning, and because of her we all die." (Sirach 25: 24; also 15: 14) And 2

Baruch declares: "Adam sinned, and death was decreed against those who were to be born." (2 Baruch 17: 2-3, 23:4) Both of these texts support the view, echoed by Paul, that death—not just the death of Adam and Eve but death as a universal phenomenon in human life—is the result of the first sin. But Sirach and 2 Baruch are relatively late compositions, not part of the Hebrew bible, and written in the period of the Hellenisation of Hebrew thought; and like IV Ezra, 2 Baruch is an apocryphal work. As the Jesuit biblical scholar, John L. McKenzie observes, "in the apocryphal books of the Jews, ...the Paradise story is embellished with many additional features."[52] It is in the relatively late period of Hellenistic wisdom and of the apocrypha that the transgression of Adam, which in the "primitive" period of Hebrew thought would have been considered a case of crossing a forbidden divide between different categories of beings, is translated into the language of sin and personal guilt before God. It is only at this late stage that the story of Adam and Eve in the Garden of Eden comes to be cloaked in the language of sin.

Barr's argument is extremely valuable in pinpointing the Hellenistic influences on Paul's thinking that provided the grounds for the origin of the traditional Christian interpretation of Genesis 3. He sums up his conclusions concerning the story in Genesis 3 by saying, "Far from it being the case that Paul's thinking is deeply rooted in the thought world of ancient Israel, it is much more precisely formed by the *interpretation* of these ancient texts which took place in Hellenistic times and in a different intellectual atmosphere."[53] (His italics) A major reason for this change in intellectual atmosphere was the Greek separation of body and soul combined with the experience of religious martyrdom in the late Maccabean period: religious loyalty made hope of a future life after death more meaningful, while the destruction of the body made it necessary for such a life to be the result of the resurrection of the body.[54] Although agreeing that belief in the immortality of the soul is not a theme or topic found in the OT, Barr maintains that the world of late Judaism, out of which the New Testament came, was burning with speculation about the immortality of the soul.[55]

Barr values the narrative roles of both the tree of knowledge and the tree of life; the former he considers to refer to "the power of rational and especially ethical discrimination."[56] The tree of life he considers to be borrowed by Israel from older mythology, with the most pertinent example being that in the *Gilgamesh* epic.[57] Of the connection between the two trees, he says:

Undoubtedly these two are not identical, for their very names and their parts in the story expressly distinguish them. In spite of their differences, however, it is likely that they have something in common. What they have in common is that both, in some degree at least, are prerogatives or attributes of God. "You will be as gods, knowing good and evil," said the snake, and God himself admitted that this prediction had come true... If humanity had come this close to deity, it was only one further step for it to partake also of the tree of life, and, it is implied, if immortality were added to knowledge, the approach of humanity to the status of deity would become intolerably close. In the event, therefore, humanity is left with knowledge, but immortality is denied it. Man has come close to God in the one regard, but not in the other.[58]

On man and the animals, Barr refers to the different talents or faculties acquired by man in comparison with the animals and goes on to note how in Genesis 2-3 this difference "lies in the knowledge of good and evil, which belongs to the world of the gods and removes humanity from the ambience of animal behaviour."[59] One result of his acquisition of knowledge, Barr observes, is that Man became conscious of his own mortality; death had dominion over Man.[60]

Of the "angel marriages" in Genesis 6, Barr notes how no major current of Christianity found much use for them since they did not appear to explain anything within our experience and their occurrence "strained belief."[61] This, he points out, contrasts with their importance in the early post-biblical stages of Judaism when they were regarded as enormously important, since they stressed that *violence* was the fundamental sin. He connects this to biblical attitudes to death. Death in the ancient texts is not regarded as at all unnatural, but death connected to violence and war is regarded as repugnant to God and contrary to his will. By contrast, within the later Greco-Roman world, death itself, death "generally and universally" is feared and this led to a widely shared view among early Christians that all death was unnatural and introduced through sin; this went along with the view that war was natural after "the Fall." Barr believes this combination of attitudes has had "very serious moral consequences in our tradition" and points out how prophetic passages in which God declares his opposition to death run alongside expressions of disgust with war and longing for peace.[62] The view widely held among Christians, deriving from Paul, that "sin brought death into the world is likely to be the product of a Hellenistic interpretation of the Old Testament rather than the self-understanding of the Old Testament texts themselves."[63] But Paul was not offering an interpretation of the story in

Genesis 3 "in and for itself; he was really *interpreting Christ* through the use of images from this story."[64] As for the widely shared view that humanity is fallen, Barr argues convincingly that this is not dependent on the story of Adam and Eve in the garden, but is something that most human beings arrive at from their knowledge of the world around them. "For most of Christianity, the story of the garden of Eden has been, not the ground on which the idea of a Fall was based, but the mode through which that idea was symbolized."[65]

It would be wrong to suggest that Barr insists on adherence to whatever is most ancient in the biblical texts. He maintains that immortality is a significant New Testament concept and that the immortality of the person, by-passing death, is an important part of the heritage.[66] Nevertheless, he claims that Paul's anthropology, including his belief in a physical resurrection, is alien to the Old Testament; classical Hebrew had no word corresponding to Paul's *soma* (body), except marginally.[67]

Above all, Barr seizes on the image of the tree of life as one that bears in itself the very First Promise (the Protevangelium) in the bible. "The tree of life," he says, "is made inaccessible to the humans; but it remains in existence."[68] He draws attention to Revelations 22.2, where there is mention of the tree of life "whose leaves are for the healing of the nations," and notes how the word "nations," a reference to the non-Israelite nations, referred to "the units par excellence of *war*." He concludes with a rather magnificent, if restrained, credo:

> Immortality, then, was on the biblical agenda from the very beginning, with Adam and Eve. In the Garden of Eden there was the tree of life. The human pair might just have got to that tree, but they did not, because God stopped them; no one was to enter the Garden, and the cherubim with the flaming sword stood there to guard the gate. Humanity was not fit to come near the tree. Nevertheless the tree remained there in the garden. Later one came to redeem the defect of humanity. Immortality was brought to light.[69]

COMMENTARY ON BARR

I have gone into considerable detail in this account of James Barr's argument because I believe that on point after point it carries conviction. It is the product of almost an entire life-time's dedication to the study of the Old Testament, and I for one am grateful to have the support of so eminent a scholar for much of the interpretation I am presenting in this book and, in particular, for the attention he draws to the two trees, their association with God and the relationship that exists between them. Barr's account of Genesis 3 tallies with the interpretation being put forward here on most points. Such disagreements as I have with him stem more from what Barr does not say rather than from what he says. For example, he says that God's prediction that man will die if he eats the forbidden fruit is not fulfilled, but fails to explain why; I have indicated why I believe the prediction was fulfilled, an issue I shall shortly explore further. Barr shows how Man's acquisition of knowledge distanced him from the animals but does not draw attention to Man's new anomalous status. He brilliantly illustrates the violence at the heart of the evil that breaks out after the so-called "angel marriages" because they represented the crossing of a boundary that should not be crossed, but fails to connect the evil that breaks out in the world from Genesis 4 onwards with the more notable crossing of a boundary in Genesis 3.

It is the hiatus that Barr opens up between Genesis 3 and the consequent evil in the world in the succeeding chapters that must count as the most serious shortcoming of his interpretation. The traditional interpretation, which he traces to St Paul, may have been misguided but it surely did not entirely miss the point in seeing Genesis 3 as being connected to what follows in Genesis 4. It is also difficult to see from his account why the human beings were *punished* for their action in Genesis 3 if there had been no transgression. Indeed, Barr shows a tendency to attribute to the "angel marriages" in Genesis 6 the role of fomenting evil in the world that the traditional interpretation has assigned to the actions that take place in Genesis 3[70], and this appears to be a rather forced part of his argument (for example, how could the "angel marriages" in chapter 6 account for the crime of Cain in chapter 4?). Barr is surely right in his claim that Paul, in his references to Genesis 3 in the epistle to the Romans, was mainly interested in *interpreting Christ* through images from the story, but he does not advance on this to discuss whether or not Paul ultimately proposed the notion of original sin. Finally, while he helps us contextualise the thought of St Paul on original sin, Barr refrains from any definitive comment on the value of original sin as a Christian doctrine or on what the knock-on effects the loss of this doctrine might be on other Christian doctrines. Nevertheless, Barr's short and condensed account (it was, after all, essentially a series of lectures) takes us a long way on our journey of interpretation, and is one that can profitably be filled out, amplified and enriched.

"IN THE DAY THAT YOU EAT OF IT, YOU SHALL DIE" (Gen 2:17)

These words of the Lord God to the man in the garden proved to be one of the key elements in Augustine's argument for Original Sin. Because of these words Augustine took issue with the Pelagians, who believed that man was created mortal, and he made the claim that God had created man immortal. Mortality, he claimed, was his punishment for having sinned against God. The "proof" of Augustine's position could be found in these words in scripture which he understood to be a kind of deal offered to Man by God with the meaning that if man did not eat from the tree of knowledge he would not die; if he did, then he would die. It was on account of his disobedient action that, in Paul's words, "death entered the world"—not just the death of the parents of the human race but death *per se*, death as a phenomenon in human existence. And since clearly the man and the woman were mortal, Augustine's argument went on, it is clear that they must have sinned; and because the rest of us are also mortal it is clear that we must have been implicated in the sin of our first parents. In fact, Augustine's argument for original sin is based on two inferences: the first, that Man had the opportunity to achieve immortality but lost it; from this he inferred that Man *must* have sinned since the loss of immortality was clearly a punishment for wrongdoing. The second inference is that since all of us are in fact born mortal, inheriting the punishment inflicted on Adam, then all of us *must* be guilty along with Adam.[71] The two logical "musts" are both inferences of Augustine's; they are not based on any explicit statement or comment in Genesis itself. The traditional doctrine of Original Sin hangs on these two inferences.

Commenting on the words in Genesis, James Barr makes the important point that death was not seen as an unmitigated evil in the Old Testament and was not by any means considered to be punishment for sin.[72] On the contrary, death not marked by violence was seen as normal and natural and was often presented as completion of a full and satisfying life.[73] Such comments as "Abraham breathed his last and died in a good old age, an old man and full of years" (Gen 25: 8) or, "And Isaac breathed his last; and he died and was gathered to his people, old and full of days" (Gen 35:29) do not suggest anything other than that death was seen as normal and natural. Barr goes on to make the point that this is an attitude that has continued into Christian culture when someone dies a peaceful death, "their life's work complete, their faith in God calm and untroubled."[74] On such occasions we do not think of death as a punishment or as contrary to the will of God, and neither did the ancient Hebrews.

When he considers the words in Genesis 2, "of the tree of knowledge of good and evil you shall not eat, for in the day that you eat of it you shall die," Barr maintains that God's warning is not delivered at a high philosophical level as one concerning the human condition—it is not a statement about death in general, but is about the immediate consequences that will follow if the man eats from the tree; it is a warning about death now, soon.[75] Barr believes that it did not happen since Adam continued to live, but he gives no reason why such a clear warning or threat by God should go unfulfilled. It is here, I think, that the thinking of Mary Douglas about what I have called the "Primitive Tradition," which Barr does not include in his reflections, can lead to a more satisfactory interpretation. For it is surely unsatisfactory that such a clear warning should appear to be unfulfilled; and it was the fact that Adam continued to live that led Augustine, and after him practically the whole of the Western Christian tradition, to interpret the words spoken by God in Genesis 2 in a highly generic sense, in keeping with the prevailing attitude to death in Greek thought,[76] as referring to death as a basic feature of human existence rather than as a warning to Adam in his specific situation in Eden. For if we take heed of what Mary Douglas says about how primitive people viewed the transition from one state or status to another, God's warning was fulfilled: Man died to his old self, his old status, and was re-born to a new self, to the status of a human being endowed fatefully with intelligence and freedom. As presented in Genesis 3, this change is every bit as sudden and immediate as God had indicated: at the end of Genesis 2 the man and his wife "were both naked and were not ashamed"; but as soon as they ate from the fruit of the tree of knowledge, they were ashamed of their nakedness, their eyes were opened, they made clothes to cover their nakedness and hid from God. They had changed completely from the state they were in before—they had become human. Their old selves were gone for ever, dead. As I have said already, rites of passage are as much about leaving the old behind as they are about embarking on the new.

In the thinking of primitive people human beings were strange anomalies, like the other animals but unlike them also in very striking ways.[77] In the Hebrew myth, the period of transition from what today we would call the hominid to the human state—the mutation into the intelligent life of humankind—was fraught with dangers. For Man to shatter the basic order of the cosmos by trespassing on what was strictly speaking God's property, thereby acquiring the divine attribute of knowledge, was to bring about a highly dangerous situation. And the danger unleashed on the world on account of this violation of the boundaries is seen in what follows in Genesis, with Cain's fratricide and the violence that fills the earth. It is not surprising that God's warning in Genesis 2 about the dangers of eating from the tree of knowledge is highly dramatic and full of foreboding. The "transitional period" from Genesis 4 to Genesis 8 is filled with danger and violence until the occurrence of the Flood, which symbolically obliterates what has gone before and initiates a "new creation," when Man and the whole earth experience a new birth and the start of a new covenant between God and humankind.

The condition and situation of humanity after the Flood are totally different from what preceded it; the race descended from Noah totally different from that descended from Adam. Man is now no longer an animal like the other animals, albeit one into whom God has breathed his spirit. Rather Man is an evolved animal, possessed of freedom and intelligence, capable of self-determination, and hence capable of discriminating between good and evil. Man is now a historical being, capable of making and unmaking his relationship with his environment and his fellow humans and, in so doing, of shaping his own identity and his relationship with God. And Man is now a carnivore, feared by all other animals (Genesis 9: 2-3)—further evidence of the loss of his former innocence. It is with this post-Noachic race that God agrees an historical alliance through which he will tutor humankind and show it how to be perfect as he is perfect. As I argued in the last chapter, Mary Douglas's account of the mentality and ways of thinking of primitive people throws a sharp light on the account in Genesis of Adam's mutation into a recognisable human being and on the transformation of the God-Man relationship that occurs between Genesis 1 and Genesis 8. In particular, it shows how God's words of warning addressed to Adam that "in the day that you eat of it, you shall die" are, in fact, fulfilled.

James Barr is surely right in seeing God's words to Adam as being a warning in the here and now rather than some grand philosophical pronouncement about death in general; this interpretation is much more in keeping with the concrete particularity of the narrative style found in Genesis 3. Mary Douglas's comments on the structure of a rite of passage reveal the truth in God's warning despite the fact that biologically Adam and Eve go on living—for they also undergo a profound transformation, a death and re-birth experience, a prototypical phenomenon that serves as the template for many such occurrences in the historical narrative that is to follow, and which will be most vividly illustrated in the death and resurrection of Christ.

IMMORTALITY AS RESURRECTION

There can surely be no doubt that in the gospels Jesus is presented as believing in immortality and specifically in immortality gained through resurrection. In John 11, where we read of him raising Lazarus from the dead, Jesus is presented as saying to Martha, Lazarus's sister, "I am the resurrection and the life; he who believes in me, though he die, yet shall he live, and whoever lives and believes in me shall never die." (Jn 11: 25-26) This is the clearest affirmation of belief in the resurrection that we find on the lips of Jesus himself. In addition, there is the central Christian belief in the resurrection of Jesus himself that is conveyed in the gospels through the narration of the empty tomb and the subsequent appearances of Jesus (Mt 28:5f; Mk 16: 2f; Lk 24:1f; Jn 20: 4f; 21:4). In Acts and Paul's letters it is abundantly clear that the resurrection was a primary component of the earliest Christian preaching (Acts 1:22). It is also clearly stated that Christ is the firstborn of those who will rise from the dead (Colossians 1: 18); that he who raised Jesus from the dead gives life to our bodies through the spirit who possesses us (Romans 8:11) and will also raise the Christian (2 Corinthians 4:14). What is singularly missing in the gospels is any hint or suggestion that Man was created immortal but had lost immortality through some fault of his own.

NOTES

1. Northrop Frye, *The Great Code: the Bible and Literature*, (New York: Harcourt Inc., 1982) p. 109.

2. Sir James G. Frazer, *Folklore in the Old Testament*, 3 Vols, (London: Macmillan and Co Ltd, 1918). Frye describes Frazer as an "early investigator who is indispensable for a book like this." See Frye, op. cit., p. 35.

3. Frazer, op. cit., Vol 1, p. 46.

4. Ibid., p. 47.

5. Ibid., p. 52f.

6. Ibid., p. 76.

7. Ibid., p. 7.

8. *The Epic of Gilgamesh*, translated by Danny P. Jackson (Wauconda: Bolchazy-Carducci Publishers, 1997). Unless otherwise indicated, this is the version referred to in this section. The episode of the flood is in Tablet XI, columns 1-3; in Genesis, the story of the flood occupies chapters 6-9.

9. Tablet 1, column 2, line 88.

10. Ibid., Tablet I, column 4 and 6; Tablet II, column 2, 3 and 4.

11. Ibid., Tablet 1, column 3.

12. Ibid., column 2.

13. Ibid., column 5.

14. For an account of the contrast between the open and fully explained presentation of reality typical of the (Greek) epic tradition and the more obscure and cryptic style of the Hebrew bible, see the opening chapter of Erich Auerbach, op. cit., p. 3ff; also, the comments of Robert Alter referred to in Chapter One.

15. See John L. McKenzie SJ, op. cit., entry under "Babylon, Babylonia," p. 76.

16. *Gilgamesh*, Tablet II, Column 2, line 33.

17. Introduction, *The Epic of Gilgamesh*, op. cit., p. XVII.

18. *The Epic of Gilgamesh*, op. cit., Tablet X, Column iii, lines 149-153.

19. James G. Keenan, "*Gilgamesh*: An Appreciation," *The Epic of Gilgamesh*, op. cit., p. XLIII.

20. The first of these short quotations is taken from the verse rendition of Danny P. Jackson, op. cit., the second from the translation by Andrew George (London: Penguin Books, 1999), and the third from the 1946 translation made by Alexander Heidel, contained in *The Gilgamesh Epic and Old Testament Parallels* (Chicago: University of Chicago Press, 1949) p. 29.

21. A great admirer of the poem, the German poet Rainer Maria Rilke, referred to *Gilgamesh* as "the epic about the fear of death."

22. See below, Chapter Five, p. 127f.

23. While I have used the plural form, "authors," when referring to the authorship of the Genesis story, this is with reference to the likely editing work done on it in the post-exilic period when the Israelites made a concerted effort to preserve their literary heritage; however, the actual composition of the story in Genesis 3 most probably occurred at a much earlier date.

24. Storytelling as an art form developed much earlier than the vocabulary of moral reasoning. It is significant that the great Greek tragedies of Aeschylus, Euripides and Sophocles were written well before the philosophies of Plato and Aristotle.

25. See *The Epic of Gilgamesh*, (Balchazy-Carducci Publishers, 1997) p. XII.

26. See for example the comments by R.J. Clifford S.J. in the chapter on Genesis in the *New Jerome Biblical Commentary*, op. cit., p. 8.

27. Alexander Heidel, op. cit., p. 14.

28. Ibid., p. 142-143.

29. Ibid., Preface, p. v.

30. Although he was unique in resorting to Latin, Heidel was not alone in finding the explicit descriptions in *Gilgamesh* offensive; other early translators adopted euphemisms or simply omitted certain lines in order to avoid offending their readers.

31. Alexander Heidel, op. cit., p. 268.

32. The phrase used by James G. Keenan, op. cit., p. XLV.

33. *The Epic of Gilgamesh*, Tablet X, Column iii (my italics).

34. Ibid., Tablet XI, Column iii, lines 85-99.

35. There is in fact a further tablet, Tablet XII, which speaks of an afterlife, but most commentators see this as a later addition that is in many ways at odds with the more coherent tale that forms Tablets I-XI.

36. Ibid., Tablet XI, Column I, line 9; Column iv, lines 179-80.

37. Alexander Heidel, op. cit., p. 12. Heidel does observe that immortality is conferred on Utnapishtim and his wife "by divine favor."

38. For the significance of the flood as an image of death and re-birth, see above, Chapter Three, p. 54. The great flood can be viewed as a return to the disorder and chaos on the earth before God imposed order upon it at creation.

39. Interestingly, the term used by the Greek Orthodox Church for the Resurrection of Jesus is "the Metamorphosis."

40. Mary Phil Korsak, op. cit.

41. Fergus Kerr, reporting the views of Henri de Lubac, supported by Aquinas and some Church Fathers, in *Twentieth Century Catholic Theologians* (Oxford: Blackwell Publishing, 2007) p. 72.

42. The agreement of my reading of Genesis 3 with long established theological teachings is one of its most powerful vindications.

43. Robert Alter, op. cit., p. 23.

44. James Barr, op. cit.

45. Ibid., p. ix.

46. Ibid., p. 5.

47. Ibid., p. 6.

48. Ibid., p. 7.

49. Ibid., p. 11-13. The view being contested by Barr here has had many powerful backers, including Aquinas who claimed that the principal element in Man's sin was in seeking to be like God by determining for himself which actions were good and which bad.: *Summa Theologiae*, 2-2, 163, 2. This is a view that tends to be regularly trotted out as if it were the transparent meaning of the action of eating from the tree of knowledge. See, for example, the theologically

informed "bestselling" religious novel, *The Shack*, by William Paul Young (London: Hodder and Stoughton, 2008) pp. 133 and 146-7.

50. Ibid., p. 12.

51. Quotations from these texts in Barr, op. cit., pp 16-18.

52. John L. McKenzie, op. cit., under "Adam," p. 12.

53. James Barr, op. cit., p. 18.

54. Ibid., p. 53-56.

55. Ibid., p. 52-53. There is further discussion of these points in the context of Paul's thinking in Chapter Six.

56. Ibid., p. 62.

57. Ibid., p. 61.

58. Ibid., p. 60.

59. Ibid., p. 72.

60. Ibid., p. 73.

61. Ibid., p. 84.

62. Ibid., p. 85.

63. Ibid., p. 87.

64. Ibid., p. 89, Barr's italics.

65. Ibid., p. 92.

66. Ibid., p. 112.

67. Ibid.

68. Ibid., p. 115.

69. Ibid., p. 116.

70. Ibid. See especially p. 83-84.

71. For Augustine's account of mortality as punishment for the original sin, see *Ad Simplicianum*, 1.4 and 1.11; also *City of God*, 12: 22.

72. James Barr, op. cit. See especially the whole of chapter 2, "The Naturalness of Death, and the path to Immortality."

73. Ibid., p. 28.

74. Ibid., p. 27.

75. Ibid., p. 11.

76. Ibid., p. 87.

77. "Man is certainly different from the animal world. He is apart, *holy* (Lev 11:44), because of his ontological link with God who is the supremely Other. But man has also an intimate link with the animal world, felt intuitively in the Old Testament, expressed more scientifically in the modern epoch." Joseph Blenkinsopp, *A Sketchbook of Biblical Theology*, (London: Burns and Oates, 1968) p. 98.

Chapter Five
A Tale of Two Trees

I have already made the point that the most authoritative biblical commentary on the events described in chapter 3 of Genesis is that delivered by the Lord God at the end of the chapter. (Gen. 3: 22-24) The reason given there for the expulsion of the human couple from Eden is not their transgression, their act of disobedience, but God's fear that they will go even further, go beyond eating from the tree of knowledge of good and evil and eat from the tree of life itself. It is this second step, which he seems to consider a natural sequel to eating from the tree of knowledge, that God deliberately prevents. That Man has become more like him by eating from the first tree is clearly acknowledged: "Behold, the man has become like one of us, knowing good and evil." Although the common theological term for the incident in the garden is the "Fall of Man," the evidence in Genesis is that Man's violation of the boundary separating him from God results in his becoming greater than he was before. What is more, God's expulsion of the man and woman from the garden is to prevent them becoming even more like him by gaining eternal life, the life of Yahweh himself.

By introducing *together* the two trees growing in the middle of the garden, and by extending the divine prohibition to both, the authors of Genesis have created a strong association between them. In the story, as soon as the human couple have eaten from the tree of knowledge, God takes action to block their access to the tree of life. We are not even told that the man and the woman intend to approach the tree of life but there is a presumption by God that they will do so—that having tasted of the tree of knowledge, the couple will naturally gravitate to the tree of life. The tree of life is seen to complement the tree of knowledge.

This relationship between the two trees is accomplished very skilfully by the Yahwist authors. In typical biblical style, at no point do they *explain* the relationship between the two trees, but *through the description of the action* taken by the Lord God the reader is made aware of the nature of this relationship. This is similar to the artistry by which the authors indicate the powers of the first tree. Again the authors do not explain these powers but rather, upon hearing that the human couple are in hiding because they are naked, God asks the question, "Who told you that you were naked?"—and then, *without waiting for an answer*, he goes on to ask, "Have you eaten from the tree of which I commanded you not to eat?" Once more, the powers of the tree are not explained but they are clearly implied by the fact that God moves on to ask his second question without waiting for an answer to his first question. The presumption is that the couple are newly conscious of their nakedness because of some power gained or acquired from their eating of the tree of knowledge. The scolding manner of God's interrogation of the human couple is reminiscent of a parent who has caught their child doing something beyond the behavioural boundaries long established in the household.

This is story telling of a high order. The dynamic relationship between the two trees is beautifully revealed: by eating from the tree of knowledge, the couple have become like God through their acquisition of the divine attribute of knowledge; but this step is presented as leading inexorably to the human couple's desire to eat also from the tree of life. It is this further step that God deliberately and ruthlessly prevents. Not only are the couple expelled from Eden but the tree of life is guarded by a revolving flaming sword. It would be hard to miss the meaning of this divine action: there is no way back for Man. Eden has gone. Human history is about to start, beginning with the birth of Eve's children. (Genesis 4:1)

With hindsight it is possible to see that the divine command that Man should refrain from eating from the tree of knowledge and, along with it, the tree of life is motivated by more than God's wish to inculcate "wholesome obedience," as Augustine would have it, but reflects the fact that these trees are "reserved" or set apart because they are divine; they denote properties or attributes that are God's and not his creatures'. The proto-humans have to transgress the boundary between themselves and God in order to acquire reason and free will but God steps in quickly to prevent them acquiring the fullness of divinity: their acquisition of the freedom and status of rational persons is on their own terms but the attainment of eternal life and union with God will be strictly on God's terms. Man is quickly reminded of his mortality and finitude: thus far and no further. Again, God's manner is not unlike that of a parent who makes a concession to their child who is beginning to act in a sanctioned "adult" way: this will be allowed but not that! The lines separating the childish from the adult world are being probed and crossed and the parent takes action to set out what is and what is not allowed "from now on." The household rules may have been re-affirmed but they have also been re-drawn.

THE BASIC HUMAN SITUATION

I have already indicated how Man's eating from the tree of knowledge of good and evil signals the transformation of humankind from its hominid status to the status of "homo sapiens"—as the ascent by Man into full human consciousness. Rather than the Augustinian fall from a previous elevated spiritual state, with a consequent deterioration of intellect and will, an ascent to rational consciousness takes place. But it falls short of its natural completion since Man is prevented from eating from the tree of life. Man is prevented from attaining the union with God that his eating from the first tree has caused him to desire and this act of prevention defines his new state, the human way of being in the world. Man becomes a creature *manqué*, someone incomplete, unfinished, deprived of the very thing his new human status yearns for. If the eating from the tree of knowledge made the animal human, the failure to eat from the second tree caused the human animal to be incomplete, in need of God to complete its humanity. So Genesis 3 reveals the tragedy of the human condition as defined by the tension between the two trees in the Garden of Eden, when Man succeeds in eating from one but is debarred by God from eating from the other which would be its natural completion and fulfilment. Man has achieved the power to reason and to act freely, divine attributes, but he has been debarred from achieving full union with God and hence from achieving immortality. Man has been left wanting.

The human species remains incomplete, only half finished; humans are still in process, *en route*, seeking, searching, aching, striving for

completeness, but the main prize of life—the very name Yahweh is ety-
mologically associated with life—has still to be attained. The story in
Genesis 3 defines and explains human *existence* in the existentialist
sense. Man is always becoming, always waiting, always hoping, always
reaching out for what is to come. The literary critic, George Steiner, asks
how it is that Man, who is "bio-socially ...a short-lived mammal made
for extinction" nevertheless remains on the whole hopeful and oriented
to the future:

> What, then, is the well-spring of our ineradicable hopes, our intimations
> of futurity, of our forward-dreams and utopias, public and private?
> Whence the radiant scandal of our investments in tomorrow, in after-
> tomorrow? Which is the source of the "life-lie," the gamble on improb-
> ability which makes most individuals and societies, despite recurrent
> exceptions, reject the logic of despair and of suicide? In short: from
> where rises the high tide of desire, of expectation, of an obsession with
> sheer being defiant of the pain, of the treadmill of enslavement and in-
> justice, of the massacres that are history?[1]

Steiner suggests as answer to his questions the phenomenon of language,
claiming that our hope stems from the "subjunctives, optatives, counter-
factual conditionals and...futurities of the verb,"[2] but this is surely rather
a safe and shallow option. In the final analysis, it is much more likely
that language reflects rather than forms or shapes reality. And the phenomenon reflected in language is, I would suggest, that humans are incomplete beings yearning for completion, creatures *manqué* looking for
God. Such a theological explanation penetrates more deeply than
Steiner's references to language. It explains our basic restlessness and
rootlessness, those qualities that have fascinated European and American
artists for most of the past two centuries: at the base of our psyche, in the
very core of our personality, we are unfinished, broken off, forever seeking that which will make us whole again. We experience the need for
wholeness, which is just another way of saying that we experience the
need for the holiness that is Yahweh's quintessential attribute. To become holy, to become Godlike, to be divinised—that is the most radical
and complete form of fulfilment that human beings can achieve. "To be
whole, or holy, is to be healed of the wounds inflicted by every kind of
estrangement we experience in life: estrangement from ourselves, from
our fellow human beings, and from the environment in which we live.

Estrangement from God occurs on one or another, or all, of these fronts."[3]

The bible gives widespread testimony to the unfinished state that men and women find themselves in. It sees a void in the human heart. Made for God, women and men spend their lives longing and pining for the fulfilment that only God can provide. As we read in the Psalms:

> O God, you are my God, for you I long;
> For you my soul is thirsting.
> My body pines for you
> Like a dry, weary land without water. (Ps 62)

> Like the dear that yearns
> For running streams
> So my soul is yearning
> For you, my God.

> My soul is thirsting for God,
> The God of my life;
> When can I enter and see
> The face of God?

> My tears have become my bread,
> By night, by day,
> As I hear it said all the day long:
> "Where is your God?" (Ps 41)[4]

St Augustine himself gives eloquent testimony to the same central human characteristic in his much quoted comment at the beginning of his *Confessions*: "You have made us for Yourself, Lord, and our hearts are restless until they rest in You."[5]

A THOMISTIC COMMENTARY

That God is not simply an object of longing alongside other objects, but *the* object of longing because men and women are utterly incomplete, utterly deprived and in their inmost being quite derelict without union with God stems directly from Man's graduation to the status of a rational being, from the human acquisition of mind. Modern Thomism helps us to understand why this is so.[6] For Thomism sees human consciousness as oriented in various ways. Consciousness is not simply amorphously "there," but is structured, shaped and pointed. First, it points to the truth: we are all of us as humans oriented to the truth, we aspire to know the truth and we cannot *not* seek to know the truth. Any denial of such an orientation of human consciousness ends up in contradiction: for such a denial is presumably intended to be taken as true and hence creates a contradiction between the denial and the performance of the denier. Human beings continually ask questions, and behind every question lies the search for truth. Just as some military weapons are heat-seeking weapons, so the human animal is a truth-seeking animal. Evolutionary biologists who wish to understand the phenomenon of religion should dwell on this remarkable characteristic of humankind, which remarkably is rarely remarked upon.

Furthermore, human consciousness points to the morally right; we are not consciously neutral between right and wrong but are spontaneously oriented to what is morally right. This orientation of consciousness actually precedes our orientation to the truth since to seek the truth is simply the cognitional sub-division of the search for what is right. In English and most other European languages, words like "true" and "honest" cover behaviour as well as what is said. So it is that we are not only required to provide proof or evidence to support our truth claims but we are also expected to give reasons to justify our actions: some actions are rational or reasonable while others are not. Among adult human beings, actions that cannot be justified or supported by reasons are considered either stupid or irresponsible. There is in fact a close link between the truth and right action: in South Africa a "truth commission" was set up to find out what happened under apartheid on the understanding that without the truth being known justice could not be achieved. The same point is established by the fact that dictators and tyrants tell the most egregious lies in order to cover up their abuse of human rights. In fact, human beings have to lie to themselves before they can do wrong: they have to pretend that what they are doing is for this or that reason perfectly right; my wrongdoing is preceded by my lying to myself.

So it is not just the case that some human beings seek the truth and pursue justice, sometimes heroically, but rather that all of us as human beings are constitutionally oriented to the truth and the right: our very consciousness is inherently pointed at or striving for these goals. This does not mean, of course, that we cannot deny or frustrate what we are by nature—we all too easily find reasons to obscure or falsify the truth and to overlook the claims of justice. But such actions do not leave us unaffected. Because of the nature of human consciousness, when we plan and act in ways that frustrate the quest for truth and justice we do harm to our natures, our personalities suffer. The reason lie detectors work is because of this basic, irresistible orientation of human consciousness to telling and living the truth.

But human consciousness does not stop at this orientation to the truth and the right: it is, by virtue of the same orientation, also pointed to God. God on this reckoning is not a first order explanation of things in the world, in the way that the passing of the moon between the sun and the earth is an explanation of an eclipse of the sun. God is not a thing among other things in the universe, a cause among other causes. Rather, as the source of the universe's intelligibility and goodness, God is the explanation of explanation; God explains why explanation is possible, why there is any explanation at all, why our intellectual questioning and probing sometimes meet with successful answers. God is the source of the possibility of explanation and hence of verification, the source of the possibility of justification, in human reasoning and acting. Without God there would in the final analysis be no intelligibility and no moral order in the universe and hence there could be no explanation of human explanation and no possibility of justifying human attempts at justification. According to Thomism, God is the necessary pre-condition for explanation being successful and moral judgment valid.

While this account of the Thomist understanding of reason's orientation to the divine is doubtless excessively condensed, it may be enough to suggest why it is that there is a void in the human heart. As the precondition for true knowledge and valid moral judgment, God is later, in terms of what we come to know, than either knowledge of this world or judgment about the rightness or wrongness of particular human actions. But as the precondition for such knowledge God is, in ontological terms, prior to such knowledge. Hence we are, ontologically, oriented to God before we are oriented to the world around us and the people around us—it is just that we catch on to this fact later. But at the very root of our being, in the core of our personality, we are pointed to God, we are God-directed. God is an essential part of the full definition of what it is to be human. Our tragedy, however, is that we cannot by ourselves achieve union with God, even if we can know about him; left to ourselves, we cannot live the life of God himself; union with God is entirely dependent on the action of God himself. As Aquinas says in his commentary on Boethius on the Trinity, "Although man is naturally inclined towards the ultimate end, nevertheless, he cannot attain it naturally, but only through grace."[7] Joseph de Finance conveys Aquinas's opinion by saying, "The highest glory of man is to be predisposed to an end which exceeds his own power."[8] It is in this way that Thomism helps to explain how the entry by Man into rational human consciousness gives rise to the longing for God in the human heart.

God is every bit as much a human imperative as are the truth and the morally right. We can, of course, attempt to escape or evade the spontaneous summons of our human nature to know the truth and to do what is right. But we cannot avoid the demand to make ourselves whole, the call to completeness, the summons to fulfilment.[9] What we can do is attempt to make ourselves whole while evading the summons to divine holiness. There are many well tried stratagems for doing this; they always involve the substitution of an idol for God. We choose to worship something other than God—just as the ancient Israelites did. First, there are the "usual suspects": we worship fame or power or money or pleasure or social status. We seek the fulfilment that only God can bring to the human personality in drink, in drugs, in reputation, fine food or sex. There is, of course, nothing wrong with any of these in themselves. The biblical notion of blessing finds it natural for Man to enjoy the good things of life. It is when these other things take the place of God in our lives that they become harmful to us.

There is no shortage of the substitutes for God that human beings can come up with: it might be the American People, or the German People, or the British Empire, or the Church, or the Papacy, or the Party, or the State, or the Market, or Science, or Technology, or the Cause. It might be our profession or ambition to succeed, our race or our religious creed, a skill or an achievement, or some group with whom we identify, and so forth. So long as these take the place of God, so long as they become the ground of meaning or the supreme value in our lives, so long as they become the over-riding norms that determine our behaviour or our treatment of others or the opinions of others, then we are worshipping idols. It is a paradox of human nature that that which makes us human also makes us prone to sin. Endowed with rational consciousness and the freedom and powers that go with it, Man is a godlike creature who can all too easily topple into the belief or attitude that he is, in fact, God, the centre of the universe.

The deceptive attractiveness of idols is recognised in the Book of Wisdom, which describes idols as "traps for the souls of men and a snare to the feet of the foolish." (14:11) It is when we attempt through some extension of ourselves to achieve the completion of ourselves that our natures crave that we come a cropper, that we find ourselves dissatisfied, unhappy, miserable; that we become conscious of the void in our heart. By contrast, to centre our lives on God is to turn away from idols. (1 Thessalonians 1:9) This is no happy-clappy, sanctimonious claptrap. For example, it is the hard-headed truth at the heart of the Alcoholics Anonymous programme of recovery, the most successful recovery programme available in our society, one that has rescued innumerable people from the degradation of alcoholism and to which many former alcoholics attribute their return to happiness and even their lives. As the late Cardinal Basil Hume was fond of saying, there is a God-shaped space in the human heart.

The human failure to reach the tree of life represents the continuing emptiness that it is the human destiny to attempt to fill. It is this void or blank that makes it easy to become decentred from the one, true God and to put some other good, or god, in his place. As Sirach expresses it, "The beginning of man's pride is to depart from the Lord; his heart has forsaken his Maker." (Sirach 10: 12) Or as William Temple puts it: "As consciousness advances to self-consciousness, so that the self, distinguishing itself from its environment, not only chooses what appetites it shall satisfy but even what ends it shall pursue, self-centredness becomes self-assertion."[10] This is the original sin, or perhaps more accurately the original sinfulness of human beings, the basic human situation. We are decentred from God and centre our lives on a false god of our own making; and from this situation sin flows.

BIG BANG OR STEADY STATE?

The traditional understanding of original sin as an act of disobedience against God's commandment is the Big Bang interpretation of sin—a single catastrophic event brought about Man's corruption and introduced moral evil into the world. What I am proposing is more akin to the Steady State theory—the *basic human situation* causes Man to become decentred, uncoupled from God and sin follows from this situation. You might say that it is an inherited situation, but in saying so you would not be required, as Augustine felt himself to be, to explain how humans came to inherit it. The reason is quite simple: it is the *basic human situation*. We have not achieved perfect unity with God and we cannot claim that we deserve such unity; it is not something that is ours by right. It is a gift that is beyond our capacity to merit. But until we achieve this gift we are incomplete, broken off, unfinished and prone to complete ourselves through the manufacture of idols. It is this tendency that constitutes the source of moral evil and sin in the world. (See Romans 1: 22-23). The words of Simone Weil can deepen our understanding of this point, for she believed that "sin was not a matter of individual acts, but of a state, the original state of mankind." She says, "Sin and virtue are not acts, but states. Acts are only the automatic consequences of the state. But we can only understand them in the shape of acts. Hence the symbol of sin prior to any act."[11] Dietrich Bonhoeffer expresses the same point in his own way, by arguing in a lecture given in 1933 that if one's *Gestalt* is centred on a false idol, then the consequences are evil. If, however, Christ has become the point of reference of the human being, then the voice of conscience becomes the voice of Christ.[12]

This explanation of moral evil and sin places a strong emphasis on interiority, on what goes on in the human heart. It sees commitment to God's will as the source of righteous behaviour and its opposite, the absence of genuine commitment, as the source of sinful action. The Old Testament word for the heart—*leb*—is a powerful word pointing to what the Hebrews believed was not only the centre of the emotions but also the centre of all thought and intellectual activity. In much of the Old Testament, the call of the prophets is for a change of heart, for interior conversion to Yahweh. Burnt sacrifices were not enough—Yahweh preferred a sincere heart. (1 Samuel 15:22; Ps 51:16-17; Isaiah 1:11; Hosea 6:6) It was this emphasis on interiority that gave rise eventually to the Wisdom tradition in the Old Testament. This was a logical outcome of the prophetic tradition and, indeed, of the emphasis on the cultivation of knowledge of good and evil. For in the Old Testament, knowledge of good and evil was something that occurred in the heart of Man.

GENESIS 4

The same emphasis on interiority is to be found in the account of the very first sin in the Bible—the first sin to be recounted as an event in history, albeit the history is mythological history. When Cain kills his brother Abel, it is hard to divine his motive. We are simply told that Cain, who was a tiller of the ground, brought to the Lord an offering of the fruit of the ground while Abel, who kept sheep, "brought of the firstlings of his flock and of their fat portions." To all outward appearance, there is no difference between the offerings of the two brothers. But we read, "And the Lord had regard for Abel and his offering, but for Cain and his offering he had no regard." (Gen. 4: 3-5) It is this response from the Lord that angers Cain and we are told that "his countenance fell." So the Lord said to Cain, "Why are you angry, and why has your countenance fallen? If you do well, will you not be accepted? And if you do not do well, sin is couching at the door; its desire is for you, but you must master it." This is the first mention of "sin" in Genesis and it is described as lying in wait for Cain. It is at this point in the story that Cain leads his brother out into a field and murders him. If commentators have found it difficult to explain Cain's motivation adequately, this is surely because the Genesis authors wish to direct attention to Cain's inward disposition—the description of sin "couching at the door" and of it being a "desire" that Cain should master points to an internal struggle. Cain's offering was slighted by the Lord because his inward disposition was wrong and it was this same inward disposition that led him to commit sin. It was, significantly, a sin of violence, the type of sin, James Barr tells us, most repugnant to God in the Old Testament.

So it is that Cain commits the first sin out of envy because his brother Abel appears to be more favoured by God than he is. His motivation is as we would expect of someone who sought to complete his nature by finding favour with God only to find that God was displeased with what lurked in his heart. The fact that the first sin is committed out of a frustrated desire for God's approval is surely consistent with the explanation for moral evil I have suggested above. For when he fails to find favour with God, who is the object of his soul's yearning, Cain's impulse is to wipe out what he sees as the obstacle to his achievement of this favour, his rival for God's affection, and so he kills his brother. It is the classic case of murder based on envy. And it is entirely consistent with the human search for completeness and wholeness—which when frustrated can lead to envy and violent, sinful action.

THE SOURCE OF SINNING

It may seem paradoxical that I have presented Man's tendency to sin as resulting from idolatry, from his tendency to usurp the place of God in his life and to replace it with himself or some other creature—but then, on reflection, this may not appear such a strange idea. After all, the commandment, "You shall have no other gods before me," accompanied by the prohibition against the manufacture and worship of idols of Man's

own making, is the very first of the Ten Commandments in both formu-
lae, that in Exodus 20:1ff and that in Deuteronomy 5: 6ff. What is more,
the tendency of the Israelites to worship man-made images or the gods of
other nations is regularly condemned in the Old Testament and drew the
withering scorn of the prophets. (For example, Isaiah 2: 6-11; Hosea 2:
8-11; Zephaniah 1: 4-5; Jeremiah 2: 26f; 7: 18-20).

Not only is the worship of idols condemned, but the making of idols
is presented in the Book of Wisdom as the underlying *cause* of sin and
corruption:

> For the idea of making idols was the beginning of fornication,
> and the invention of them was the corruption of life,
> for neither have they existed from the beginning
> nor will they exist for ever.
> For through the vanity of men they entered the world,
> and therefore their speedy end has been planned. (Wisdom 14: 12-13)

The same idea of idol worship as the *source* of sin and evil is repeated a
few verses later:

> For the worship of idols not to be named
> is the beginning and cause and end of every evil. (Wisdom 14: 27)

At the core of this condemnation is the imperative that Man worship
only the one, true God. Idol worship is so reprehensible because it is the
opposite of righteousness, of fidelity to God and the covenant, and is a
radical form of alienation from God. St Paul shares the prophets' deep
loathing for the worship of idols:

> Claiming to be wise they became fools; and they exchanged the glory
> of the immortal God for images resembling a mortal human being or
> birds or animals or reptiles. (Romans 18: 22-23)

Just as righteousness, fidelity, is not a one-off action but a state of being,
so the worship of idols is condemned so roundly because it reflects an
on-going and enduring false stance or attitude. To identify sin with idolatry highlights the fact that individual sins are rooted in a sinful state of
the human being. To see sin as rooted in Man's attempt to place himself
or some other creature at the centre of his universe is to see it not as a
single act but as a state or condition from which single acts of sin occur
or emerge; it is to see it as consisting essentially in some "fundamental

option" or steady affective tendency.[13] Sins do not occur "out of the blue," so to speak, with no prior preparation, but rather they are rooted in some basic orientation or lifestyle which one has opted for, or they reflect a tendency in one to move towards such an orientation or lifestyle. For this reason sinning cannot be truly cured or healed without a change in this fundamental option. Reversal of the fundamental option requires that the sinner needs to change not just this or that sinful deed but to effect change at a radical level by placing God at the centre of his life. As William Temple puts it: "Life cannot be fully integrated about the self as centre; it can only be fully integrated when it becomes God-centred. For God is the real centre of the world; ... only in Him therefore can all creatures find a centre which brings them all to harmony with one another and with themselves."[14]

The first of the ten commandments can readily be seen to be the source or foundation of the other nine that follow since to break a commandment is, at root, to go against God or, to express the same point another way, to prefer something else before God. All sin is a form of idolatry. By contrast, to turn away from idols and do the will of God is to remain in God's friendship, to retain one's God-centred fundamental option. When our fundamental option is for self, we become so full of ourselves that we have no room in our hearts to receive anything as a gift, whether it be a gift from God or from our neighbour: to create room requires us to empty ourselves, to remove the clutter of all the false gods to which we have become attached. Openness to God and to our neighbour requires a degree of purification and self-emptying, for such self-emptying creates the conditions both for receiving and for giving in return. All of this is in the spirit of the First Letter of John, which concludes with the words: "Little children, keep yourselves from idols (1 Jn 4:21)." James Danaher catches the essential message very well when he speaks of those who are venerated as "saints": "Unlike the rest of us, the saint is more acutely aware of the sinister nature of the idols of the world and therefore lives in a more constant state of repentance and turning back toward God. The saint is different from the rest of us, not in being sinless, but in her awareness of her sin and need of repentance. Unlike the rest of us who try to cover or excuse our sin in order to appear sinless, the saint exposes her sin in order that she might become evermore aware of God's forgiveness and love."[15]

This interpretation is spared the problem of explaining how it was possible for two innocents to sin, since the conditions for sin were put in place as soon as Man crossed the boundary between the created realm and the divine, and it also avoids the problem of implicating God in human sinning. The only thing that the human protagonists are denied is union with God himself and that is not something that human beings could possibly be entitled to. In terms of the relationship that exists between God and human beings, union with God could only take place as God's gratuitous gift to his creatures. With the dawning of human intelligence and freedom, the conditions were created that made sin possible. Genesis 3 is an analysis of the basic human situation that makes sin possible, for it shows Man acquiring knowledge and freedom but failing to achieve life, the life of eternal union with God. That is the basic human situation: Man achieves knowledge but not life; he is left wanting and all too easily he will attempt to fill the void with some extension of himself. What I refer to as the basic human situation exposes the radical nature of sin. It is the source of idolatry and it is idolatry or self-worship that lies at the root of all sin.

This explanation of the moral evil in the world in no way attempts to underplay the depth or pervasiveness of evil in the world. It goes along with the words of the Psalmist:

> For I know my transgressions,
> and my sin is ever before me...
> Behold, I was brought forth in iniquity,
> And in sin did my mother conceive me. (Ps. 51)

Moral evil is a primordial fact of human life because Man is born decentred from God, his true end. The source of sinning is the false stance represented by idolatry and idolatry has its roots in Man's condition of *privatio Dei*—of wanting God, of needing God, of lacking God. But because this interpretation does not accept or posit a first, originating sin (*peccatum originale originans*), it avoids seeing humanity as a *massa damnata* while continuing to see it as a *massa salvanda*. Man still stands in need of the completion that only God can give but the default setting for humanity is vehemently not damnation, as Augustine's interpretation would have it. This interpretation goes along with the notion that God wills all human beings to be saved, in accordance with 1 Timothy 2: 3-4, where we read how God our Saviour "desires all men to be saved and to come to the knowledge of the truth."

THE DEVELOPMENT OF THE HEBREW NOTION OF SIN

At this point, it would be well to deepen our understanding of what exactly the bible means by sin by exploring how the transition from the "primitive mentality" to the "wisdom mentality" affected the Hebrew notion of sin.

Primitive consciousness does not conform to modern notions of "morality." Those described by anthropologists as "primitive" do not think in the same moral categories as people who live in what they also describe as "more advanced" cultures. That is why it has taken anthropologists many years and many different approaches to understand the way that primitive people think.[16] The point made by Mary Douglas and other anthropologists is that primitive people have distinctive ways of classifying objects in the world and that this classification determines what is appropriate and what is inappropriate action for human beings. That is why the confusion of categories, crossing some forbidden line, results in the transgressor being deemed unclean, polluted, defiled. What is more, the transgressor becomes a source of pollution for the rest of society. In Greek mythology, Oedipus, who unwittingly breaks the taboos of killing his father and marrying his mother, is himself unclean and the source of the pollution that afflicts the city of Thebes. The pathos and dramatic irony of Sophocles' play, *Oedipus Turannos*, stem from the fact that the more Oedipus attempts to escape his fate the more he brings it upon himself; the audience can see what he is doing in its true light but Oedipus remains in ignorance until it is too late. Primitive societies are not lacking in norms of behaviour but the norms are puzzling to those brought up in a tradition where actions are thought of as the responsibility of individual human agents and blame is attached to people on grounds of personal culpability. Such a way of thinking, based on the development of "interior" concepts such as "responsibility" and "accountability," took some time to develop; they were also dependent for their development on the notion of the "person," the individual who carries responsibility. This also took time to develop. For in primitive cultures social mores are uppermost, the individual self is not strongly differentiated from society but rather "the self is seen as a passive arena in which external forces play out their conflicts."[17]

The covenant made between God and the Hebrew people helped to develop their sense of responsibility. But at first and for a long stretch of their history, the Hebrews understood the covenant as a corporate agreement—an agreement between God and the whole people of Israel.

Moral defect or defilement was conceived not as the violation of a cosmic order imposed by a rigid system of classification, as in primitive society, but as violation of the terms of the agreement between Israel and Yahweh. Moral defect was personalised in being conceived of as an offence against God but was not yet something that was conceived of as the result of an individual's action unless that individual was the king whose actions always implicated the whole community. When the Hebrew prophets urged repentance it was at first and for the most part the community of Israel that they addressed. Hosea's command is typical: "Return, O Israel, to the Lord your God." (Hosea 14: 1) Amos warns: "Prepare to meet your God, O Israel!" (Amos 4: 12) It was the community of Israel that transgressed, worshipping idols and breaking the terms of the covenant, and hence it was the community that was addressed.[18] The notion of individual repentance and conversion to Yahweh emerges in the writings of Jeremiah, in the last days of the Kingdom of Judah just before the Babylonian exile. The return of the whole people to the ways of Yahweh was a lost cause by that stage and so Jeremiah urges each good Israelite to turn again to Yahweh whose ancient covenant of Sinai will be crowned with a new covenant to come.[19] (Jeremiah 18:11; 25:5; 36:3) In the Psalms too conversion to Yahweh is almost always a personal matter. (See, for example, Psalm 51).

The experience of exile in Babylon reinforced the notion of individual responsibility since in that period it was individuals who had remained faithful, and after the exile the emphasis on individual conversion is associated with the need for purity of heart. (See Ezra 9: 6-15; Nehemiah 9: 6-37; Baruch 1: 15-38).[20] The same emphasis is found in Ezekiel, the prophet of the exile: the individual must shoulder responsibility for his own deeds, "the soul that sins shall die." (Ezekiel 18: 4) Through the experience of exile which prompted a good deal of soul searching and revisionist thinking among the Jews, when access to Temple worship and sacrifice was not possible, a shift took place away from a system of penitential sacrificial rituals to a deeper concept of what is involved in returning to Yahweh with one's whole heart. A more interior and personal understanding of sin and conversion developed in this way.[21] God's covenantal relationship with the Hebrews can be seen as a gradual education and movement away from external, behavioural observance of precepts and commandments towards an interior conversion to God, that enables the individual to do what is right because she has understood in her heart what it is that God wants.

It was by these means that the notion of sin as personal guilt before God emerged and this is the notion that we find being developed in the wisdom tradition and which is current by the time of Jesus and the emergence of the Christian era. It is important to grasp that the association between sin and the notion of pollution entertained in primitive cultures is not completely lost. In the bible sin is never merely a matter of morality and always remains a religious concept, the violation of a personal relationship. It is not primarily a transgression of the moral law or the breaking of one of the commandments; it is much more personal than that. As Jaroslav Pelikan explains,

> Forgiveness of sin…was not the act of God by which He forgot a given number of deeds against the Ten Commandments, but the act of God by which I was made worthy of His fellowship. The root of moralism has been the assumption that the sense of sin was moral rather than religious in its derivation, and that therefore the religious sense of profaneness was based upon the moral sense of transgression. Such a definition of sin has been the obverse side of the identification of the Holy and the Good.[22]

He goes on to add that God is primarily concerned with making us holy, making us capable of union with him, preparing us for fellowship with him; sin is our refusal to let God rule over us, holding him off and thereby making ourselves profane before him.[23] It is this understanding of sin that is evident in Paul's writings.

So the biblical notion of sin is not a moral but a religious notion: sin is what gets in the way of Man's friendship with God. Contrary to the claims made by Matthew Arnold [24], the ancient Hebrews were not preoccupied with conduct, action and practical affairs, and Christianity is not concerned first and foremost with conduct and behaviour. (As Arnold famously expressed it, "Religion is ethics heightened,…lit up by feeling…, *morality touched by emotion*."[25]) The reduction of Christianity to a system of morality is suggested and reinforced by the traditional Augustinian understanding of original sin, which reflects Augustine's preoccupation with his own past sexual misdemeanours and the question that haunts his *Confessions*—Whence comes evil? There is more than a suspicion that Augustine incorporates Genesis 3 into his own personal and deeply felt inquiry into the origin of moral evil in the world, his almost desperate search for the answer to that nagging question. However, Genesis 3 is not primarily about a sin nor about the origin of moral evil, but about humanity, what is distinctive about it, and in exploring this question the ancient Hebrews found it necessary to illustrate and explain Man's relationship with God. The early, mythological chapters of Genesis are about those key relationships—between man and woman, with the other animals, with other human beings, and above all with God—that make Man Man.

And with the metamorphosis that makes these relationships possible. That is the central message of Genesis 3, which can surely no longer be considered to be an historical document. The fact that it begins by introducing a talking snake suggests to the reader that we are dealing here with a product of the human imagination. And that it is a work of fiction and not an historical record is strongly confirmed by the literary debt it owes to the *Gilgamesh* epic. Genesis 3 is best understood as a parable, as a commentary on the human race that seeks to interpret the species by explaining how it came into being. As in all parables, the question to ask is not "Did this happen?" but rather "What does this mean?" And, to sum up, the meaning of the story is that two things happen together. First, Man achieves human reason, becoming self-directing and self-determining, capable of merit and demerit (sin); as such he embarks upon history, the story of Man's making of the human world—civilisation, art, artefacts etc.—and with it of Man's making of Man, within the covenantal arrangement provided by God (unity with God through obedience, or sin and separation from God). Second, the basic event, the momentous incident, is that in acquiring reason Man crossed the boundary between the human and the divine. That is the fact that is reinforced by the only commentary on the event we have in Genesis 3 itself—the powerful concluding passage of that chapter, "Behold, he has become like one of us." It is not a situation created *ab initio* by God but is an evolved situation that creates the conditions needed for the drama of salvation, salvation history, to begin. With the dawning of human freedom—basic or radical freedom to determine his own actions—Man also becomes inclined to fall into the slavery of sin, of self-sufficiency and alienation from God.

THE CHRISTIAN UNDERSTANDING OF SIN

The biblical notion of sin is well reflected in Jesus's parable of the Prodigal Son, who wishes to go it alone, leave his father and spend his inheritance elsewhere. Having left his father's house, he soon dissipates what he has inherited (all of which is a gift from the father) and finds himself an exile in a foreign land, standing in pigswill (highly offensive to Jewish sensibility) and thoroughly miserable. This image of sin as *exile from the father, as alienation from God,* conveys much more accurately than Augustine's moralistic reflections on lapsation of the will just what the bible means by sin. And what the bible refers to is a religious situation, the state of the people's or, later, of the individual's relationship with God. Sin in the bible is not a one-off disaster, a tragic mistake with untold consequences; it is a religious state of affairs. And reparation of sin is equally a religious state of affairs, the reparation of our relationship with our father God.

In the parable of the Prodigal Son, the father does not spend his time condemning his exiled son but rather he daily scans the horizon, hoping for his son's return. It is little wonder that the suggestion has been made that the story should be more accurately known as the Parable of the Prodigal Father. In the parable, upon the son's return and confession of having sinned, there is no calling to account, no calculation of the damage or suffering caused to the Father, no reckoning of the shame brought on the household by the son's self-inflicted exile; the language of the moral calculus is totally absent and in its place we read of a welcoming embrace, merry-making, feasting, rejoicing and celebration, because the son that was dead is alive again, he who was lost has been found. (Lk 16: 32) A relationship of friendship and love between father and son has been restored.

NOTES

1. George Steiner, *Errata: An examined life*, 1997, (London: Phoenix edition, 1998) pp. 84-5.

2. Ibid., p. 85.

3. Gabriel Daly, op. cit., p. 89.

4. The *Grail* translation of the Psalms, (London: Fontana Collins 1963).

5. St Augustine, *Confessions*, Book 1, Chapter 1. There are many editions.

6. Bernard Lonergan SJ, "Natural Knowledge of God" in *A Second Collection*, (London: Darton, Longman and Todd, 1974) pp. 127-8. Karl Rahner has a similar insight which he expresses somewhat differently. See Karl Rahner SJ, *The Spirit in the Church*, (London: Burns and Oates, 1979) pp. 14-15. See Jer-

emy Blackwood, "Lonergan and Rahner on the Natural Desire to see God" in *Method: Journal of Lonergan Studies*, New Series, Vol 1, No 2, Fall 2010.

7. Aquinas, *In Boetium de Trinitate, in fine* (q. 6, art. 4, ad 15m), quoted in Henri de Lubac, *Augustinianism and Modern Theology* (New York: Crossroads Publishing, 2000) p. 175.

8. Ibid. Bernard Lonergan's notion of "vertical finality" is pertinent to this idea: see Jeremy Blackwood, op. cit.

9. This statement is supported by Aquinas's ruling that freedom of the will pertains to willing the means but not to willing the ultimate end; here there is no question of freedom. See Bernard Lonergan, *Grace and Freedom*, op. cit., p. 419 and elsewhere.

10. William Temple, *Nature, Man and God*, (London: Macmillan, 1934) p. 366.

11. Ibid., p. 151.

12. Ibid., p. 150.

13. The notion of "fundamental option" is set out by Maurizio Flick S.J. in *De Gratia Christi* (Rome: Gregorian University, 1962) p. 183 ff.

14. William Temple, *Nature, Man and God*, op. cit., p. 373.

15. James Danaher, "The Saint," in *New Blackfriars*, Vol 90, No 1027, May 2009, p. 301.

16. See E.E. Evans-Pritchard, op. cit.

17. Mary Douglas, *Natural Symbols: Explorations in Cosmology* (London: The Cresset Press, 1970) p. 28.

18. John Power, "The Call to Penance in the Old Testament" in *Sin and Repentance*, Ed. Denis O'Callaghan, (Dublin: Gill and Son, 1967) p. 11-12.

19. Ibid., p. 8.

20. Ibid., p. 15.

21. Bernard Lonergan, summarizing the views of Paul Ricoeur, comments: "among the Hebrews, moral defect was first experienced as defilement, then conceived as the people's violation of its covenant with God, and finally felt as personal guilt before God, where, however, each later stage did not eliminate the earlier but took it over to correct it and to complement it." *Method in Theology*, p. 88.

22. Jaroslav Pelikan, *Human Culture and the Holy*, (Philadelphia: Muhlenberg Press, 1955; London: SCM Press, 1959) p. 72-3.

23. Ibid., p. 82-3.

24. Matthew Arnold, *Culture and Anarchy*, (first published in 1869, in revised form in 1875. The edition used here is that edited by J. Dover Wilson, Cambridge: Cambridge University Press, 1950). Here Arnold sets up a contrast between Hebraism and Hellenism, the latter concerned with ideas, intelligence, flexibility and openness of mind, and the former with practicality, duty and self-control. In *Literature and Dogma* (first published in 1873, in a shorter, popular

edition in 1883) and his other religious writings, Arnold suggests that the Judaeo-Christian religious tradition, properly understood, is concerned not with doctrines but with righteousness and right conduct.

25. Matthew Arnold, *Literature and Dogma*, (1883 edition) p. 15-16.

Chapter Six
Restoring Roots

One of the unfortunate consequences of Augustine's interpretation of Genesis has been the loss to the later Christian tradition of the deep symbolism of the image of the tree of knowledge of good and evil and of the image of the tree of life. It is true that the tree of knowledge has featured in many artistic depictions of Adam and Eve in the garden, but they have been depictions of what the artists, operating within the Augustinian tradition, believed to be the moment of "original sin," where the tree is usually presented as an apple tree and is accompanied by the snake![1] Under Augustine's influence, any connection the tree might have with knowledge has tended to be lost or ignored and the focus has been almost exclusively on the supposed act of disobedience, as a naked Eve proffers a bright juicy apple to her naked husband. Compared with depictions of the "apple tree," depictions of the tree of life are relatively rare and the significance of the tree of life as *that to which God deliberately blocked human access once knowledge had been attained* tends not to be conveyed.[2] Yet there are good grounds for claiming that the images of the tree of knowledge and of the tree of life have strong positive associations in both the OT and the NT. Christians have been alive to the theme of wisdom in both testaments and to the notion of the spirit of God being associated with truth and life. But they have tended not to link these themes to the two trees mentioned in Genesis or indeed to other biblical references to these two trees. And this has been a considerable loss.

When an interpretation of a foundational biblical image, concept or event goes awry, then the loss to the tradition is bound to be both considerable and unfortunate.

Augustine, because he saw the major significance of the incident in Genesis 3 as consisting of Man's sinful disobedience of God's command and the fall that followed from this, interpreted the image of the tree of knowledge in a reductive manner. For him the knowledge our first parents achieved did not refer to any power inherent in the tree, but was the knowledge that resulted from the sinful act, the post-factum knowledge that they had done wrong. It did not refer to any knowledge or power deriving from the tree or to any property the tree might be thought to possess. The reference in Genesis to the couple's eyes being opened once they had eaten from the tree of knowledge was likewise reduced to an association with the act of wrongdoing—the couple's eyes were opened to the shame of their sinful action. He never entertains the possibility that the couple might have gained something, acquired some new powers; he has thoughts only for what he believes they have lost. Augustine's unsatisfactory interpretation of the significance of the two trees is of a piece with his unsatisfactory understanding of the divine command that the human couple should not eat from the tree of knowledge. For Augustine, the divine prohibition is simply authoritarian, the inculcation of the message that the human couple owed a duty of obedience to God.[3] Augustine is quite blind to the "primitive tradition" view that the prohibition was related to the fact that knowledge and life were attributes of God, divine prerogatives that lay beyond the rightful reach of the couple.

If Augustine's interpretation of Genesis 3 is accepted then a good part of revelation in scripture might be expected to be concerned with the action taken by God in association with his Chosen People to undo the sin of Adam and put the Hebrew race—and through them the human race—on the right track. In short, it would have been action aimed, first, at countering or undoing and, then, at redirecting. But this is not the picture that emerges in the biblical narrative. Rather, what we find in scripture is a picture of God's action—once the initial impulse to wipe Man out has been reversed—aimed at perfecting the divine asset of knowledge of good and evil that our first parents acquired; and of doing so for the reason that such knowledge is the pathway to eternal life with Yahweh. In both Testaments, the emphasis is on refining and fine-tuning Man's grasp of what is right and what is wrong; of developing what came to be called Wisdom; and, through Wisdom, of bringing Man closer to God. With reference to the symbolic significance of the two trees, we can say that in the bible narrative that follows Genesis 1-11, God strives to educate Man in the use of the "knowledge" he had acquired from the first tree so that he might gain access to the "life" associated with the second tree, access to which God had deliberately blocked in the Genesis tale. The biblical theme or movement known as the "Wisdom Tradition" is the first of the ideas in salvation history I wish to *reconnect* with Genesis 3; the second is the general cast or character of Paul's religious thinking; the third is the revelation of Christ's mission in the gospel of John; fourthly and finally, I shall reconnect Genesis 3 with the image of the tree of life found at the end of the Book of Revelation.

A: WISDOM

The association of the words used in Genesis 3: 22, "knowing good and evil," with wisdom and good judgment is well brought out in a number of passages in the Old Testament. Several commentators have noted the close similarity of the words used in Genesis with the words used by Barzillai in 2 Samuel 19: 34. Barzillai was an old man of eighty who went to meet King David at the river Jordan after David's army had suppressed the rebellion instigated by Absalom, David's son. In an earlier episode Barzillai had fed David and his followers after they had fled from Absalom, so he was someone the King looked on with favour. Invited by King David to cross the river and join him at court in Jerusalem, Barzillai excuses himself on the grounds of his advanced years, saying he has lost the power of telling the difference between good and evil, using a form of words reminiscent of Genesis. Bible commentator Pauline Viviano draws the reasonable conclusion that Barzillai is being invited by the King to come to the court as a trusted adviser or counsellor. In making his excuses, the aged Barzillai in fact is referring to the loss of his ability to make wise judgments.

Viviano ably supports this interpretation by referring to other biblical texts, such as 1 Kings 3:9 and 2 Samuel 14: 17, where the meaning of the phrase "good and evil" is linked to the ruler's ability to make wise and honest judgments on behalf of the people. 1 Kings 3:9 refers to the wisdom of Solomon, which became legendary among the Hebrews. In this text the young King Solomon is asked in a dream what he would like God to give him, and replies: "Give thy servant therefore an understanding mind to govern thy people, that I may discern between good and evil." In verse 12 we read how God is pleased with Solomon's prayer and responds by giving him "a wise and discerning mind." In 2 Samuel 14, King David is petitioned by a "wise woman" and is challenged to make a complicated judgment, and the woman says of the king that he is "like the angel of God to discern good and evil." A few verses later, she says of David, "my lord has wisdom like the wisdom of the angel of God..." In both of these passages, the phrase "to discern good and evil" is clearly taken as synonymous with "having wisdom" while the comparison in the second with the "angel of God" indicates the Hebrew association of wisdom with divinity. What is more, in Deuteronomy 1: 39 and Isaiah 7: 15, the phrase "knowing good and evil" can be seen to refer to knowledge of an adult kind, not possessed by children, knowledge that has been acquired over time through experience. In summary, the phrase "knowing good and evil" refers to the ability to make wise judgments in an independent, adult way, without requiring the permission of some higher personage.[4]

Finally, in Sirach, a late deuterocanonical work authored by Ben Sira that contains the longest portion of Israelite wisdom to come down to us,[5] we read in chapter 17 a poem dealing with the gifts that God has bestowed on human beings:

> The Lord created man out of earth...
> He gave to men...authority over the things upon the earth...
> And made them in his own image.
> He placed fear of them in all living beings,
> And granted them dominion over beasts and birds.
> He made for them tongue and eyes;
> He gave them ears and a mind for thinking.
> He filled them with knowledge and understanding,
> And showed them good and evil. (Sirach 17: 1-7)

In this poem, with its clear echoes of Genesis, knowledge of good and evil is included along with other priceless gifts and blessings—speech, sight, hearing, mind, knowledge and understanding—that the Lord has bestowed on Man. It is clearly something positive, something to be prized; and, coming at the end of such a list, there is no suggestion whatever that this was something that Man acquired illicitly or wrongly—on the contrary, like the other gifts mentioned it is something that God wanted Man to have. In this way it is clearly linked with wisdom, which the Wisdom tradition conventionally treats as something precious that God has freely bestowed on humankind. The other feature that is common to many of the gifts listed here is that they distinguish Man from the other animals, which do not accumulate knowledge nor can they pass it on to their offspring through the gift of speech. Indeed, God entrusts Man to have dominion over the beasts, using his ability to discriminate between good and evil to negotiate moral complexities and respond creatively to life's challenges. He "lets go," thereby enabling Man to grow up and achieve maturity.

This wealth of Old Testament texts would seem to confirm the association between the words used in Genesis about knowledge of good and evil and wisdom, along with an emerging emphasis in the bible on the need for rulers and kings to exercise wise judgment; and to dispose of the arguments of those who are inclined to interpret the Genesis words as referring to the dawning of sexual awareness manifested in the human couple's consciousness of their nakedness.[6] Rather than referring to the dawning of sexual awareness, the phrase "knowing good and evil" or "telling good from evil" as used in these passages clearly refers to the attainment of knowledge, judgment and powers of discernment of a mature, grown up kind—in a word, to the attainment of wisdom and the status of adulthood. And these texts also surely make it clear that the reference to the attainment by the human couple of the knowledge of "good and evil" in Genesis 3 can no longer be understood as a reference to their wish to determine for themselves which actions are good and which are evil.[7] That line of argument is simply not sustainable.

The cultivation of wisdom was, in fact, a dominant theme in the literature of the ancient Near East. Egypt produced wisdom writings in all periods of its history. Proverbs, fables and poems about human suffering came also from Mesopotamia. Wisdom was prized by rulers and public administrators as well as by those belonging to the clerical classes. It reflected the ambitions of those who wanted to "get on" at court, of those who wished others to think well of them, and placed a strong emphasis on enlightened self-interest while stressing the desirability of honesty, moderation, kindliness, chastity and other social virtues. Consisting largely of exhortations, warnings and hymns in praise of wisdom, it knew no national boundaries, and Israelite Wisdom literature shows many examples of "borrowings" from the writings of other nations.[8]

Wisdom literature is unusual in making few references to Israelite history, such as the exodus or the promise made to Abraham or the conquest of Canaan, and the like. Wisdom is more interested in reason and the solutions to life's problems that reason can devise. It is a tradition that is at once intellectual, placing a strong emphasis on human reason, and practical, oriented to discovering the art of living well. For the Israelites Wisdom is not like Greek knowledge but more akin to a skill: it is the skill of the craftsman, the sure touch of the skilled administrator, the prudence and good sense of the leader. In Greek, wisdom is *Sophia* and not *Episteme*. The Hebrew books in the Wisdom tradition, such as Proverbs, Ecclesiastes and Job aim at teaching men how to live with their problems rather than achieve intellectually satisfying solutions. Wisdom focuses on the craft of living a good life, on the skills and values that lead to happiness, on how to achieve a good outcome through our conduct. For example, in Proverbs 3: 29f, we read, "Do not plan evil against your neighbour/who dwells trustingly beside you./ Do not contend with a man for no reason,/ when he has done you no harm./ Do not envy a man of violence and do not choose any of his ways;/for the perverse man is an abomination to the Lord,/ but the upright are in his confidence."

So highly prized did Wisdom become in the culture of the ancient Hebrews that a whole literature grew up not only to communicate it but to sing its praises: Wisdom became the object of deep veneration and unstinting praise, recognised as the secret of a good life. So in Proverbs 3: 21f, we read: "My son, keep sound wisdom and discretion;/ let them not escape from your sight,/ and they will be life for your soul/ and adornment for your neck./ Then you will walk on your way securely,/ and your foot will not stumble./ If you sit down, you will not be afraid;/ when you lie down, your sleep will be sweet."

The Israelites' cultivation of wisdom is made distinctive through the association that they recognised between Wisdom and Yahweh; for Wisdom is one of Yahweh's greatest attributes:

> The Lord by wisdom founded the earth;
> By understanding he established the heavens;
> By his knowledge the deeps broke forth,
> And the clouds drop down the dew." (Pr. 3: 19-20)

Only Yahweh is truly wise and it is he who grants wisdom to humans: because the Nephilim, the giants of old, were denied wisdom, they perished through their folly (Bar. 3: 26-28). Similarly, it was because Cain departed from the path of wisdom, slaying his own brother, that "he perished"—in deliberate contrast to Adam, the first human, who interestingly was delivered from his "transgression" by wisdom and given the strength "to rule all things"! (Wisdom 10: 1-3)[9] This depiction of wisdom as quintessentially divine chimes with those Old Testament passages that depict knowledge of good and evil as a divine attribute and one of the greatest gifts humankind ever received from God. (See above, the prayer of the young King Solomon in Kings 3:9-12, and Sirach 17:7).

The height of wisdom is understanding the judgments of Yahweh and it is said that "fear of the Lord is the beginning of wisdom" (Proverbs 9: 10; Job 28: 28). In Deuteronomy there appears the notion of wisdom that is to dominate all later ideas: that wisdom is the observation of the Law (Dt 4: 6). The observation of the Law is seen to be the Israelite route to prosperity and esteem among the nations; failure to observe the Law can only lead to ruin. Folly is the opposite of wisdom, the fool the opposite of the wise man. The fool is not indulged in the Old Testament because, where wisdom leads to prosperity and blessing, folly leads to ruination and disaster. To depart from the pathway laid down by wisdom is to end up ruined and miserable.

The Hebrew cultivation of wisdom is the result of a prolonged reflection on the importance of the role of wisdom in its own tradition. As the grandson of Ben Sira, the author of Sirach, says in the Prologue, his grandfather, "after devoting himself especially to the reading of the law and the prophets and the other books of our fathers, and after acquiring considerable proficiency in them, was himself also led to write something pertaining to instruction and wisdom, in order that, by becoming conversant with this also, those who love learning should make even greater progress in living according to the law." So the Wisdom tradition is seen to come out of the prophetic tradition and the insistence of the prophets on the need for Israel to adhere to the law. Ben Sira was most probably a religious Jew living in the Jewish quarter of the Hellenistic city of Alexandria, who was anxious that his fellow Jews should be mindful of their heritage and guided in their decisions about how to live by the customs and examples of their forefathers.[10]

However, even in the Old Testament the limitations of wisdom, its inability to answer all of life's questions, are explored. Both Ecclesiastes and the Book of Job question the somewhat complacent belief that a life dedicated to wisdom will inevitably be rewarded with happiness and prosperity. These two books in particular reflect on the injustices in the world and on the human suffering and misery that are experienced even by very good people, revealing the limitations of human reason and of the Wisdom tradition itself. While both Job and Qoheleth, the author of Ecclesiastes, are ultimately resigned to the mystery of suffering and submit to the inscrutable will of Yahweh, they nevertheless point up the limitations of Hebrew wisdom and suggest that the riddle of human existence requires as a solution something deeper and greater than mere wisdom. Notwithstanding this subversive element within the wisdom tradition itself, however, wisdom continues to be prized and even Qoheleth never quite abandons his belief that "wisdom excels folly as light excels darkness." (Ecclesiastes 2: 13)

The prevailing Old Testament position is that there is a strong association of wisdom with Yahweh, and this is seen most powerfully in the personification of wisdom in several of the books in the wisdom literature. Wisdom was the first thing created by God:

> Wisdom was created before all things,
> And prudent understanding from eternity...
> The Lord himself created wisdom;
> He saw her and apportioned her,
> He poured her out upon all his works.
> She dwells with all flesh according to his gift,
> And he supplied her to those who love him. (Sirach 1: 4-10)

> The Lord created me at the beginning of his work,
> The first of his acts of old.
> Ages ago I was set up,
> At the first, before the beginning of the earth.
> When there were no depths I was brought forth,
> When there were no springs
> Abounding with water. (Proverbs 8: 22-24)

Proverbs goes on to speak of how wisdom was with God when he created the earth: "then was I beside him, like a master workman." (Proverbs 8: 30) It is in this way that the feminine *Sophia*, sometimes referred to as "Lady Wisdom," the Wisdom of the Old Testament, acts as the template for the masculine *Logos* (meaning both Reason and Word) mentioned in the Prologue of St John's gospel: "In the beginning was the Word, and the Word was with God, and the Word was God. He was in the beginning with God; all things were made through him, and without him was not anything made that was made." (Jn 1: 1-3) It would be hard to think of a closer tie between the Old and the New Testaments than this.[11] The Hebrew notion of Wisdom was the culmination of a very long tradition and, once we grasp its link with the acquisition of the knowledge of good and evil by our first parents, we can see how in the bible the emphasis was—is—on bringing this knowledge to a refined level of perfection and prizing it as something good.

Knowledge of good and evil may have played a role in the events of Genesis 3, but it is far from being disowned and is cherished as something precious. It is not presented as the result of a sinful action, as something illicitly stolen from God. Rather, if we see it in the context of the "Primitive tradition," while the acquisition of knowledge may have represented a crossing of the boundary separating God from the created realm, once that boundary was crossed the divine plan of salvation was to enable Israel to develop its divine asset so that, by its means, the chosen people would be drawn ever closer to God himself. That is why, I believe, it is quite legitimate to see the prohibition against eating from the tree of knowledge in Genesis 3 as part of the mechanics of the plot rather than as a strict moral prohibition. If God truly wanted humanity to have wisdom it is difficult to understand the prohibition in any other way. In terms of narrative function, the divine prohibition sets up anticipations in hearers or readers: what will become of the man and the woman if they cross the line separating God from his creatures—the ultimate *taboo*? In a society committed to the categories of "clean" and "unclean" that must have been the epicentral issue. The rest of the unfolding drama hangs on the divine response.

THE LITERARY ARTISTRY OF THE TALE

This leads me to reflect on what I firmly believe to be essential to a correct understanding of the early chapters of Genesis, namely their artistic composition. Whenever we are tempted to read the story in Genesis 3 as a *moral* tale—as the tale of human disobedience of a divine command—we need to remind ourselves that the notion of sin as personal guilt before God, and the kind of moral reasoning that goes with this, developed among the Hebrews some considerable time after this ancient tale was first composed; storytelling as an art form for the communication of complex ideas by means of metaphor, image and symbol was in existence long before the vocabulary of moral reasoning had been developed. The greatest danger of reading the story the wrong way occurs when we view it through spectacles not only of later generations but of later epochs, when we impose on it thought categories belonging to a much later age. If the story is seen more appropriately as the artistically crafted tale of a rite of passage, our response is likely to be truer to the *narrative intention* of the storytellers. In a rite of passage the focus is on the transformation of the protagonists, and that this is the focus of this tale is brought out by its artistry as a piece of literature, by the fact that the moment of high drama in Genesis 3 occurs, not when the couple eat the fruit—this is treated in flat, muted language—but when God abruptly asks the couple the question: Who told you that you were naked? That is the point of confrontation, the moment of greatest dramatic tension.

The question jolts the reader with its very strangeness. Human nakedness had already been signalled and highlighted by the Yahwist storytellers' strong, flamboyant placement of the couple's *unashamed* nakedness at the end of Genesis 2. But when in Genesis 3 we read of how God calls on them in Eden in the cool of the day, the man tells him that he was afraid because he was naked and so hid himself. A "before and after" comparison in respect of the couple's response to being naked has been set up. It is at this point that God asks him who told him he was naked and then, without waiting for an answer, goes on to ask the next question, Have you eaten of the tree of which I commanded you not to eat? (Gen 3: 11) This latter question pinpoints the reason or grounds for the difference between "before" and "after." Augustine, who completely misunderstands the meaning of the Hebrew word for "shame" in this story, places the emphasis on the second part of this second question, on the subordinate clause referring to the prohibition; but the true artistry, and the point of high drama, resides in the fact that God asks such a question and then *does not wait for an answer but provides his own answer in the form of a question.* This reveals the incisive wisdom and sure insight of the Lord God who addresses the couple like a wise parent confronting a pair of erring children. *It also draws attention to the fact that a profound change has occurred*: the couple now know that they are naked when not clothed, something that was not the case before they ate from the tree of knowledge. The writing very deliberately ensures that the climactic moment of Genesis 3 is not the act of eating from the tree but the resultant transformation of the human pair. That is the main point of the story. One of the characteristics of Hebrew narrative, as we noted earlier, is communication by means of implication rather than by explicit explanation, and the implication behind the fact that the second question is asked before any answer to the first question has been received is enormous.

The storytellers' brilliance is seen in the formulation of the first, "strange" question and the combined effect of the two questions coming together. The formulation of the "strange" question—"Who told you that...?"—is unexpected. A more conventional and predictable question by the Lord God, upon discovering that the couple were hiding because they were naked, would have been: "Why are you ashamed of being naked?" or "Why are you afraid of being seen naked?" Such a line of questioning could have lent weight to the Augustinian emphasis on the guilty shame brought about by the couple's knowledge of their sin, of their supposed wrong-doing. But the actual question asked—"Who told you that you were naked?"—avoids any such implication and puts the spotlight clearly on a change in the couple's self-understanding or self-awareness; it speaks not of shame, even in the sense of simple embarrassment, but of cognition, of a new self-knowledge. The question suggests that some third party might have imparted information to them about their condition, leading them to see themselves in a new light, suggesting that they could not have worked this out on their own, as they had come from the hand of their creator; as we read, the thought that the Lord God is here alluding to the cunning snake comes to mind. But this thought is dispelled by the question that quickly follows: "Have you eaten from the tree...?" This second question changes the focus, illustrating how the Lord God's thinking moves rapidly on, and enforces the point that this new self-understanding is not due to some third party but has been caused by a change that has been brought about in the couple themselves: their new self-knowledge is down to their eating from the tree of knowledge. To suggest so much with two questions is a superb illustration of the storytellers' art, and it also makes clear that what is being revealed in this story, that what the story is about, is not some act of wrongdoing or sin, but *the change* that has been wrought in the couple. Their consciousness has been radically altered and is now fundamentally different from the consciousness of the other animals, none of whom experience any embarrassment about being naked.

If the *transformation of the human couple* is the central fact revealed by the tale in Genesis 3, we also need to bear in mind that it is only the first part of a three part story. If I am right in seeing this tale as the opening stage in the narrative of a rite of passage, we need to treat it as just that and, for the sake of narrative integrity, accept that the story is not completed until after the dangerous interim stage described in Genesis 4-8 and after the final stage, the stage of re-integration and renewal, which comes with the Flood and the inauguration of the covenant in Genesis 9: this last part of the narrative is the divine response to the human act of transgression and the taboo the couple have incurred; it is the tale's denouement, without which it is incomplete. The artistic integrity of the narrative requires us to see it as consisting of these three stages; to isolate any one stage is to do damage to the tale's narrative structure. From the point of view of literary art, Genesis 3 is an integral part of a story that runs until the end of Genesis 9: 17, and so long as we accept this we are unlikely to mistake the tale's narrative intention. A major mistake of Augustine, who shows no understanding of what is meant by a "rite of passage," is to treat Genesis 3 as an isolated incident, as a story in its own right, wrenched from the larger narrative leading up to the covenant; around this incident he then feels free to weave his own private speculations based on his guilt about his past sexual experience and his Greek Neoplatonic philosophy.

WISDOM AND THE DIVINE

It is hard to appreciate the Hebrews' deep and prolonged veneration of Wisdom unless we see it as the veneration of something divine in Man. The author of Proverbs comes close to proclaiming this when he describes Wisdom as "a tree of life to those who lay hold of her." (Proverbs 3: 18) It is suggested in this passage from Isaiah:

> The spirit of the Lord shall rest on him,
> the spirit of wisdom and understanding,
> the spirit of counsel and might,
> the spirit of knowledge and the fear of the Lord.
>   (Is. 11: 2)

The Wisdom tradition, the Israelite pursuit of Wisdom, I am suggesting, was perceived as an extension of the divine attribute of wisdom that Man had acquired in Eden; this is hardly surprising since we are told that "the woman" in the story saw that "the tree was to be desired to make one wise." (Genesis 3: 6) It is also implied by the fact that in a good many other passages written by Hebrew biblical authors the phrase used for wisdom is "knowledge of good and evil." As we have seen, Sirach considers such knowledge to have been one of the greatest gifts God has made to men: "He filled them (men) with knowledge and understanding,/And showed them good and evil." (Sirach 17: 7)

If the wisdom tradition in the Old Testament is the fruit of questing and questioning, something achieved over time through experience, then the wisdom mentioned in the New Testament is revealed as the answer to Israel's searching. There are not many references to wisdom in the gospels, but in the Gospel of Luke, in one of his more fiery exchanges with the Pharisees, Jesus presents himself as the true interpreter of Divine Wisdom, and goes on to accuse the Pharisee lawyers of having "taken away the key of knowledge" before telling his disciples that "Nothing is covered up that will not be revealed, or hidden that will not be known." (Lk 11: 49—12: 2) Jesus is here presenting *himself* as the one who will unlock the wisdom of God for all to come to know. *He* is the knowledge that Man was searching for when he first ate from the tree of knowledge in Eden.

In chapter 5 of the Epistle to the Hebrews, the author, usually considered to have been an educated Jewish convert to Christianity with a Hellenistic intellectual background who wrote some time after Paul had completed his last epistle, makes the distinction between those who, like children, live on milk and are "unskilled in the word of righteousness" and "the mature" who are capable of eating solid food because their faculties have been "trained by practice to distinguish good from evil." (Hebrews 5: 13-14) This is yet another passage, this time from a relatively late period in the New Testament writings, where a clear equivalence is made between wisdom, the fruit of experience, and the ability to distinguish good from evil. Like the passages quoted from the Old Testament, it suggests that in eating from the tree of knowledge of good and evil our first parents gained something positive, acquired something precious, something that set them apart from the rest of the animal kingdom and marked them as mature adults capable of taking on the responsibilities that life presents, a divine asset whose cultivation was positively salvific.

B: ST PAUL

In his writings, St Paul presents Jesus as the final revelation of God's wisdom. At the beginning of his letter to the Ephesians, he speaks of how God has "made known to us in all wisdom and insight the mystery of his will, according to his purpose which he set forth in Christ as a plan for the fullness of time, to unite all things in him, things in heaven and things on earth." (Eph. 1: 9-10) In 1 Corinthians Paul makes a still bolder claim when he defines Christian wisdom as Christ nailed to the cross, which confounds the wisdom of this world but is the revelation of God's hidden wisdom and secret purpose, his plan of salvation for humankind (1 Cor 1: 18 and 2: 7-10). Defying the somewhat complacent link between wisdom and human prosperity frequently proclaimed in the wisdom tradition of the Jews, he goes on to say that the wise of this world must become fools to acquire the true wisdom of God: "For the wisdom of this world is folly with God." Christ is presented as the fulfilment of the wisdom of God, as the means of salvation who has superseded the law of the Old Testament.

It is in this way that Christ is related to the first mention in the bible of the tree of knowledge of good and evil. It is surely not too fanciful to see the tree of knowledge of good and evil being transformed in the Christian era into the tree of the cross, since in Acts and the epistles the cross is frequently referred to as a tree[12]—that the knowledge Man took from God now finds its completion in the cross, understood as the great symbol of loving self-giving; and that the human quest for knowledge of good and evil, for wisdom, finds its answer in the commandment to love God above all things and our neighbour as ourselves. And just as the tree of knowledge of good and evil is presented in Genesis as the gateway to the tree of life, so the cross of Christ is the gateway to the resurrection and a sharing in the eternal life of Yahweh. And just as God raised Jesus from the dead (Rom 8: 11) so will he raise from the dead those who have put on Christ Jesus; and in this way the barrier that Yahweh placed on the way to the tree of life (Gen 3: 24) will be definitively removed. Deprived of this association with the images of the two trees in the Garden of Eden, our appreciation of the saving actions of God in Christ, as set out in Paul's writings, is greatly impoverished. It is hard to believe that Paul, with his references to time and "the hidden wisdom of God," did not grasp these associations and intend his readers to grasp them also.

THE EPISTLE TO THE ROMANS, PAUL AND ORIGINAL SIN

Augustine provides a different interpretation of Paul's writings. As is well known, he found in Paul, and in particular in his references to Adam and Christ in the Epistle to the Romans, further confirmation for his doctrine of original sin. In *Ad Simplicianum*[13], where he reflects on the Epistle to the Romans, Augustine first uses the term *peccatum originale* (original sin), a phrase not found anywhere in scripture, and supports his understanding of it by reference to Romans 5: 14. In a later work, *De natura et gratia*[14], he again quotes from Romans 5, this time citing verse

12 against Pelagius, claiming that "death passed to all men" through Adam, "in whom all have sinned." This is a famous mis-translation in the Latin Vulgate bible of the Greek *eph ho pantes hemarton* which reads in the Vulgate as *in quo omnes peccaverunt—in whom all have sinned*. The correct translation should rather be *in as much as* all have sinned, or *in that* all have sinned, or *because* all have sinned. The mistake made by Jerome, the translator of the Vulgate edition whose prowess as a translator Augustine greatly admired, was to translate *eph ho* as if it were *en ho—in quo, in whom*. It is a major mistake that Augustine inherited from Jerome (and defended against his own critics) and no doubt underpinned the supreme confidence Augustine had in his understanding of original sin, since the verse appears to state clearly that all of us have sinned in Adam and must, for that reason, share his guilt. It has been described as Augustine's "trump card"[15] in his debates with his opponents.

Notwithstanding this error, a defender of Augustine might well claim to find in Romans 5 sufficient evidence to support Augustine on original sin. For the passage draws a clear parallel between Adam and Christ, claiming that Adam brought sin into the world and, through sin, death, which spread to all men; and goes on to add that "if many died through one man's trespass, much more have the grace of God and the free gift in the grace of that one man Jesus Christ abounded for many...Then as one man's trespass led to condemnation for all men, so one man's act of righteousness leads to acquittal and life for all men. For as by one man's disobedience many were made sinners, so by one man's obedience many will be made righteous." (Rom 5: 12-19) A neat schematic summary of Romans 5 would look like this:

Adam—Christ
Disobedience—Obedience
Sin—Grace
Condemnation—Justification
Death—Life.

From this powerful passage in Romans 5, some theologians have been led to draw several conclusions: first, that just as Christ is a real person, so Adam must be understood as a real person; second, and most importantly, that Paul clearly sees Adam's action of eating from the forbidden tree as an original trespass or sin responsible for all subsequent moral evil, a sin in which all of us are implicated; and third, that as a consequence of these two, the incident described in Genesis 3 must be interpreted as a fall from a higher to a lower state since it has called forth Christ's saving act of redemption aimed at restoring us to something approaching our former status.

In answer to these arguments, I would say, first, that to understand Christ's role in deliberate contrast to Adam's is not thereby to grant historical status to Adam. One of the functions of myth in Genesis is to provide mythical prototypes which are the pattern of the historical figures or incidents written about later. So when Paul speaks of Adam as "a type of the one who was to come" (5: 14), there is no necessity either to believe that Paul understood Adam to be an historical person (though he may well have done) or for us to understand Adam as an historical person. The significance of Christ's action, which it is Paul's main aim to convey, is just as adequately served by the notion that Adam was a type of Christ—a model or image or pattern—in a purely figurative sense. The antithesis between Adam and Christ drawn by Paul can be understood, therefore, as nothing more than a literary device.

This is the crucial point. If we can agree that, whatever Paul may have believed, modern scholarship makes it well nigh impossible to read Genesis 3 as the record of an actual historical event, then the possibility of the event described in Genesis 3 having an actual impact on events in human history—on human nature and human behaviour—can be discounted. If the link between the events in Genesis 3 and history are severed, then the Augustinian understanding of these events is negated and nullified. Gabriel Daly, a Catholic theologian who finds the traditional Western teaching on original sin extremely problematic, observes, "The task which faces the Christian theologian today is to show how one can and must accept the reality of the situation which the phrase 'original sin' was designed to cover, but to do so without an appeal to what Newman called 'some terrible aboriginal calamity'."[16] Chapter Five of the present work was devoted to showing how there is, in fact, an alternative explanation for the situation which the phrase "original sin" was designed to cover—namely sin as rooted in idolatry and idolatry as rooted in the basic human situation—and Chapters Two, Three and Four were devoted to showing that Genesis 3 is not about a first or original sin. The arguments deployed in these chapters also support the view that it is simply no longer tenable to consider Genesis 3 to be the record of an historical event. Neither could Genesis 3 be considered to be a fictional recreation of an historical event, like the so-called historical novel. The form of literature known as the "historical novel" works by weaving a story—or stories—around established historical events, but in the case of Genesis 3 there is no established historical event and, indeed, what is to be considered as fact is the issue in question.

Neither is there any need to understand Paul's reference to "one man's trespass" with a realism compelling the judgment that Adam's action, as described in Genesis 3, was anything more than a literary illustration of the nature of sin (and temptation as an integral element of sinning). If, as seems likely, Paul's main intention is to draw out the universality of Christ's action by drawing a parallel between Christ and Adam (as opposed to a more strictly "Jewish" figure such as Abraham or Moses), then this intention can be achieved just as well even if Adam is regarded as a non-historical mythical man. Historical realism is not required for the significance of Christ's action to be grasped. Paul is presenting Christ as the new Adam and, as such, the new head of humanity, the firstborn of the new creation. This is a general point that Paul makes several times in his epistles and is not dependent on any Adam-Christ comparison. For example, Paul makes the same point in his epistle to the Colossians without making any reference to Adam, speaking of Christ as "the image of the invisible God, the first-born of all creation...He is the head of the body, the Church; he is the beginning, the first-born from the dead, that in everything he might be pre-eminent." (Col. 1: 15-18) On other occasions, such as in Romans 5 and 1 Corinthians 15, Paul finds in the fact that Adam was presented as the first of many, the head of humanity, a useful analogy for illustrating the universality of Christ's redemptive action.

In other words, the comparison with Adam made by Paul can be understood as no more than a convenient literary device drawing attention to the fact that Christ's saving action was a "new deal" for *all of humanity*. Those who are born of Christ through baptism are born into this new humanity and in this way become "sons of God": we become by adoption what Christ is by nature.[17] The Adam-Christ contrast mirrors Paul's comparison of the "flesh" and the "spirit," two distinct and often opposed orders of being central to his thinking; Adam represents the order of nature, the natural order of the universe, or the "flesh," and Christ represents (and extends) the meaning of the supernatural order, the order of salvation, which is summed up by Paul in his frequent use of the word "spirit." The point I would stress here is that when he compares Christ with Adam, whether in Romans 5 or in 1 Corinthians 15 (the reference to Adam in 1 Timothy 2: 12-14 does not consist of an Adam-Christ comparison but of an Adam-Eve comparison, to Eve's disadvantage), Paul is seeking to explain Christ and not Adam. As James Barr says, here Paul is *interpreting Christ*.[18] Paul's intention is not to offer a commentary on Genesis 3 but rather he refers to Genesis 3 in order to illustrate a feature of Christ's act of redemption, its universal scope; Adam was not central to Paul's thinking but Christ certainly was. This view of Paul's references to the image of the "two Adams" is supported by the following comments of the highly respected Catholic scholar Raymond Brown on Romans 5: 12-21:

> Paul's interpretation of Genesis may have been shaped in part by the interpretations of his time, but what dominates his picture of Adam is his theology of Jesus. In other words, he did not read Genesis and come to understand Jesus; he understood Jesus and read Genesis in that light. *This retrospective approach means that Paul really has nothing novel to teach us about the historical origins of the human race. Paul's view of the universality of sin and death stems from observing the existing world, and he uses the Genesis story to explain that.*[19]

The answer to the third argument follows from the answers to the first two. There is no reason to see Christ's act of redemption as a restoration of Man to his former higher state.[20] Indeed, Paul makes no comparison between Man's new status and the condition of Man before the "Fall," nor does he for that matter ever speak of a "Fall."[21]

It is in the "later strata" of the Old Testament, those influenced by Greek thought, that references occur to the sin of Adam and its consequences. As we saw earlier, such references do not occur in the Hebrew Old Testament. This is a view confirmed by the eminent Protestant biblical scholar James Barr as well as by the Catholic biblical scholars, Herbert Haag[22] and Joseph Blenkinsopp[23], and it is strongly reinforced by the Hebrew Bible expert James Kugel who in his book, *The Bible as It Was*[24], spells out the changes in interpretation of certain key episodes in the Hebrew Old Testament that occurred between 200 BC and 100 AD. One of these episodes is that described in Genesis 3.

As a religiously educated Jew, hailing from the cosmopolitan city of Tarsus and speaking Greek as well as Hebrew, Paul was doubtless influenced by the Hellenistic wisdom tradition of his day. It was under the influence of this tradition that Paul wrote as he did in Romans 5 and 1 Corinthians 15. In trying to reach a judgment about how we should take Paul's account in these texts, it is best, I believe, to accept that Paul was drawing on the Greek influenced wisdom tradition of his time in his remarks about death entering the world through the sin of one man (Romans 5: 12); but at the same time we need to bear in mind that he was not primarily offering an interpretation of the story of Adam and Eve in Eden but rather offering us an insight into the nature and scope of Christ's redemption and the superabundance of Christ's grace; he was simply using a story that was to hand, so to speak, for the sake of illustration. It was St Augustine, taking his interpretation from Paul and, supporting it with his own brand of Neoplatonic Greek thought, who imposed the Greek inspired interpretation on the story in Genesis 3. As I have previously observed, Augustine's argument is based to a large extent on the inference he draws from the words of the Lord God in Genesis 2: 17, "for in the day that you eat of it you shall die." From this he inferred that Man was created immortal and that death—which to the Greeks but not the Hebrews was regarded as a "terrible thing"[25]—was introduced as a punishment for sin. But whereas Paul's aim in Romans 5 and 1 Corinthians 15 was to help his hearers or readers to understand Christ, Augustine took these passages to be offering an interpretation of the deeds of Adam and Eve, and he undoubtedly felt his argument to be supported by Jerome's erroneous and misleading translation of Romans 5: 12.

The Church in the West has supported Augustine's interpretation and, in so doing, endorsed the comments found in a few texts in the Greek Old Testament as well as in some of the intertestamental apocryphal texts. However, the gospels are silent on the subject of Adam's sin; at no point do we find Jesus making reference to what for Augustine was a key component of his whole theological system, and the silence of the gospels on this matter is fully in harmony with the silence about it we find in the books of the Hebrew bible. Despite being highly conscious of human sinfulness, at no point does the Hebrew Old Testament refer back to the incident in Eden to explain this or to suggest that death is a consequence of sin[26]. The silence of the Old Testament and of Jesus himself on the subject of original sin surely weighs strongly in favour of this doctrine not having the importance which the Western Christian tradition has attributed to it, at least since the time of Augustine. If Jesus's mission had been to undo the sin of Adam and restore us to the state of innocence we were in before the "Fall," then his silence on the subject is quite baffling.

Nor do we find in the gospels or the Hebrew Old Testament any sense of "a lost world," any nostalgia for a world that might have been if Adam had not sinned, a hankering after an age of innocence and virtue now long gone. There is longing, wanting, yearning in the Old Testament, but this is directed at Yahweh and is oriented to the future rather than the past:

> As the hart longs
> for flowing streams,
> so longs my soul for thee, O God.
> My soul thirsts for God,
> for the living God. (Ps 42)

There is also the widely acknowledged and telling fact that, despite having the scriptures many hundreds of years before the arrival of Christianity, the Jews never formulated anything like the Christian doctrine of a first or original sin. And we should also recall that among the Fathers Augustine's was not the only interpretation of Genesis 3 but, on account of his stature and the accessibility of his Latin writings in the West, his was the view that dominated Christian thinking throughout the medieval period and at the time of the Reformation and the Counter-Reformation.

THE GENERAL CHARACTER OF PAUL'S THOUGHT

If we move beyond Romans chapter 5 to consider the line of reasoning to be found in the epistle *as a whole*, it is remarkable how the epistle appears to be a trenchant commentary on chapter 3 of Genesis as we have interpreted it here. For the Epistle to the Romans takes up and amplifies the theme that is central in Genesis 3, the theme of the relationship between knowledge and life. Paul brings out vividly the fact that knowledge—in this case knowledge of the law, whether that be the law "written on their hearts" which the Gentiles know (2: 15) or the law of Moses which the Jews know (2: 17f)—does not translate into life, that knowledge by itself cannot confer life, in that peculiar biblical understanding whereby life is associated with God, freedom and righteousness and death is associated with sin and slavery. The condition of Man under the law of Moses, Paul may be understood as saying, is not such an advance as Jews like to think on the condition of Man depicted in Genesis. In fact, Paul goes further and sees knowledge as positively dangerous, since it makes sin possible while failing to provide an effective antidote. This again mirrors the picture that emerges in Genesis, where Man achieves knowledge but this fails to lead on to living righteously but rather creates the conditions needed for sin. The Epistle to the Romans, I would suggest, is the best Christian commentary we have on the first book of the bible, and is clearly written with Genesis in mind.

First there is Paul's startling comment: "For no human being will be justified in his sight by works of the law, since through the law comes knowledge of sin." (3:20) This is clarified by the extensive comments on the law and sin in 7: 7-25:

> What then shall we say? That the law is sin? By no means! Yet, if it had not been for the law, I should not have known sin. I should not have known what it is to covet if the law had not said, "You shall not covet." But sin, finding opportunity in the commandment, wrought in me all kinds of covetousness. Apart from the law sin lies dead. It was once alive apart from the law, but when the commandment came, sin revived and I died; the very commandment which promised life proved to be death to me. (7: 7-11)

An interesting distinction is made here by Paul between the law, which is good, and the sin which knowledge of the law makes possible. The parallel with Genesis 3 is fairly clear: the achievement of knowledge is not in itself a sin but it opens the way for sin, it creates the preconditions for sin. What Paul—a Jew brought up in the Mosaic covenant with a thorough familiarity with the law—wishes here to emphasise is that in the face of sin's power, mere knowledge is puny:

> For I know that nothing good dwells within me, that is, in my flesh. I can will what is right, but I cannot do it. For I do not do the good I want, but the evil I do not want is what I do… For I delight in the law of God, in my inmost self, but I see in my members another law at war with the law of my mind and making me captive to the law of sin which dwells in my members. (7: 18-20)

Contrasting with the feebleness of the law when confronted by sin's power is the power that comes from Christ's victory over death:

> But you are not in the flesh, you are in the Spirit, if the Spirit of God really dwells in you. Any one who does not have the Spirit of Christ does not belong to him. But if Christ is in you, although your bodies are dead because of sin, your spirits are alive because of righteousness. If the Spirit of him who raised Jesus from the dead dwells in you, he who raised Christ Jesus from the dead will give life to your mortal bodies also through his Spirit who dwells in you. (8: 9-11)

Here then is the final answer to the riddle of human existence, the in-completeness of Man exposed in Genesis. Man's separation from God has been partially overcome through God's initiation of the covenant with Moses. But the Mosaic covenant, and the system of Law that devel-oped within and through it, have not been able effectively to bridge the gap between God and Man; they have provided knowledge but not life. In many ways, Paul is saying, the gulf between God and Man remains, the law does not provide true union with God; rather in a sense it simply serves to taunt us, to tease and torment us by showing how far from such union we are. In some ways Paul is pointing up the ultimate bankruptcy of the wisdom tradition since the knowledge provided by the law is not efficacious. Paul introduces a new element into salvation history, affirm-ing that Christ replaces the law with the Spirit of God and that it is the Spirit that makes knowledge efficacious, for to live the life of the Spirit is to achieve true union with God.

> When we cry, "Abba! Father!" it is the Spirit himself bearing witness with our spirit that we are children of God, and if children, then heirs of God and fellow heirs with Christ, provided we suffer with him in order that we may also be glorified with him. (8: 15-17)

The last sentence is significant. We are to live lives that are like Christ's—certain moral imperatives follow from our status as sons and heirs of Christ of the glory that is to come, in which we set our hope (see 8: 23-25). The moral imperatives flow from our relationship with Christ and are set down in chapters 12-15: "Bless those who persecute you...do not be haughty but associate with the lowly...Repay no one evil for evil, but take thought for what is noble in the sight of all" etc. These words are a filling out of Christ's command that if anyone would come after him they should take up their cross daily and follow him. They are Paul's realisation that in this life the tree of the cross is the route to the tree of life, that the way to the tree of life is the *via crucis*. We are em-powered to follow this way "because God's love has been poured into our hearts through the Holy Spirit who has been given to us." (5:5)

Being filled with the Spirit of God or living the life of the Spirit is the final and conclusive manifestation of what is meant by "divinisation" in this book. It is the state of being in love with God, the gift of the Spirit, that reveals itself in acts of kindness, goodness, fidelity, gentle-ness, and self-control. (Galatians 5: 22) The action of the Spirit in us causes us to overcome our natural egotism, to allow God's spirit to take command of our spiritual faculties, and to grow as human beings by bridging the gap between knowledge and life. What is most illuminating in Paul, and it is a point of the utmost importance grasped by the Reformers, is that it is by being absorbed in the Divine Life and purposes through faith that human beings become capable of sustained good works.[27] Just as sin enters the world as a consequence of Man's state of estrangement from God—and not as the result of a single wrong action—so good works are the fruit of those who live the life of God in faith. In both Genesis and Romans *esse* precedes *agere*, ontology comes before action. What comes first in both accounts is the relationship between God and humankind; actions are grounded in this relationship. It is because we are as we are that we act as we do.

The larger categories in which Paul deals in the first half of the epistle to the Romans are the flesh, death, sin and the slavery that sin invariably brings with it, on the one hand, and the spirit, life, grace and freedom, on the other. And the solution to the problem of moral evil in the world that is definitively achieved by Christ's death and resurrection partakes of the homeopathic pattern we first encounter in Genesis, where the divine attribute of knowledge, which Man's trespass on the divine has enabled him to acquire and which on the surface looks like an unmitigated disaster, becomes the means under God for Man's sanctification and salvation. The comparison of Christ with Adam which Paul makes brings out the cosmic significance of Christ's death and resurrection, the universality of the new covenant that Christ establishes, the fact that it is open to all humankind, which Paul was perhaps the first to appreciate. In Romans, as we have said, Paul is not trying to interpret the sin of Adam but rather to interpret Christ through his references to Adam: his central focus is on the abundant grace of Christ, on the new relationship opened up between Christ and all of humanity, on Christ as the new head of the human race, the new Adam. We are all of us raised up with Christ through faith and joined in his victory over death. Death has no more dominion over us; life has triumphed over death. With this goes a new way of relating to God and a new way of being in the world. To follow Christ is to take up one's cross daily and the way of the cross is the way of Christian love, the way back to the tree of life. The cross is the cross-over point between knowledge and life, translating knowledge into life in union with God, life as it should be lived. Redemption brings about a new way of being in the world because it brings about a new way of being with God—or rather, since the initiative is always with God, a new way of God being with us.

Man's acquisition of knowledge gave human beings the freedom and creativity to be co-creators of the world with God; redemption gives human beings the grace to be co-redeemers of the world with Christ by means of the cross—by means of self-denying Christian love which has the power to bring good out of evil. On this account, Man's original transgression of the Human-Divine divide, his trespass onto God's territory, is indeed a "felix culpa," to borrow Augustine's phrase, for it was the first step in the divinisation of Man, the raising of Man to new life with God that reaches its completion in and through Christ and the action on Man's spirit of the Spirit of Christ. Augustine's arresting phrase sits more easily with this interpretation than with the somewhat pessimistic tradition he fathered.

The Epistle to the Romans is the most mature and comprehensive statement of Paul's understanding of redemption as an act of atonement initiated by God the Father and completed by his son, the man Jesus, with the power of the Holy Spirit. In his reflections Paul is clearly addressing what was for him a contemporary issue: what was it that Christianity added to Judaism, the religion of his fathers? Why was Christ needed to complete the revelation to the Jews? In presenting his answer, Paul penetrates to what he considers to be the major fault line of Judaism: that it taught adherence to the Law but that the Law was insufficient of itself to deliver the life of unity with God that humankind needed and most desired. This is a contemporary issue for Paul but, in diagnosing it, it is likely that Paul recognises that behind it stands one of the oldest truths in scripture: the inadequacy of the law mirrors the inadequacy of mere wisdom, of mere knowledge of good and evil, for the attainment of life. In addressing this issue Paul is surely aware of the fact that he is reaching back into the first book of the bible and addressing the basic human fault line which was revealed in the story, telling of how Man ate from one tree but was prevented from eating from the other, thereby causing a fissure to open up in the human heart: Man wishes for union with God but cannot command it nor can he effect it by his own actions. It must come as a gift from God. There is good evidence for thinking that Genesis 3 provides the template for one of the major arguments put forward by Paul in Romans.

If this is Paul's thinking, then I believe that Paul's Epistle to the Romans, so often cited in support of original sin, should be seen for what it is: a powerful endorsement of the interpretation of the cause of human sinfulness that was set out in Chapter Five (though, of course, not of the support of twentieth century thinkers for this interpretation). Paul would not have spoken of Christ and the Spirit as he did, would not have addressed the issue of redemption in the manner that he did, had he not grasped the significance of knowledge that falls short of achieving life, where "life" implies union with God.

OTHER PAULINE WRITINGS

It would be a mistake to think that these views of Paul on the limitations of the law are confined to the epistle to the Romans. The futility of the law and of mere wisdom when compared with the power of God's Spirit is a theme that is developed in chapters 2 and 3 of 1 Corinthians, and much of Paul's Epistle to the Galatians concerns the inability of the law to deliver salvation or bring justification. In Galatians Paul reaches heights of eloquence on this theme that are surpassed only in Romans:

> We ourselves who are Jews by birth and not Gentile sinners, yet who know that a man is not justified by works of the law but through faith in Jesus Christ, even we have believed in Christ Jesus, in order to be justified by faith in Christ, and not by works of the law...For I through the law died to the law, that I might live to God. (Gal 2: 14f)

And in the following chapters Paul continues:

> Now before faith came, we were confined under the law, kept under restraint until faith should be revealed. So that the law was our custodian until Christ came, that we might be justified by faith. But now that faith has come, we are no longer under a custodian; for in Christ Jesus you are all sons of God, through faith....And because you are sons, God has sent the Spirit of his Son into our hearts, crying "Abba! Father!" (Gal 3: 23-26; 4:6)

In these passages in Galatians Paul might be understood as saying that "we"—Jews like him—were de-centred from God, despite the best endeavours of the Law; but now "we" have become, through the power of the Spirit of Christ that is given to us, truly and lastingly centred on God our Father, just as Christ is; that through the power of Christ the "compass needle" of our conscious being has found its true direction, and we have become Father-centred; and that this has brought us freedom from the slavery of sin in the form of a wholeness and completeness, a human integrity, that the Law could not provide.

Paul in his preaching is incapable of talking of Christ without placing him in the context of the history of Israel; as he says in Galatians, "And if you are Christ's, then you are Abraham's offspring, heirs according to promise." (Gal 3: 29) Paul, of course, does not attempt to win over his fellow Jews to a *new* religion, since by his day Christianity was not yet recognised as a religion separate from Jewish religion; rather Paul's argument is an internal Jewish argument as he seeks to demonstrate who is the true Israel.[28] Paul sees Christ as the culmination or end-point of Jewish religious history and those who are annexed to Christ through faith are also perforce annexed to the history of salvation centred on the Chosen People. Hence the attraction that continuity between Genesis 3 and the mission of Christ holds for Paul. As I have argued in the context of the epistle to the Romans, Paul sees the coming of Christ as making up for what was till that point the inadequacy of the Jewish religious tradition, a view that chimes with the inadequacy of mere wisdom and law for salvation and is supported by the interpretation of Genesis 3 put forward in the last chapter.

James Barr sketches the changes in the interpretation of Genesis 3 that took place during the intertestamental period. He suggests that under the influence of Hellenistic thought, death (*thanatos*) "as a metaphysical generality" came to be regarded as "a terrible thing"[29] and that this led to a belief that death was some kind of punishment, traceable back to Adam. Where I would take issue with James Barr is in his contention that "Paul's thinking is not deeply rooted in the thought world of ancient Israel."[30] This strikes me as accurate if it suggests no more than that by Paul's day Jewish thinking about death had been influenced by Greek thinking about death. It is also worth pointing out that by Paul's day an accurate understanding of the "primitive" notion of "a rite of passage" had probably been lost; in that case, it would have been perfectly natural for Jewish men and women, already influenced by Greek thought, to infer that since God's words of warning to the man in Genesis 2: 17 ("in the day that you eat of it you shall die") did not take immediate effect, then the reference of God's words *must* have been to death as a generic fact of human existence: they would not have grasped the point that a rite of passage entails death and re-birth. That much is true. However, if taken as a generalisation—which may well not be Barr's intention—then Barr's statement about Paul's thinking would appear to go beyond what is warranted by the evidence. For Paul's religious vocabulary shows him to be someone who shared many of the central concepts of "primitive" Hebrew religion. For example, in language reminiscent of Leviticus he says in 1 Thessalonians, "for God has not called us for uncleanness, but in holiness." (I Thes 4:7) And again, "so that he (the Lord) may establish your hearts unblamable in holiness before our God and Father." (1 Thes 3: 13) And we should not forget that Paul put himself forward as someone who had advanced far in the study of the religion of his fathers. (Galatians 1: 14; Acts 22: 3)

It is, of course, perfectly possible that Paul wrote as he did without recognising the threads of connection between what he was saying about redemption and what is revealed in Genesis 3 on this point. That is possible though, I believe, unlikely in the light of what I have indicated concerning Paul's manifest intention of interpreting the significance of Jesus's life and death within the unfolding religious history of the Jews and of his particular focus on Genesis, and on the Adam-Christ typology in particular, in both Romans and 1 Corinthians. Paul's reflections on the inadequacy of the law for salvation following his life-changing encounter with Christ and the Spirit on the Damascus road may well have been grounded in his previous understanding of the inadequacy of mere knowledge for the attainment of life revealed in Genesis 3. There is the view that Paul read salvation history backwards: that from the fact that Jesus was the completion of Jewish salvation history he inferred that up till the coming of Jesus Jewish salvation history *must* have been incomplete and inadequate. This view is rendered redundant, however, if it is conceded that Paul grasped the relative inadequacy of Judaism from his study of the Hebrew scriptures and, in particular, by grasping the connection between the message of Genesis 3, concerning knowledge that falls short of life, and the inadequacy of the law for salvation.

But even if it were the case that Paul did not see these connections, or did not imply them, it is possible for us to recognise them and in this way deepen our appreciation of the significance of Christ's redemption. For it can surely not be denied that Paul's reflections on redemption and justification take on greater depth when we recognise the links they suggest with the basic depiction of Man found in Genesis 3. For these links make it clear that it is something *fundamental in Man's constitution as Man* that Christ's redemption is addressing; redemption can be seen as introducing the reign of the Holy Spirit in Man's heart—in the Hebrew sense of *leb*, the centre of intellectual activity as well as the seat of the emotions—and hence as bringing about genuine ontological change by closing the gap between knowing and being, between wanting and doing, between wisdom and life; the split or fissure in the human psyche that is the underlying cause of sin is healed and closed up through the power of the Holy Spirit. The human inclination to sin is countered by our becoming temples of the Holy Spirit, as Christ was (1 Cor 3: 16; Jn 2: 21): it is not a matter of one deed cancelling out another—the action of Christ versus the action of Adam—but rather of one state of being or basic situation replacing another. We are healed from within, and in this way made whole, through the action of the Spirit. For this reason it can hardly be denied that Augustine's reductive interpretation of the image of the tree of knowledge and his relative indifference to the image of the tree of life have contributed to an impoverished appreciation of the importance of these two images in Christian theology.

C: St John's Gospel

Although it has become fashionable in some quarters to claim that Paul "invented" Christianity, a little thought reveals that what he has to say is the result of his reflections on the Jewish religious tradition in the light of Jesus's earthly mission; and while Paul wrote before the gospels were written down, his reflections can be seen to be developments of themes and ideas that we find in the accounts of Jesus's mission in the gospels. For the sake of brevity, I shall confine myself to a consideration of the interpretation of that mission that is presented in the gospel of John, but a similar understanding could also be obtained from a consideration of any of the synoptic gospels.

What is remarkable about John's gospel is how time and again we encounter two major themes: first, that Jesus is the climax and conclusion of Jewish salvation history[31]; and second, that Jesus is presented as the bringer of new life, as the source of life in accordance with the Father's will and in association with the mission of the Spirit. My purposes will be served by a series of quotations—my commentary on their connection with Genesis 3, as I have interpreted it, will follow.

> Jesus said to Nicodemus: "...God so loved the world that he gave his only Son, that whoever believes in him should not perish but have eternal life." (Jn 3:16)

> In one of his long altercations with "the Jews," Jesus said, "You search the scriptures, because you think that in them you have eternal life; and it is they that bear witness to me; yet you refuse to come to me that you may have life... Do not think that I shall accuse you to the Father; it is

Moses who accuses you, on whom you set your hope. If you believed Moses, you would believe me, for he wrote of me." (Jn 5: 39-46)

Jesus said to them, "Truly, truly, I say to you, it was not Moses who gave you the bread from heaven; my Father gives you the true bread from heaven. For the bread of God is that which comes down from heaven, and gives life to the world." They said to him, "Lord, give us this bread always." Jesus said to them, "I am the bread of life; he who comes to me shall not hunger, and he who believes in me shall never thirst." (Jn 6: 32-35)

"For this is the will of my Father, that everyone who sees the Son and believes in him should have eternal life." (Jn 6: 40)

"It is the spirit that gives life, the flesh is of no avail; the words that I have spoken to you are spirit and life." (Jn 6:63)

On the last day of the feast (of Tabernacles), the great day, Jesus stood up and proclaimed, "If any one thirst, let him come to me and drink. He who believes in me, as the scripture has said, 'Out of his heart shall flow rivers of living water.'" Now this he said about the Spirit, which those who believed in him were to receive; for as yet the Spirit had not been given, because Jesus was not yet glorified. (Jn 7:37-39)

"Truly, truly, I say to you, if any one keeps my word, he will never see death." (Jn 8: 51)

"Your father Abraham rejoiced that he was to see my day; he saw it and was glad...Truly, truly, I say to you, before Abraham was, I am." (Jn 8: 56 - 58)

So Jesus again said to them, "Truly, truly...I came that they may have life and have it abundantly." (Jn 10: 10)

In his farewell discourses with his disciples, Jesus told them that "he who has seen me has seen the Father...Do you not believe that I am in the Father and the Father in me?" (Jn 14: 9-10)

He assured them that he would not leave them desolate. "The Counsellor, the Holy Spirit, whom the Father will send in my name, he will teach you all things, and bring to your remembrance all that I have said to you." (Jn 14: 26)

"I am the vine, you are the branches. He who abides in me, and I in
him, he it is that bears much fruit, for apart from me you can do nothing. If a man does not abide in me, he is cast forth as a branch and with-
ers." (Jn 15: 5-6)

These quotations could be extended, but there is no need. The case is
clearly made: Jesus is the completion of God's revelation, the climax of
Jewish salvation history, the bringer of new life, the one who reveals the
Father to mankind and acts as the mediator between God and Man. The
Spirit will be sent to those who believe in Jesus after his resurrection
from the dead, and will lead believers to the truth. It can surely not be
doubted that Jesus is the source of that life, the life of union with God,
that God himself prevented humankind from acquiring by blocking the
way to the tree of life in Genesis 3: " 'and now, lest he put forth his hand
and take also of the tree of life, and eat, and live for ever'—therefore, the
Lord God sent him forth from Eden..." (Genesis 3: 22-23) That act of
prevention was not the end of the story but the beginning. As the whole
thrust of John's gospel makes clear, through the associations it creates
between knowledge of the truth, eating and drinking and living forever,
the mission of the Spirit who will lead the disciples to the truth, and the
Father whose will it is Jesus's mission to fulfil, on the one hand, and life,
coming alive in God, eternal life that overcomes death,[32] on the other,
the movement of divine revelation, as seen from the perspective of the
Christian gospels, is a movement towards the attainment of life—and
hence the attainment of that which God denied humankind in Genesis.

   What emerges into the full light of day in John's gospel is something
that could only be adumbrated and rather vaguely alluded to in the Book
of Genesis: that it is God's plan not to deny forever humankind access to
life with him, the source of life, but rather to enable women and men to
attain to such life, in the normal course of events, only when they have
acquired the wisdom or holiness so to do. Man can acquire eternal life,
the life of union with God, only on God's terms and not on his own, as it
were, simply by reaching out and plucking it from the tree. Augustine's
interpretation has the effect of severing the work of our salvation, as revealed in the gospels, from its roots in Genesis 3, and such severance
amounts to an impoverishment of salvation history.

D: THE BOOK OF REVELATION

As James Barr points out, the image of the tree of life, outside of Genesis, appears mainly in the wisdom literature of the Old Testament, where it is associated with the cultivation of wisdom.[33] Indeed, wisdom herself is referred to as "a tree of life to those who lay hold of her" (Proverbs 3:18); this and other references reflect the strong association celebrated in the wisdom tradition between wisdom and life, including eternal life. References to the tree of life in the New Testament are rare but the image does make one highly significant appearance, referred to by Barr, in the final chapter of the final book of the New Testament. Some myths are about beginnings and some are about ends and it is noteworthy that the Christian bible is flanked by mythical writings at either end, the one concerned with protology ("In the beginning") and the other with eschatology (the end of time). The Apocalypse or Book of Revelation, the final book of the Christian bible, is basically an eschatological vision graphically depicted in terms of symbols and allegories, which contains many echoes of the Book of Genesis. Its allegorical nature and its concern with the last things—the *eschata*—has made it a favourite text of the prophets of doom school of scripture commentators who love to interpret its images as clues to the actual historical events—mostly lurid catastrophic events—that will occur in the run up to the end of the world. A more sober and scholarly approach would tend to agree with the Catholic theologian, Yves Congar, that what we find in scripture is not a literal account of events but a theological interpretation of the meaning of history.[34] In this last book of the bible, the significance of human history is illumined by a theological reflection on the last days, on what it will mean for us when time itself runs out and the world we know ceases to be. Understood in this light, we can see how the book, while allegorising certain events in Jewish and Christian history, is basically a meditation on salvation history that builds on and responds to themes first developed in Genesis.

The author of Revelation recounts a vision of the final things, in which he is shown around or directed by an angel, rather in the way that Dante in the *Inferno* is shown around by Virgil. The last chapter of the book follows on a vivid and detailed description of the splendours of the heavenly Jerusalem, described as coming down to earth to become the home of all those who are saved. The arrival of the heavenly Jerusalem on earth is the final arrival of the Kingdom of God, or the Reign of God, which Jesus taught his disciples to pray for and to which he makes many references in the gospels. Having described the city in some detail, the author opens the last chapter of the book with these words:

> Then he showed me the river of the water of life, bright as crystal, flow-
> ing from the throne of God and of the Lamb through the middle of the
> street of the city; also, on either side of the river, the tree of life with its
> twelve kinds of fruit, yielding its fruit each month; and the leaves of the
> tree were for the healing of the nations. (22:1-1).[35]

A little later we read:

> Blessed are those who wash their robes, that they may have the right to
> the tree of life and that they may enter the city by the gates. (22: 14).

The picture presented here is nothing less than the completion of the story begun in Genesis. Described in Genesis as being driven out from paradise and barred from access to the tree of life, the human species— or at least that portion of it who have washed their robes, the fornicators and idolaters and murderers being kept outside along with the dogs and the sorcerers (22: 15)—now finds itself having the right to enter through the gates of the city and to be empowered to eat the fruit of the tree of life. The emphasis throughout is on life, on abundant and plentiful life, as the water of life from its source in the throne of God flows right through the middle of the city with the tree of life on either side. The tree of life is no longer confined to the middle of the garden, as it was in Eden, but is now on either side of the river, publicly and freely available, and "its leaves are for the healing of the nations," for the healing of the forces that cause humankind to make war and commit acts of violence.

The image of the tree of life frames the Judaeo-Christian narrative: in Genesis the tree of life is denied Man but in Revelation it is revealed as our eschatological hope and as shaping the whole direction and meaning of salvation history. Between them, Genesis and Revelation establish the protological-eschatological framework within which the history of salva-tion is to be understood; and they do so principally by revealing the tree of life as the goal of Man's deepest desires and the "inspiration" of God's saving action. Everything else flows from this.

According to Augustine, the two points between which we live our lives are Adam, the bringer of death, and Christ, the bringer of new life: the Fall followed by grace. In the interpretation presented here, the two points are (1) the prevention by God of Man's access to the tree of life at the centre of the Garden of Eden, described in Genesis 3; and (2) Man's free access to the tree of life at the centre of the New Jerusalem, the Kingdom of God, described in chapter 22 of Revelation. In this interpretation, the driving force in the biblical narrative is the quest for life, which also means the desire to be at one with God—or, more accurately, since the initiative always lies on God's side, the driving force is God's quest for unity with Man. It is this motif, which is firmly in the hands of God, that weaves the narrative together and gives it direction and momentum. And in relation to this overarching motif or theme, the motif of "sin and redemption"—the Adam-Christ typology—stands as a part to the whole. It happens. It happens frequently in human life. There are times when we have to face up to the failures in our relationships, when alienation sets in, when we face the need to make amends, to address our failings, to achieve a reconciliation. But we do that so that the narrative of life can flow freely once more. Sin and reconciliation are not the point of life but incidents that occur, a means for achieving a fresh start—but a start to being able to live again and enjoy the life-enhancing power a loving relationship provides. The cry of "Repent!" in the New Testament is a call to return to life.

One of the startling features of the heavenly Jerusalem come down to earth (the image of the Kingdom of God, a central theme of the synoptic gospels) is that it has no temple ("I saw no temple in the city," 21:22)—there is no need for a temple for there is no need for Man to worship God in faith any more, since God is now finally and immediately present. All the covenants are superseded, the faith relationships are over, for the human journey is complete as humankind at last finds union with God. And the heavenly Jerusalem comes down to earth. As Tom Wright puts it: "Think of the vision at the end of Revelation. It isn't about humans being snatched up *from* earth to heaven. The holy city, new Jerusalem, comes down from heaven to earth. God's space and ours are finally married, integrated at last."[36] The human journey is not towards some other, non-earthly destination; its completion occurs on this earth with the complete penetration by God of human history and society; union with God is not some replacement of human nature with something else, but the bringing of that nature to its true fulfilment and perfection. It is on this earth that union with God is finally to be achieved, on this earth that the Kingdom of God will be established. At the end, it will be life on this earth that will be transformed when the reign of God comes into its own. Man and God will share the same space because Man will be holy as God is holy—whole and complete. Man will be divine. As we read in 1

John 3: 2: "Beloved, we are God's children now; it does not yet appear what we shall be, but we know that when he appears *we shall be like him*, for we shall see him as he is."

NOTES

1. The reason for the traditional identification of the fruit of the tree with an apple lies in the coincidence, in Latin, of the word for "apple" being the same as the word for the noun "evil" (*malum*), which can also mean a disaster, while "evil" as an adjective (*malus)* also means "apple-tree."

2. For example, in Hans Holbein's didactic painting, *An Allegory of the Old and New Testaments*, the Tree of Life stands at the centre of the canvas, at the divide the painter is suggesting between the two testaments, with its branches dead and withered on the side of the Old and flourishing and thrusting on the side of the New. Clearly in this painting the Tree of Life has lost its connection with Genesis—Adam and Eve are depicted as belonging to a distant past—as well as with the Book of Revelation.

3. This view is cited with approval by Marguerite Shuster, *The Fall and Sin*, op. cit., p. 50-51.

4 Pauline A. Viviano, "Genesis" in *The Collegeville Bible Commentary, Old Testament* (Collegeville: The Liturgical Press, 1988) p. 44.

5. See the commentary on "Sirach" in *The New Jerome Biblical Commentary*, op. cit., p. 498f.

6. See, for example, P. Kyle McCarter, in *The Anchor Bible*, (New York: Doubleday and Co, 1984) p. 422, note 36.

7. As maintained by Aquinas, for example, in *Summa Theologiae*, 2-2, 163, 2.

8. *Jerusalem Bible*, (London: Darton, Longman and Todd, 1966) p. 723.

9. It is worth mentioning here that in such books as the *Wisdom of Solomon* and *Sirach* (49: 14-16), Adam is not regarded as a "hate object" or a "bad man" who did incalculable harm to humankind, but is rather celebrated as a very fine fellow. See James Barr, op. cit., p. 81-82.

10. R.A.F. MacKenzie, "Ben Sira as Historian," in *Trinification of the World: A Festschrift in honour of Frederick E. Crowe*, (Toronto: Regis College Press, 1978) p. 316.

11. This is perhaps the best response to the divide between old and new suggested by Holbein's distinctively Lutheran interpretation of the divide separating the Old, the realm of the Law, and the New, the realm of grace. The *Sophia-Logos* link suggests continuity and development rather than division.

12. For example, Acts of the Apostles 5:30; 10: 39; Galatians 3:13; 1 Peter 2: 24.

13. St Augustine, *Ad Simplicianum de diversis questionibus,* written in AD 396; Vol VI of "The Library of Christian Classics," translated with introduction by JHS Burleigh (London: SCM Press, 1953).

14. St Augustine, *De natura et gratia,* written in AD 414; Vol 86 (Washington: Catholic University Press of America, 1992) translated by JA Mourant and WJ Collinge.

15. N.P. Williams, op. cit., p. 379.

16. Gabriel Daly, op. cit., p. 117.

17. Daniel A. Keating, *Deification and Grace* (Naples: Sapientia Press, 2007) pp. 21-25.

18. James Barr, op. cit., p. 89 (his italics).

19. Raymond E. Brown, *An Introduction to the New Testament,* (New York: Anchor Bible, 1997) p. 580 (my italics).

20. On this, Ben F. Meyer comments that "the defining note of the eschaton was not Paradise regained (*gan'eden*) but the fulfilment of God's will," in *The Aims of Jesus,* (London: SCM Press, 1979) p. 171.

21. It is true that the Jerusalem Bible English translation of 1966 speaks of Adam's "fall" in verses 15-17, but this is a rather free translation of the Greek word *paraptoma* which most other English translations render as "misdeed" or "wrongdoing" or "fault" or "trespass" and which the Latin Vulgate translates as "delictum."

22. Herbert Haag, op. cit., p. 93 ("As has frequently been noticed, the story of the Fall in Genesis 3 finds no echo in the entire Old Testament").

23. Joseph Blenkinsopp, op. cit., p. 55 ("There is no reference in the Hebrew Old Testament to an original sin of Adam").

24. James L. Kugel, *The Bible As It Was,* (Cambridge: Harvard University Press, 1998).

25. James Barr, op. cit., pp 27, 87.

26. James Barr, op. cit., pp. 6, 47.

27. The point is well made by Emil Brunner in *The Divine Imperative* (London: Lutterworth Press, 1937), in Book I, chapter 9, "The Definition of the Christian Ethic." Much of what is being said here relates to Bonhoeffer's notion of *Gestaltung* (restructuring) mentioned in chapter 3.

28. Geoffrey Turner, "Paul and the Old Testament—his Legacy and Ours," *New Blackfriars,* Vol 91, No 1032 (March 2010).

29. James Barr, op. cit., p. 87.

30. Ibid., p. 18.

31. As has been well said, "In the Fourth Gospel, unlike the other three, Jesus is, notoriously, the object of his own message: what he reveals is himself." John Ashton, op. cit., p. 171.

32. For a profound reflection on the meaning of "eternal life" in the fourth gospel, see C.H. Dodd, *New Testament Studies*, (Manchester: Manchester University Press, 1953) chapter 8.

33. James Barr, op. cit., 61.

34. Hans Urs von Balthasar, *Word and Redemption: Essays in Theology 2* (New York: Herder and Herder, 1964) p. 153, footnote 1.

35. The links with Genesis in this passage are clear enough but it is worth noting that the more proximate template for the passage is Ezekiel 47: 1-12, where the image is drawn of life-giving water issuing from the side of the temple and nourishing the trees growing on either side, whose leaves will be for healing. St John also alludes to this passage in Ezekiel when he speaks of the water issuing from the wound in the side of the crucified Christ (Jn 19: 34).

36. Tom Wright, *The Lord and his Prayer*, (London: SPCK, 1996) p. 24.

Chapter Seven
Some Loose Ends

I am aware that what I have argued for in the preceding chapters will not be welcomed by some readers or some Christian schools of thought. In particular, there will be many Christian theologians of numerous religious backgrounds who have invested heavily in the traditional "Augustinian" interpretation of original sin, who will take issue with what I have written. I am thinking in the first instance of those in the Protestant tradition who have subscribed to the notion that human nature was totally corrupted by Man's fall. For Martin Luther, original sin was not just a weakening of human intelligence and will but "the readiness to do evil, the repugnance for good, the distaste for light and wisdom, the love of error and darkness, the avoidance of and supreme contempt for good works, the unrestrained drive towards evil...It is...a weakness of the senses and of all the powers..."[1] John Calvin was also committed to the radical depravity of human nature as a consequence of original sin. Chapter 3 of book 2 of Calvin's *Institutes* is entitled, "Only Damnable Things Come Forth from Man's Corrupt Nature," and asserts that "the soul ... is not only burdened with vices, but is utterly devoid of good."[2]

Not only is this not the language of Jesus, it is also quite alien to the Old Testament. Behind the severe language of Luther and Calvin stand not the Jewish or Christian scriptures but the figure of Augustine, who "calls the line of Adam a mass of slime; a mass of sin, of sins, of iniquity; a mass of wrath, of death, of damnation, of offense; a mass totally vitiated, damnable, damned."[3] Even the most severe language of the Old Testament avoids the "wholesale" quality found in Augustine's words of condemnation, that is then picked up and magnified by Luther and Calvin—his efforts to glorify God and praise his mercy by stressing the corruption and sinfulness of humanity. As James Barr observes, far from being obsessed with sin the Old Testament is as much about the righteous and righteousness as it is about sinners and sin. And Yahweh's dealings with the Israelites, even when he is displeased with them, are always tinged with merciful indulgence. (See, for example, Psalm 103: 8-14).

But the words of Augustine denouncing the iniquity of human nature resulting from Man's fall have become the model for scores of fundamentalist Christian preachers who seem to compete with each other in finding new ways of expressing their loathing for human depravity and sinfulness. The Augustinian view of original sin probably bears the stamp of its author's personality as much as any of his teachings, reflecting his low regard for human nature, which was doubtless influenced by the shame he felt when he recalled his own lifestyle as a young man[4]: the doctrine of original sin is made in the image of Augustine.

It is relatively easy to find fault with extremes, including the extreme language of the early Reformers, which can prove embarrassing even to some of their most admiring disciples. But the interpretation of the Fall provided by Augustine can lead to a series of reflections that, while avoiding the excesses of the Reformers, nevertheless are focused too much on the negative. Such is the interpretation provided by another disciple of St Augustine, Joseph Ratzinger, later Pope Benedict XVI, in his book *In the Beginning*.[5] These are, in fact, homilies first preached by the then Cardinal Ratzinger in Munich in 1985. Besides saying a great deal that is good and pertinent to today's world, Ratzinger in these homilies can only interpret the deed of Adam in Genesis 3 as a sinful act of rebellion, a refusal by Man to accept the limitations of his creatureliness. A few quotations will convey the general trend of his commentary in the fourth homily entitled "Sin and Salvation":

> With this we have arrived at the real heart of the matter. People today know of no standard; to be sure, they do not want to know of any because they see standards as threats to their freedom.... They (Adam and Eve) make the decision not to accept the limitations of their existence;...they decide not to be bound by the limitations imposed by good and evil, or by morality in general, but quite simply to free themselves

by ignoring them...They do not free themselves, but place themselves in opposition to the truth. And that means that they are destroying themselves and the world...Here we can at once say that at the very heart of sin lies human beings' denial of their creatureliness, inasmuch as they refuse to accept the standard and the limitations that are implicit in it...They are living in untruth and in unreality. Their lives are mere appearance; they stand under the sway of death. We who are surrounded by a world of untruths, of unlife, know how strong this sway of death is, which even negates life itself and makes it a kind of death.[6]

While allowance must be made for the fact that these are extracts from a homily, nevertheless they are the words of a leading theologian who has consented to their publication with the sub-title of "A Catholic Understanding of Creation and the Fall." They are representative of a current of thought that stems from Augustine and are offered here simply as such. And what is clear is that the understanding of what occurred in Eden that they convey is that it was nothing more nor less than the rejection by Man of the limitations of his existence, and hence a rejection of his Creator, and that it was thoroughly and unambiguously bad. Ratzinger takes for granted the view, now shown to be mistaken, that the first humans wished to determine right and wrong for themselves. The language is more tempered than the language of Luther or Calvin, or of Augustine for that matter, but the message is just as wholeheartedly negative as far as human nature is concerned.

But Genesis 3, as interpreted in this book, is not a straightforward tale of human rebellion and to present it as such, I believe, is to distort its meaning and to impoverish theology by denying the salvific outcome of Man's acquisition of the knowledge of good and evil. While the Augustinian interpretation allows one to indulge in wholesale condemnation of Adam and, by some kind of extension, of the modern scientific and technologically inclined world (worries about technology seem to lie at the centre of Ratzinger's concerns), the interpretation offered here requires one to strike a balance, and that is less easily achieved. As I have attempted to suggest in the title of this book, Man falls and rises simultaneously. It is the genius of the Yahwist authors to bring this out both in the words pronounced by the Lord God about the incident in the garden ("Behold the man has become like one of us.. And now lest he put forth his hand..."—in which we can sense the swing back and forth, from an affirmation of Man's divinity to words of restraint and containment, from something approaching admiration at Man's audacity to a deliberate act of prevention), as well as in the sober and generous action, focused on the long term, the Lord God eventually takes.

The upshot is that God is not, emphatically not, totally condemning of what Man has done but rather, upon mature reflection, reverses his first impulse to wipe Man out and initiates the plan to educate Man and provide him with the opportunity to cultivate and develop his divine attribute. God confounds the conventional wisdom of the world by turning a negative into a positive, a pattern that prefigures other events in the OT as well as the central event in the NT. The words applied to Christ in 1 Peter 2: 7 could, *mutatis mutandis*, be applied to God's action in response to the event in Genesis 3: " The very stone the builders rejected has become the corner stone." That Man's action in the garden provided the capacity and inclination to sin must surely be recognised along with all the consequences of human misery and suffering that this has entailed. But the movement is not all one way. Man also gained something very precious and valuable, namely human consciousness. As well as imposing limitations God was providing, through the instrument of human evolution, a framework for creativity and for a loving relationship with himself. The original transgression of the animal-divine divide was utterly transformed by God to Man's immense advantage. It is true that this outcome reflects more on God's bountiful mercy than on Man's merits but the human blessings that flowed from the incident in the garden should not be ignored.

Clearly the view of human nature that this interpretation presumes and promotes is far from being a static one—one of nature as fixed, changeless, once-for-all. Rather human nature is conceived as dynamic, open to change and development, to progress and decline. Human beings are seen to be historical and social creatures whose opportunities for growth occur in their dealings with others in the course of time. It is over time that we encounter the opportunities and challenges that will enable us to grow closer to or more distant from God; and we will do this by the inevitable changes that will occur in the course of our dealings and interactions with others in our spiritual capacities of knowing, valuing, loving, deciding and acting. As is suggested by the binary opposites contained in the phrase "knowing good and evil," human wisdom derives not only from the good we encounter and embrace but also from our detection and overcoming of evil—as modern psychologists will confirm, we grow in truth and wisdom through suffering and by overcoming adversity as well as through the human confirmation and affirmation we occasionally enjoy, just as we grow towards wholeness by recognising and accepting the darker side of our natures, the impurities and darker impulses that lurk there. Human life is characterised by darkness and light, by misfortune as well as good fortune, and we need both in order to grow and develop as sane and balanced people.

Life's trials are opportunities for the human spirit to grow; without them, development and maturation would be much slower and less profound. The operations of the human spirit require a context of personal freedom to take place, and it is by means of these operations that Man makes the world around him and, in so doing, also makes himself. Grace in this interpretation is not something added to human nature but something normal that occurs as part of daily life. Nor is grace, as it is for Augustine, something that is required to restore us to our original integrity,[7] to the state of Adam before the Fall, but rather something that is required to help us achieve the wholeness that will, by uniting us to God, complete our humanity: grace is at all times a sharing in the divine life, an integral part of the divinisation of Man. According to this interpretation, God is not an onlooker on the human drama, but an active participant, one who shapes our ends and provides us with the grace and strength to meet the challenges we face. He calls each of us to wholeness and completion—to holiness—and, having called us to this end, he will provide the means to enable us to reach it.

MASSA DAMNATA

If there was never any original sin, as the term has been understood in Christian theology, there can of course be no inherited guilt. In this case it would be absurd to claim that the descendants of the first humans are born with the stain of guilt upon them—there is no guilt. From this it follows that it is misguided and wrong to talk of humanity, as Augustine does, as a *massa damnata*—damnation cannot be considered the default setting of humanity since there is no inherited sin deserving of punishment. It does not follow that human beings do not need to be saved since, in the interpretation put forward here, human beings are sinners from birth and depend on the grace of God to be made whole and to achieve the level of holiness that would fit them to be admitted to union and friendship with God. While humanity should no longer be considered a *massa damnata* it does remain a *massa salvanda*.

The ability of the interpretation being put forward here to absolve humanity of any primeval guilt has some very important consequences.

For, as long as humanity was conceived of as a *massa damnata* Christians with a mind to the conquest of non-Christian races had the excuse that what they were doing was for the good of the people against whom their aggression was directed; these people were, after all, children of darkness, unbaptised, and hence destined to hell. Their conquest by a foreign Christian power was no doubt painful for them but it provided them with the opportunity of salvation, of being spared the eternal torment of hellfire, and that was well worth the temporary inconvenience of being robbed of their wealth, and in many cases fettered, imprisoned and even tortured and killed. The mission to "baptise the pagans" has provided Christian aggressors down through the centuries with a perfect cover story for their selfish and cruel impulses and actions. And it has not only been non-Christians who have been victims of the doctrine of original sin; even in so-called Christian nations the doctrine has been the excuse for accepting practices like slavery and serfdom as well as for tolerating a variety of cruel practices and social evils that might otherwise have been put right.[8] One has to ask, for example what role the traditional teaching on original sin played in the belief system of the priests, nuns and religious who, over decades, regularly beat and abused children in care, some of them very young.[9] The doctrine of original sin has a lot to answer for. When it was pointed out that all human beings without exception were made in the image of God, a point unambiguously stated in Genesis, and were therefore worthy of being treated with respect, it allowed the Christian oppressor to answer that the image of God had been tarnished and defaced by sin—an unfortunate consequence of Adam's original act of rebellion—and hence certain punitive measures were required to restore a sense of righteousness and maintain order and the rule of law. It was, after all, for the good of the natives—or, even, the young children.

In the interpretation of Genesis being put forward here, all human beings without exception, by virtue of being human, are seen to be divine not merely by virtue of being created in the image of God but also because of their status as rational, free beings. Hence each and all, no matter how lowly, are of greater value than any material resources, possessions or things, or indeed than any other kind of animal, and deserve to be treated with the respect owed to the divine. To recognise that God is, quite literally, in all human beings provides a sound basis for the recognition of one's own dignity and, simultaneously, the dignity of others, for seeing oneself in others and others in oneself. The divinity of the human is a doctrine that could become a bedrock of human rights and humane codes of conduct. It transcends all ethnic, cultural and religious divisions and blends well with the best values associated with the Enlightenment, which are a powerful force in contemporary European and American society. At a time when respect for the human is a crying need throughout the globe, the doctrine of the divinity of the human could help to break down the barriers of suspicion and enmity between peoples and become a powerful force for unity, peace and goodwill

ANIMA HUMANA NATURALITER CHRISTIANA

It is because of the divine element in human beings that all are called to union with God—because by virtue of their humanity, of the spiritual capacity that makes them human, all are capable of being united with the one and only God. The basic concept underlying this way of talking is that only that which is of God, who is Spirit, can become one with God—hence the Hebrew belief that at death Man's spirit returns to God (Ecclesiastes 12:7; also Psalm 104:29-30).[10] This does not mean that only a part of Man, the "spiritual" or "divine" part, can achieve union with God, but rather that the whole Man, Man as incarnate spirit, as a living *nephesh* (Gen 2:7), can be brought into union with God by virtue of the divine element in his make up. Some important consequences follow from the realization of this fact.

For example, the Church is called to serve, not just its own members, but all of humanity. It should not be a narrow, inward-looking institution that looks after its own. Rather, it needs to think of the needs of all human beings, of all who have the spirit of God within them by virtue of their rational powers and conscious freedom—their need for holiness and wholeness, for integrity and dignity, for justice and truth, and for the freedom required for such wholeness to be achieved. The Church should not be a refuge from the world. It has a duty to reach out to all. It is quite right to talk about the natural human virtues since human nature itself is capable of being virtuous—honest and truth telling, thirsting for justice, searching for integrity and authenticity. Fortitude, patience, self-control, temperance, kindness, love, perseverance, humility etc.—these are basic virtues, which all human beings are called to pursue. Grace does not replace nature but helps to bring it to perfection. But in the first instance all human beings are called by God to union with him. For this reason, all that is truly human should be valued and Christians can say with the pagan Roman poet Terence: *Homo sum: nihil humani a me alienum est* (I am Man: nothing that is human is alien to me). As one Christian rather shockingly has said, "Jesus did not come to make us into Christians; he came to fulfil us as human beings."

The covenant God made with Noah was a universal covenant, made with all of creation with Man at its head. All subsequent covenants are built on this first covenant between God and all of creation and that first covenant is not wiped out or annulled by the later Mosaic, or for that matter, the Christian covenants. Similarly God's special covenant with the Jewish people is not wiped out or annulled by the Christian covenant and Christians owe their Jewish ancestors a great debt of gratitude and reverence for the heritage they have passed on to them. As I said earlier, Paul was incapable of thinking of Jesus outside of the context of Jewish salvation history and we Christians are perforce, by virtue of belonging to Christ, also partners in the same salvation history. All of us are, by extension, religious Jews, children of Abraham (Galatians 3: 29; Ephesians 3: 6).

Salvation is a gift from God but it is achieved by bringing to maturity and perfection the divine attribute of knowing good and evil that is in all of us, helping us to be truly wise, truly holy, truly centred on God as our final end and the goal of our lives. The way of salvation is not the way of the world, the way of violence, conquest and domination of others. That is a false way, based on the idols of self-worship and self-glorification. The way of salvation is the way of the cross, the way of self-sacrificing human love. "Whoever would save his life will lose it; and whoever loses his life for my sake and the gospel's will save it." (Mk 8: 35) Or, as we read in John's gospel, "Unless the grain of wheat falls into the ground and dies it remains alone; but if it dies it bears much fruit." (Jn 12: 24)

The ability to sacrifice one's own selfish interests out of love is the criterion of moral and spiritual maturity, which we have seen both St Paul and the author of Hebrews cite as the defining characteristic of Christ. By virtue of our human inheritance of knowledge and freedom all of us can become co-creators of the world with God. By virtue of God's redemptive action those who allow the Spirit of God to reign in their hearts can become co-redeemers of the world with Christ, capable of bringing good out of evil. Christian love does not annul or destroy our basic human nature since that is already divine, but rather strengthens it, ennobles it, purifies it and brings it to perfection and maturity. Christianity is a natural religion, one grounded in human nature as God has shaped it through evolution and history: *anima humana naturaliter Christiana* (the human soul is naturally Christian).

EVOLUTION

The book of Genesis and the theory of evolution have had a long and strained relationship. Even today, some 150-odd years since Charles Darwin first put forward and defended his account, there are Christian creationists who believe that the scientific theory of evolution is inimical to the word of God set forth in the bible's first book; that it is pernicious and evil, untrue in fact and anti-religious in intent. Contrasting with this is another group, more common in the past than today, who have sought to find the theory of evolution already established in Genesis. Neither camp is convincing. It would be to travesty the kind of literary text Genesis is to suggest that it could possibly contain an account of a scientific theory such as the theory of evolution. The authors of Genesis were not in any sense scientists; they would not have been able to formulate a scientific question. They had no inkling of evolution, no idea that Man might be descended from animal ancestors, no knowledge whatsoever of dinosaurs, no sense of the evolution of the planet.

But the authors of Genesis certainly were able to recognise Man's affinity to the animals (this is brought out in Genesis 2: 20 which portrays the Lord God considering if the man might find a helpmate among the animals). Man as described in Genesis has all the appearance of being organic to nature, as emerging in the final analysis from the dust of the earth. And in seeking to explain how Man might have become different from the other animals, it would appear that the authors put this down to a mutation in human consciousness which caused a new type of human to emerge, one capable of a covenantal relationship with God, and also of sin. To convey this mutation they told the story of Man's eating from the tree of knowledge of good and evil. The change that is described in this story is more than a cultural change, a change in the habits or customs or beliefs of a particular people, but a change in Man's basic constitution, the ascent of Man to a new form of intellectual consciousness, and alongside this, a passage to adulthood and a change in the basic human situation, the human way of being in the world; Man became a creative, historical animal, capable of changing the world about him, and himself in so doing. So while it is true that we do not and could not find in Genesis anything resembling the scientific theory of evolution, what we do find there is a symbolic tale that can easily be incorporated into an evolutionary interpretative framework. Women and men who have an evolutionary cast of mind or outlook, believing that humans are an evolved species, can fit their understanding of the tale told in Genesis 3 quite comfortably and convincingly into their evolutionary way of thinking. There is not only a compatibility but a solidarity between the interpretation of Genesis 3 put forward in this book and the scientific theory of evolution.[11]

The theory of evolution belongs to science and science is not myth and myth is not science. Darwin was a scientist who devised a theory that explained a broad range of phenomena in the natural world, a range of empirical data he had gathered over a fairly long period of time. This theory pulled all of the data into a unity by placing them within an explanatory framework—the framework of natural selection. Why was it, for example, that each island in the Galapagos archipelago seemed to be inhabited by a different species of finch?[12] Natural selection provided an explanation of this phenomenon by appealing to processes in nature. Unlike the scientist, the mythographers of Genesis 3 are not seeking to establish a theory that works by appealing to natural processes; rather, they are seeking to achieve a measure of human self-understanding, and they do this by locating human beings in relation to such things as God, the universe, other human beings and even the other animals. It is this last relationship, I am suggesting, that led the authors of Genesis 3 to the same conclusion as Charles Darwin: Man mutated or passed from the animal state to the state of being human; he ascended to a level above that of the other animals. The mythographers explained this by claiming that Man partook of the divine, becoming thereby a peculiar hybrid of animality and divinity. The finding—that Man is some kind of "higher animal"—may be the same as Darwin's, but the reasoning behind it is quite different. Myth and science have quite different rationales, they seek to answer different sets of questions, but questions in both cases that are "real," questions that human beings sincerely want answers to: we might suggest the difference between them by noting that the "tree of life" had a quite different meaning for Darwin than it had for the authors of Genesis 3. According to Mircea Eliade, "verification" in the case of myths does not consist of confirmation of a theory on the basis of observations of natural processes, but of confirmation by the broad range of experiences that life throws up. We might say that the religions of Judaism and Christianity are myths that became history, as the animal that became human was invited and assisted by God to develop his divine assets of freedom and understanding over time, thereby becoming more like God and drawing closer to him. This "covenantal" understanding of the relationship between God and his "chosen people" developed into a whole way of life, governed by a set of laws and sanctions, one that set the Hebrews apart from all other nations—the myth was verified, if you like, in the life-style of the ancient Israelites.

The notion of intentionality might help to clarify both Man's affinity with the other animals and his difference from them and in this way throw light on the different dimensions of human life that science and religion are directed towards. Intentionality indicates a capacity along with a set of aptitudes or skills that are spontaneously directed to a particular end—that are, in a word, purposeful or goal directed. All animals, Man included, enjoy a certain type of biological intentionality; they have instinctive or spontaneous orientations to the achievement of certain biological ends, understood as ends that aid and abet their survival and flourishing as biological entities. So all animals flee from danger, seek the food and drink they need to live and are strongly driven to mate and produce offspring. In addition, the different species of animals have inbuilt instincts for survival, including predators who are well adapted to scenting and hunting their prey: there can, for example, be no doubting the intentionality of the great cat that crouches in the long grass eyeing her prey, ears erect, body taut and her whole being alert, awaiting the precise moment to pounce.

Man is no exception to this general biological rule and has the same need to eat, drink and reproduce his species. But Man has, in addition to his biological intentionality, an intellectual intentionality whereby he seeks ends that cannot be reduced to the quest for survival and reproduction. His intellectual intentionality means that he belongs to a species that, quite spontaneously and irresistibly, seeks the truth, that is by nature inclined to search for justice and what is morally right (though he can, of course—because uniquely he is free—frustrate his nature in these matters) and, in a way already described, is in need of God as the necessary and sufficient completion of his existence, as the one who alone is commensurate with the infinity of his longing and capacity for wonder.[13]

According to Genesis, Man acquired this capacity when God breathed into him his own spirit (Genesis 1:26; 2:7); but this capacity was activated and actualised when he ate from the tree of knowledge of good and evil—or more strictly speaking, the moment or occasion of such actualisation is told in Genesis through the medium of the story of Man eating from the tree of knowledge of good and evil. That is when

Man's intellectual intentionality kicked in. In Genesis 1 we read that God created Man in his own image, in Genesis 2 that God breathed his spirit into the clay from which Man was created; in Genesis 3 we read about the actualisation of the potencies Man had received from God. The mutation in human consciousness recorded in this story set Man apart from the other animals, endowing him with a freedom of action and powers or reasoning that they could not match.

In terms of salvation history, Gabriel Daly sums up well the fateful ambiguity brought about by this mutation:

> With the arrival of man, nature evolves into culture. It is at once a marvellous and an appallingly dangerous development... We have a power not granted to galaxies: We can say yes or no to God's creative invitation. That awesome power is what makes salvation necessary. Emergence into freedom is emergence into a condition which the New Testament teaches us to call the new creation. Natural laws no longer suffice to bring about God's purposes. Something radically different becomes necessary when creation reaches intelligence and freedom. The garden of paradise now has its antitype, the hell of Auschwitz and all it symbolizes.[14]

From the moment of hominisation onwards, Man became a historical and creative being, a free self-determining agent of change and development, capable of sin but capable under God of being transformed and brought to the true likeness of God himself. This work of transformation is what Christians refer to when they speak of grace. Grace is the work of Man's salvation, the change wrought in Man by the Holy Spirit of God, whereby Man is purified of his wrongdoings and sins, made holy and thus worthy of enjoying the friendship of God, in whose image he was created. Like the rest of the animal kingdom, Man is an evolved species but he cannot be confined to his biological intentionality. He also enjoys an intellectual intentionality and was created for friendship with God. It is a gross error to try and reduce Man's intellectual intentionality to his biological intentionality, though there are not a few intellectual pundits today who appear intent on doing just that. They have great difficulty, however, in explaining how Man is capable of acting against his biological interests—his biological "programming," if you like—by putting himself in danger, for example, or by his willingness to go hungry or deny himself goods that are biologically desirable; and how it is that when he does these things, overcoming instinctive inclinations, on the basis of moral principle or out of love for another or others, far from being condemned by his fellow humans, he usually becomes an object of admiration. There are many times, in short, when women and men have subordinated their biological drives and instincts to their intellectual and moral natures and have been admired and honoured for so doing.

By the same token, it is totally wrong to try and absorb or flatten Man's biological intentionality into his intellectual intentionality, as Augustine attempts to do when he considers spontaneous biological reactions, such as the normal human response to sexual stimulation, as wrong and sinful—and evidence of some original sin—because not subject to rational control. Likewise, Augustine's argument that the fact that human couples spontaneously seek privacy while engaged in sexual intercourse, even "legitimate" intercourse, indicates some kind of basic human shame about engaging in such practice is open to serious objection: there are good reasons based on the evolutionary need for survival why this should be a natural and spontaneous human characteristic, and there are also important psychological and social reasons why such physical and emotional intimacy should be accompanied by the desire for privacy. In these matters Augustine seems to have drawn the false conclusion that a desire for privacy is a manifestation of shame[15], and to have been misled by his Neoplatonist beliefs, supposing that what is not subject to Man's rational will is somehow misguided and wrong, against nature. Of course, he had the excuse of living in a pre-scientific age when understanding of what today we term biology was light years away from our modern understanding, but there remain some who retain a tendency to reduce the value and significance of Man's biological intentionality because it differs from and at times appears to challenge or interfere with his intellectual intentionality. The human being is an amalgam of both intellectual and biological intentionalities; both are needed in any definition of what it is to be fully and properly human. The body is not the enemy of the soul but rather, as Wittgenstein put it, "The human body is the best picture of the human soul."[16] Bernard Lonergan conveys the same message when he speaks of Man as "incarnate spirit": "The bodily presence of another is the presence of the incarnate spirit of the other; and that incarnate spirit reveals itself to me by every shift of the eyes, countenance, color, lips, voice..."[17]

To be psychologically whole Man needs to develop a healthy balance, or better still a harmony, between his intellectual and his biological intentionalities—between the various drives and impulses that make up the human being. This is a big subject that cannot be explored at length here. What might be said is that the work of Man's salvation is very much about achieving this healthy and wholesome balance. We can see this in the saving mission of Jesus who attended to each of the physical, the psychological and the spiritual needs of the people with whom he came in contact. Salvation is not about some distant after-death existence but is involved in the making of Man in the here and now, about achieving a just and free society, about developing those virtues that go to the heart of what it is to be properly human, and about creating an environment in which human beings have a better chance of achieving a healthy balance or harmony between their biological needs, on the one hand, and their psychological, intellectual, moral and spiritual needs, on the other. The human need for wholeness extends to all of Man's physical, psychological, social and spiritual being.

These reflections lead on to others of a more strictly theological nature. In the story of Adam and Eve in the garden of Eden, Man succeeds in eating from the tree of knowledge but is prevented from eating from the tree of life. We can perhaps find in this simple fact the revelation that the eating from the tree of knowledge is part of Man's ascent from a lower to a higher form of life; it is a move from below upwards, the passage or ascent to a fuller, rational type of human consciousness, and occurs as part of a natural process of evolution. By contrast, Man does not achieve success in partaking of the tree of life as part of this evolutionary process. In the story, God deliberately prevents Man gaining access to the tree of life. Any partaking of the tree of life is reserved very much to God: the bestowal of this higher form of life—the life of union with God—is in the gift of God and, if it occurs, it will do so in accordance with God's plan. It is not something that Man can achieve by his own efforts, by the exercise of human ingenuity or by dint of hard work, nor is it the result of some natural evolutionary process. In so far as Man acquires this life it is strictly as a gift from God, by virtue of a movement from above downwards. In this way, to quote Bernard Lonergan, "human development is of two quite different kinds. There is development from below upwards...But there is also development from above downwards."[18] Lonergan speaks of "two vectors, one from below upwards, creating, and the other from above downwards, healing."[19] We are touching here on two distinct orders of being, one natural and the other supernatural, with the natural identified as the product of evolution and, at a later stage, of human decisions and actions, and the supernatural being strictly the product of the action of God.

Referring to the work of Karl Rahner, Lonergan says that within the divine or supernatural order, from an evolutionary perspective there can be seen to be "a threefold personal self-communication of divinity to humanity, first, when in Christ the Word becomes flesh, secondly, when through Christ men become temples of the Spirit and adoptive sons of the Father, thirdly, when in a final consummation the blessed know the Father as they are known by him."[20] These reflections support some of the comments I have made in my own way about the nature and course of salvation history; they also indicate something of the relationship between the two orders—the natural and the supernatural—that are, I am suggesting, hinted at or implied in the story told in Genesis 3, where we read of Man attaining the tree of knowledge but being prevented by God from reaching the tree of life, since the according of life in union with himself is something that, in the story, God reserves strictly for himself.

THE ONTOLOGICAL CONSTITUTION OF MAN

The interpretation of Genesis 3 presented in this book has implications for our understanding of what makes a Man, of the ontological constitution of the human being. Throughout European history, the most commonly held view on this question has been that Man is composed of two distinct things, namely a body and a soul. These two things are said to make up the human being. People today are less comfortable than people in the past in talking about a "soul" and some would prefer to re-phrase the statement and say that human beings consist of a body and a mind. In many ways they mean the same thing, namely that human beings have a material thing called a body and an immaterial thing called the mind, that lodges or dwells in the body. This is a view that goes back to Plato, who claimed that the soul is an intelligent agent dwelling in the body that enables us to think and act in ways that the body on its own would not be capable of, and who also believed that at death the soul, which is spiritual and immortal, is released from the body, which is physical and mortal.[21] Indeed, Plato also claimed that souls were created at the beginning of the world, and existed prior to becoming implanted in human bodies, a view echoed at times by Augustine.[22]

The Platonic division of the human being into two substances, one spiritual called the soul or mind, and the other physical called the body, appears to lie behind certain Church declarations, such as that made by the Fifth Lateran Council (1512- 1517), which declared that an "anima intellectiva," or "thinking soul," was infused or poured into the body, and was immortal. More recently, Pope Pius XII in his encyclical *Hu-*

mani Generis (1950), speaking on the subject of evolution, said that while it was quite in order for those properly qualified to inquire into the question of whether the human body "comes from pre-existent and living matter," faith requires us to believe "that souls are created immediately by God,"[23] a view that appears to assume that human beings are composites of two separate substances, body and soul. In similar vein, Pope John Paul II, in an address to the Pontifical Academy of Sciences in 1996, made the same assumption when he declared that the theory of evolution "cannot account for the appearance of the human soul" which must "be 'immediately created by God'."[24]

But while this might have been the majority view among theologians and others in the past, it has not been the only view. The alternative view holds that the human being is not a composite of two separate substances but is a single substance or a unified entity endowed with certain attributes or capacities. According to this view, the soul or mind is not a separate entity but is the form that makes a body a human being. This view finds philosophical support in Aristotle's understanding of matter and form. For according to Aristotle, who is followed on this issue by Aquinas[25], matter and form are not two separate substances but rather combine to form a single substance. So an entity like a house, for example, is made up of bricks, wood, glass, tiles and other materials; but by themselves these do not constitute the house and, to do so, stand in need of the "form" or design or idea that makes them into a house. The house is a single substance, a single entity. Though the materials it is made from are diverse, as a concept and reality it stands as a unified entity, and this on account of its form. The form is the cause of these materials making a house. They could have been made into something else—an office or stables or shop or laboratory or whatever else they were capable of becoming, but in fact they are the material component, the "matter," of a house. One way of thinking of "form" is to see it as the "meaning" of the thing in question. So in grasping that something is a "house," we are answering the question: what is the *meaning* of this building? Or, in more idiomatic language: what kind of building is it? We might say that the house is a composite of the materials it is made from and the meaning of these materials in the particular instance, but we cannot claim that the house constitutes two distinct things since, quite clearly, considered strictly as a house it is a single, unified whole. As this example illustrates, the form that makes material objects into a thing is not another thing but rather is the cause of the thing of which it is the form, which would not be the thing it is without the form. So it is that form and matter combine to bring into being a single substantive entity or thing but cannot by themselves be considered to be two things. To sum up, we might say that, when talking of matter and form, the form places or imposes a unity on the diverse components of the matter, conferring on each of these components a purpose or meaning within a larger whole. It is the form that defines the meaning of the entity composed of matter and form, the form that determines what the entity is. If the Platonic view of the human person is dualistic, considering Man to be composed of two separate things, the Aristotelian view is anti-dualistic.

The reason for this disquisition on matter and form is to show that if the human being consists of body and soul considered not as two substances but, respectively, as matter and form—if, as Aristotle claims, the soul is the form of the body, the formal cause of a body being a human being—then it is mistaken to identify the human being with his mind or soul[26], as some adherents of the dualistic view have been tempted to maintain in the past, or for that matter with his body, and it is also wrong to maintain that Man is made up of two distinct substances. Rather the human being is a single entity, a body that by virtue of its form is a human being. This is also a view that has been propounded by a Church Council in the past. In 1312 The Council of Vienne declared that "the rational or thinking soul is truly and of itself the form of the human body" and that to call this in doubt is "erroneous and inimical to Catholic truth." So there have been two views entertained in Church thinking on this matter, both of which have received strong authoritative affirmation, one consistent with the dualistic view of Plato and the other with the anti-dualistic view of Aristotle.

It should, I think, be quite clear that the interpretation of Genesis 3 presented in this book is consistent with the Aristotelian view, the view enunciated at Vienne, and quite inconsistent with the dualistic Platonic view expressed in the statements issued by the Fifth Lateran Council as well as in those made on this subject by Popes Pius XII and John Paul II. The reason for the inconsistency is this: while both the "Vienne view" and the "Lateran view" might be considered compatible with the creation story told in Genesis 2, and especially with the episode of God breathing life into the clay of the earth (which *could be* interpreted in a dualistic fashion, but *need not be*), it is simply not possible to see any notion of the human soul having to be created immediately by God as being consistent with the interpretation of Genesis 3 presented here. For in this interpretation it is very clear that it is not God who directly effects the passage of Man from his former innocent status to his new adult status, from the hominid state to the fully human state—indeed, the story suggests that this passage or transition causes God to chastise and admonish the human couple. If we stick to the data of the story, the passage from one state to another is a natural as opposed to a supernatural occurrence, a passage from below upwards rather than the result of some divine intervention. In this way, the interpretation placed on the Genesis 3 story here is consistent with an evolutionary, emergentist view of the human being, one that holds that humans, endowed with the capacities of intelligence and free will without which they could not be considered human, evolved from lower forms of life, forms of life that did not enjoy these capacities, or at least not to the degree necessary for them to be considered human. This interpretation sees the humanising of Man, the process of hominisation, as consisting of two stages, the first told in the creation narratives in Genesis 1 and 2 when Man is provided with the potentiality of ascending to full rational consciousness, and the second stage consisting of the actual mutation into this form of consciousness, which is described in the story of Man eating from the tree of knowledge in Genesis 3. For this reason this interpretation promotes the view that Man as a complete unified being evolved or emerged from lower forms of animal life.

There are strong philosophical and cultural reasons for preferring an anti-dualistic to a dualistic understanding of Man. In the realm of epistemology, dualism has fathered a whole host of errors and blunders.[27] Descartes, the father of modern philosophy, posited two completely disparate attributes, namely spatiality and consciousness, and assigned the body to one and the mind to the other. The body was a *res extensa*, the mind a *res cogitans*, and the problem was how to overcome this dualism by bridging the gap between these two dimensions of reality. The problem has remained and indeed has proved insuperable so long as the *res cogitans*, the "thinking thing," is conceived as something that does the thinking while remaining apart or separated from the body, and the world, including the body, is conceived as a *res extensa*, a thing "out there," stretched out in space and time.[28] The most serious problem has been what has been called "veil of ideas scepticism" since within this model of knowing it has proved impossible for the *res cogitans* to know with certainty anything other than the ideas of the mind, the ideas it entertains within its own consciousness; and this has meant that it cannot claim to know how or if these ideas accurately represent the *res extensa*, the world presumed to lie out there in space and time; the ideas form a "veil" or barrier making it impossible to know that what I claim to know corresponds with what is so in the world.[29] The notion that Descartes bequeathed to the Enlightenment of the self as a disembodied centre of consciousness confronting the world out there and attempting to understand it and interact with it has given rise to all sorts of dislocations—between mind and body, thought and language, meaning and behaviour, self and others—that continue to plague our culture.[30] The dualism of mind and body that the notion of the immediate creation of souls by God entails and upholds has passed to posterity a very unhappy philosophical legacy.[31] Another—theological—problem confronting what we have called the "Lateran view" is that, while the proponents of this view are in general committed to the notion of an inherited original sin, it is difficult to see how belief in such an *inherited* characteristic is compatible with the immediate creation of souls by God. Augustine had been aware of this difficulty besetting the "creationist" account of the origin of the soul.[32]

The notion of a unified human being emerging from pre-existent forms of life avoids such dualism and all the many problems—philosophical, theological and cultural/theoretical—that attend it. It overcomes Cartesian dualism by seeing Man as rooted through his senses to the physical world he inhabits. It overcomes the social isolation of the Cartesian ego by seeing the individual's acquisition of knowledge, language and culture as being social and communitarian ventures produced through teaching, sharing ideas and public discourse. It is incapable of seeing the individual as anything other than the product of the family and the wider community; and the wider community as itself the product of a process of evolution that is at once cultural, moral, intellectual and, ultimately, physical. Human beings are embodied beings and, as embodied, they are rooted in history, in society and in nature. In short, the evolutionary conception of Man, the conception of Man as an evolved being, is totally inimical to the disembodied, deracinated "thinking thing" that body-mind, or body-soul, dualism gives rise to.

What is more, the notion of Man as a unified entity is compatible with the Hebrew notion of Man as a living *nephesh*, the word used to describe Man in Genesis 2: 7, whereas body-soul dualism of a Platonic or Cartesian kind is quite incompatible with Hebrew thinking.[33] Classical Hebrew simply has no word for "body" corresponding to the Greek word *soma*.[34] Perhaps the best way we can give a modern, philosophical expression to what the Hebrews understood by *nephesh* is by means of an *integrative explanation* of what constitutes a person. In botany, for example, the laws of physics and chemistry are not negated or suspended

but are taken up and encompassed within the higher integration of botany, a science in its own right with its own laws and systems; similarly,
in human beings the laws of physics, chemistry, biology and neurology
continue to operate but are integrated into the higher levels of the conscious operations of human thinking, deciding, loving and acting. Human beings are bodies, with arms, legs, hands etc., but they are "intellec-
tualised bodies" in the sense that they frequently move their legs and
arms in order to achieve results that are freely chosen and for reasons
that are non-physical. As the Harvard literary scholar, playwright and
poet, William Alfred, wrote: "Every act of the body is an act of the
soul."

Human beings certainly need their bodies to come to an understanding of the material universe; without the sensory contact between their
bodies and the world of matter there could be no data of sense and without the data of sense understanding of the world of matter could not take
place.[35] But the data of sense only represent a first stage in knowing and
beyond the input of sensory data there is required an act of understanding by the inquiring subject. This brings us to one of Man's principal
spiritual capacities. For in understanding, the inquiring subject grasps the
universal in the particular; and the universal is an intelligibility that transcends the material world in which it is instantiated. The universal is not
capable of being grasped by our physical senses of sight, touch, taste etc
since these regard only the particular and the here and now. To understand what a chair is, for example, is to grasp the idea of "chair" and this
idea is capable of being instantiated or exemplified in any number of
material objects in the world, past, present and future—it is a universal
idea. Man has the capacity to transcend the limitations of time and space
and grasp an idea that is universal. Clearly we are touching here on a
fairly complex area of inquiry and it is not possible to do the subject justice in a book dedicated to quite another subject. But to sum up as best
we can, we might say that by virtue of their rational powers human beings enjoy a freedom from the constraints of time and place to which
their bodies and the material world are subject,[36] and it is this freedom to
transcend the spatio-temporal constraints endured or experienced by our
bodies that licenses us to describe Man as a spiritual being. Man is a unified being, a body which by virtue of the form of consciousness it enjoys
has powers and capacities that are both physical and spiritual. He can
appropriately be called an incarnate spirit since his physical powers and
capacities are unified under and at the disposal of his spiritual powers of
reasoning and making free decisions.

Further insight into the spiritual dimension of human existence is provided by Gabriel Daly's account of how we encounter God in our everyday experience, which is at heart the human experience of the need for wholeness described at some length in Chapter Five. Readers must make up their own minds as to whether or not the description corresponds with their own lived and felt experience:

> Men and women encounter God as the horizon which encompasses and draws them on beyond every concrete experience. God is the dynamic principle in life and he manifests himself in the depth experiences which come to us from life, in the mind's quest for meaning, and in the heart's restless reaching out towards a beyond which is encountered prospectively in the experience of our subjectivity but never apprehended as a graspable object. God approaches men and women in and through created beings. Men and women are made aware of this approach through their experience of transcendence as horizon and their encounter with the depth dimension of everyday human experience. The experience of creatureliness, the "sting of contingency," as von Hugel called it, is the felt presence of God as the absolute future of man. It cannot be encountered categorically or empirically. It is encountered, experienced, and lived as dependence, contingency, hunger for infinity. It is embodied in every element which points beyond itself to the being of God himself.[37]

I have tried in this sub-section to show that the notion of Man as an evolved species avoids a series of problems besetting body-mind or body-soul dualism.[38] The logic of the interpretation I have put forward would suggest that it is really a waste of time to speculate about the origin of something called the soul, since there is no such separate entity (though undoubtedly the use of the word "soul" continues to be of value); and to suggest that faith requires that we subscribe to the belief that God creates each soul immediately is a form of idle speculation since in the nature of things this is not something that can be verified by reason or supported by reference to scripture. Rather it is the product of a dualistic form of thinking that Christian philosophy should be at pains to demote and discard. By contrast, the present interpretation suggests that we should be focusing our attention on life after birth and on the divine action that is needed to complete each member of the incomplete human species in order to bring our spiritual attributes—which include the freedom of action we enjoy as rational beings—to the required level of perfection and make each of us worthy of enjoying God's friendship for eternity. The arena of divine intervention and interaction with us humans is not before we are born but after we are born, throughout the duration of our lives, and in the life hereafter.

REVERSAL IN THE WOMAN'S ROLE

We saw in Chapter One how Augustine adhered strictly to the notion that all sin proceeded from the original sin of Adam, the first man, in whom was gathered "the entire plenitude of the human race." Nevertheless, in *The City of God* Augustine presents as evidence of the devil's superior intelligence his stratagem of beginning the process of temptation by attending first to "the lower member of that human couple in order to arrive gradually at the whole," and goes on to say that while Adam was not deceived by the serpent, Eve was, with the result that Adam sinned because he "refused to be separated from his sole companion even in a partnership of sin."[39] In this, as in so much else, Augustine was simply recycling an interpretation of the events in Eden that had become quite established by the time of the Hellenistic Wisdom literature in the Old Testament.[40] For example, in Sirach 25: 24 we read, "From a woman sin had its beginning, and because of her we all die." This tendency to blame the woman can also be found in the New Testament, where 1 Timothy 2: 14 states quite baldly, "Adam was not deceived, but the woman was deceived and became a transgressor." Down through the centuries these verses provided a pretext for those so inclined to point the finger of accusation at the woman concerning responsibility for the first human sin.[41] So long as Augustine's interpretation of Genesis 3 is upheld, it is indeed hard to escape this conclusion since in the story told there the woman plays a leading role, parleying with the snake, picking the fruit from the tree, eating it and giving some to her husband to eat.

The damage done by this understanding of the Genesis tale to women's reputation and standing in Christian societies is hard to overestimate. This is well conveyed in the bitter speech put into the mouth of Anne Boleyn by author Hilary Mantel in her acclaimed novel, *Wolf Hall*:

> As I am a woman, I am the means by which sin enters this world. I am the devil's gateway, the cursed ingress. I am the means by which Satan attacks the man, whom he was not bold enough to attack, except through me. Well, that is their view of the matter.[42]

But if the Genesis tale is not about the first human sin but rather about humanity's passage to rational consciousness, the role of the woman suddenly takes on a new significance. Whatever the interpretation—a first or original sin, or the ascent to rational human consciousness—the woman in the tale can be seen to play an important role as the one who leads the way, takes the initiative and persuades the male of the species to follow her lead. With the interpretation offered here, it begins to appear that the man—and Man—was led on to achieving his full stature as a human being through the influence of the woman. What is more, it was the woman who recognised that the fruit was good to make one wise and, if we stretch our imagination forward from this episode to take in the connection between the eating from the fruit of the tree of knowledge of good and evil and the development of the cult of Wisdom among the Hebrews, once more the accolade for taking the lead in this process belongs to the woman. It is surely not totally accidental that among the Hebrews Wisdom was represented, variously, as a mother, a wife, a lover and a sister—but always consistently as a female figure, Lady Wisdom.

TRINITARIAN THEOLOGY

In attempting to achieve a limited and imperfect understanding of what the human mind is incapable of understanding fully or perfectly, namely the mystery of the Divine Trinity—of the reality of there being three divine persons but only one God—Christian theologians, going back to Augustine, have found the most helpful analogy to be the operations of the human mind. In the words of Bernard Lonergan:

> From St Augustine onwards, virtually all theologians have studied the human intellect and will in order that, rising by way of an analogy drawn from that image and likeness in which we have been made, they might proceed to speculate in some way about the triune God.
>
> The first step in this investigation is to be found in...the nature of the human mind. Unless one has a clear and accurate grasp of the rational part of human nature, one will proceed in vain to acquire an understanding, however imperfect, of this mystery.[43]

By speaking of Man being made in the image and likeness of God, Lonergan here alludes to the statement in the first creation account at Genesis 1: 26-27. However, this Genesis statement *does not specify* in what particular aspect of Man the image or likeness of God resides. In this book I have argued that at this initial stage—creation—Man simply acquired the *potentiality* to become fully human[44] and that the story of Man's passage to the status of full humanity—and in this way to human adulthood—is to be found in Genesis 3 which describes the crucial breakthrough moment, Man's achievement of full rational consciousness that enables him, with God's indispensable aid and guidance, to grow in holiness and divinity through the cultivation of his spiritual faculties. It was this breakthrough moment that *defined exactly* what is meant in the statement in Genesis 1 concerning Man being made in the image and likeness of God. This breakthrough occurrence is depicted as distancing Man from the other animals by showing him being assimilated more closely to God through his acquisition of mind and the personal freedom that mind entails. Hence it is that this interpretation takes nothing away from but rather lends additional force and significance to Christian theology's ancient practice of attempting to understand the inner life of God, the relationships that define and constitute the Trinity, by means of an analogy with the human mind.

It is not possible to separate Trinitarian theology from the theology of the Incarnation: God spoke his eternal Word and that word became flesh and dwelt among us (Jn 1: 14). The very possibility of God speaking his eternal word in human history is because human beings are already, as one might say *in embryo*, divine beings. If there were not some common ground between God and Man, some ontological link, communication between them would not be possible. It is only because human beings are already, in the sense explained, divine—by virtue of being created in the image of God and of that image being activated and coming alive through Man's passage to full rational consciousness—that it is possible for God to speak to men and women as a man, as a human being using the idiom and concepts of common humanity. Jesus is the incarnate Logos, the eternal Word of God made flesh, only because humanity shares certain aspects of God's nature. It is this fact that makes it possible for God to speak to Man, for God to communicate with Man in a human idiom. The Father spoke his Word and that word was at once human and divine. As divine, Jesus returned to the Father the love communicated by the Father in that moment of conception. This love, freely given and received, is the essence of the relationship between Father and Son (Jn 5: 20), and is called the Holy Spirit.[45] The Spirit is pure relationship and is possessed by both Father and Son. So often in scripture the Spirit is referred to as the "Spirit of…"—as God's Spirit or the Father's

Spirit or Christ's Spirit, and it is noticeable that Jesus, like the Father, has command of the Spirit, but also that he is led by or driven by the Spirit (Mt 4: 1; Mk 1: 12; Lk 4: 1). It is because of the common bond of the Spirit shared by Father and Son that Jesus in the gospels can say that he is "in the Father" and that "the Father is in me" (Jn 14: 10). This mutual indwelling is only possible because both share the same Spirit.[46] Like the Father, Jesus dispenses the Spirit and in the run-up to his death and resurrection he "arranges" for the Father to send the Spirit to take over from him in his earthly mission when he is gone (Jn 14: 26), thereby inaugurating the reign of the Spirit in human hearts and human history.

As I have previously said, the divinity of Jesus is manifested in the gospels by the references made there to his possession by the Spirit of God. Possession by the Spirit, being full of the Spirit, is the essential condition for Jesus being considered a divine being, and it is also the condition by means of which we in turn are brought into union with God, thereby fulfilling our divine nature, bringing it to completion and wholeness. Our possession by the Spirit, the bond of unity between the Father and Jesus, brings us into union with God. It is through the Spirit that we are bonded to Jesus and through Jesus and his mediating mission that we are bonded to the Father, becoming sons and daughters of God by adoption[47] (Jn 14: 20). This possession of us by the Spirit is the culmination of that sharing in the life of God himself that in Genesis 3 God is reported to have deliberately prevented: Man's attainment of that life was not to be achieved in an instant but rather was destined to become the work of God in human history. But the process was begun with Man's ascent to full rational consciousness symbolised in the story by his eating from the tree of knowledge.

REDEMPTION

Christians are probably too readily inclined to consider the saving actions of Jesus in isolation, without regard for the fact—a fact insisted on in the gospel accounts and in Paul—that Jesus is but the culmination of a long process of salvation conducted by God throughout Jewish history. In understanding Jesus's saving action, what theologians refer to as "redemption," we need to keep in mind what has gone before in the scriptural account of salvation history. In St John's gospel Jesus says of himself, "I am the way, the truth and the life," adding, "no one comes to the

Father, but by me." (Jn 14:6) This oft-quoted saying brings together three prominent images to be found in the story told in Genesis 3. First, Jesus is "the way" to the Father—this surely can be accepted as a reference to "the way to the tree of life" (Genesis 3:24) which God deliberately blocks to prevent the human couple from gaining access to the tree at that point. Jesus presents himself as the new, unblocked way to the Father, the source of life. Next, Jesus is "the truth"—and this can very plausibly be seen as a reference to the tree of knowledge of good and evil, the tree of wisdom, which Man did eat from in the story, thereby fatefully crossing the line separating the divine from the created realm, but also thereby beginning to share in that divine wisdom that came to be celebrated in the Jewish scriptures and in relation to which Jesus presents himself as the completion and summation. Finally, Jesus is "the life"— surely a reference to the life that God prevented the human couple from gaining access to in Genesis 3. In these ways, Jesus becomes the point of convergence of these three powerful motifs that run through Jewish revelation from the beginning: the way to God, the truth of Divine Wisdom and the life of union with God. In claiming to be the way, the truth and the life, Jesus is claiming to be the end-point of Jewish salvation history, and his identification of himself with "the life" cannot be understood as amounting to anything less than a claim to divine status, given the close association in Jewish and Christian religious thinking between life and God (notably Jn 5: 26).

Christian theology of redemption is so cluttered—cluttered by the products of competing theological schools, by the speculations and inclinations of the Reformers and their opponents and by so many other extraneous influences, not least the concepts and vocabulary of lawyers and jurists (particularly in the West)—that it is well to go back to the most primitive image of salvation to be found in the bible. That is Noah's ark. As we can recall, God suggests the idea of an ark to Noah and even prescribes its design and precise specifications (Genesis 6: 14-16). The ark is made by Noah but in every other respect—in its conception, design and purpose—it is the work of God. Its purpose is the salvation of Noah, his family and a selection of the other non-human animals that inhabit the world; God intends that they shall survive the destructive waters of the Flood and, having come through successfully to the other side, become the seed or foundation of a new creation. He forms a covenant with Noah and his successors. In calling Jesus "redeemer" or "saviour," we are implicitly comparing him with Noah's ark: like the ark he is to be God's medium for the salvation of humankind, mediating God to humanity and humanity to God,[48] the source of a new covenant between God and Man, the initiator of a new creation, a new beginning for human beings in their relationship with God. In a way I have already suggested in this book, Jesus is the point of union between God and Man; the clue to how this is possible is to be grasped in the fact that in being perfect God, Jesus is perfect Man. Jesus is not partly God and partly Man but fully God and fully Man. This seemingly impossible reality is only possible because Man already shares in the divine nature (2 Peter 1:4); in Jesus the divine nature is simply expressed in human form in a complete way—hence Man finds his completion, as human and as divine, through union with Christ. As St Paul expresses it: "For in him (Christ) the whole fullness of deity dwells bodily, and you have come to fullness of life in him, who is the head of all rule and law." (Col. 2: 9-10)

In Jesus, in and through the humanity of Jesus, rather like Noah's ark, God has designed a way of revealing himself, who he is, what his purposes are, what he intends for the human race. Jesus's death and resurrection are the final act in the drama of God's plan of salvation. Jesus's crucifixion is no act of substitution—Jesus is not standing in for us, the ones who ought to be punished, *iustus pro iniustis*—but evidence of Jesus's total and loving commitment to his mission, the mission given him by the Father, the mission that his Jewish enemies, as presented in the Gospel of John, are determined to put a stop to—"We have a law, and by that law he ought to die, because he has made himself the Son of God." (Jn 19:7) By undergoing death by crucifixion, Jesus shows his unyielding, unwavering love for the Father and for the human race to which he belongs. In raising Jesus from the dead, the Father also raises up all those who are, through baptism, heirs with Jesus to divine sonship. We achieve salvation, as did Noah, by passing through the waters of death—death to our old selves—to the other side, and rising to the new life, the new created order that is centred on the person and mission of Christ Jesus. As Paul puts it: "Therefore, if any one is in Christ, he is a new creation; the old has passed away, behold, the new has come." (2 Corinthians 5: 17)

The comparison with Noah's ark is a reminder that for Christians Jesus's death and resurrection are a rite of passage: that just as Noah's ark was the physical embodiment of Man's rite of passage from his previous animal state to his new human state and the establishment of the covenant, so Christ's death and bodily resurrection are the physical embodiment of Man's rite of passage from his old human state to his new divine state, when Man will live at one with the Father through the power of the Spirit dwelling in him.[49] We do not achieve this goal by our own merits, as something that is ours by right, but only as ones who are borne on the saving ark of Christ. We owe our salvation to Christ, and it is in this way, by being "at oned" with God in Christ, that the distance between God and Man, the alienation that constitutes our original sinfulness, is bridged.

What is more, this is not an account of Man becoming united with God by being taken out of this world into some other-worldly realm, but rather of Man becoming at one with God because God has penetrated human history, because God now dwells as a living and life-giving Spirit with Man in the world, because the reign of God has now been established on the earth. "Christian faith affirms that salvation is *finally* and completely expressed in a realm beyond history; but death merely places a seal on what has already been taking place in this world."[50] Although we have our own indispensable role to play, in its conception, design and purposes, the history of our salvation is the work of God, and this work is not some "restoration" of a divine-world order that was shattered by the sin or sins of humankind but an integral part of God's once-and-for all plan of creation.[51] "Creation, sin, and redemption form part of the one sweep of divine love and they should not be considered as temporally successive happenings."[52] As part of God's original plan of creation, Man attained the freedom and power to sin and, on account of what I have termed the basic human situation, human beings became strongly inclined to sin by virtue of becoming human. Redemption is the work of God in history aimed at helping human beings to become centred on him—something their humanity craves—and, in being centred on him, achieving the wholeness and balance that creates the conditions for a good and enjoyable life on earth followed by eternal union with him in the life hereafter. "Redemption" in the Christian economy of salvation is a dimension of God's offer to bring human beings to completion and fulfilment by bringing them into union with him, an offer all human beings receive but are free to refuse. "Redemption is not a new offer, but the original offer coloured by the refusal."[53] For the Christian, God is not some fixed point in the past nor is he the one who supports and sanctions a static and unchanging world order, as people in the Middle Ages tended to think, but he is the God of Man's future, the God of Man's becoming, who through revelation in history has entered into Man's making of Man.[54] In their life journeys human beings stand in continuous need of redemption since all that they do and achieve is continually marred and contaminated by failure and sin, but they need to remember that the saint is only a sinner who keeps on trying and keeps turning to

God for forgiveness and healing. Conversion can be a once-for-all experience, but redemption is on-going and life-long.

THE PROBLEM OF MORAL EVIL

One of the most common arguments against the existence of God is the fact that there is evil in the world. How could a good God, the argument goes, create a universe in which there is so much evil? I cannot hope to deal here with the problem of evil *per se*, of evil of every kind, but since this is a book about the alleged Fall of Man and Original Sin, understood as the origin or source of all subsequent sin, something ought to be said about the problem posed by the existence of moral evil, that is the evil that is brought about by wilful and deliberate human wrongdoing. How could a good God allow a universe to come into being in which there could be so much moral evil, so much sin? The challenge posed by the existence of moral evil is not so much to the existence of God as to the goodness or the omnipotence of God. If God is truly omnipotent, how is moral evil compatible with his alleged goodness?

In Chapter One I argued that despite his subtle philosophical argument, Augustine does not succeed in his efforts to remove from God all responsibility for human sinning. I argued that, on the contrary, Augustine is involved in a contradiction since he attributes the first sin to Man's sinful pride which, in strict logic, he should have cast not as the source of sinning but as a consequence of the first sin. For logically if Man was already infected by sinful pride *before* he committed the first sin—the sin allegedly recorded in Genesis 3 of eating from the tree of knowledge—then he must have come from the hand of God as an already sinful being or, at the very least, as a being already inclined to sin. The conclusion cannot be avoided that God in the traditional Augustinian account is responsible for the moral evil that exists in the world. Man may be the proximate cause of such evil but God is its remote cause, for God cannot be exempted from the responsibility of having created Man as a sinful creature or as a potentially sinful creature. Augustine's account of the original human sin fails to prevent God being implicated in human sinning.

Now it may well appear that the evolutionary account I have given of the emergence of *homo sapiens* likewise implicates God in the origin of moral evil and sin. For I have argued that the story in Genesis 3 is in fact about the acquisition by hominid Man of full rational consciousness; and there can be no doubting the fact that it is the human achievement of such consciousness that makes sin or moral evil possible. For before he achieved rational consciousness, hominid Man, like the other animals, lacked the freedom and self-reflective knowledge that are required for sin. Sin is a human accomplishment; it presupposes that the sinner is responsible for his actions; without the fact of such responsibility, sin is not possible. For sin to occur Man must knowingly and freely do something that is contrary to the will of God. It was only when human beings attained the freedom that is an essential ingredient of rational consciousness that sin became possible. In making such freedom possible it would appear that God also made sin possible.

In the evolutionary account of Man's origins, Man is not at one instant free and innocent and in the next free but a sinner, as he is in the traditional Augustinian account. Rather, before eating from the tree of knowledge, Man is innocent in the sense of not being fully rational and hence as not having the freedom to be capable of sin; after eating from the tree of knowledge—that is, after his ascent into full rational consciousness or self-consciousness—Man is both free and separated from God and hence capable of sin, indeed, on account of his radical incompleteness, inclined to sin. But hominisation, the moment when Man became capable of sinning, was not the moment of creation; rather it was part of natural history, and indeed the inception of human history. When he first came from the hand of his creator the creature that became human was as innocent of sin as all the other members of the animal kingdom because it was not yet capable of sin. It was only following the achievement of human status that this creature became capable of sin, and I have sought to show that at the moment of hominisation the conditions were created that made sin probable or likely. But hominisation is the end product of an extremely long process of evolution, which witnessed vast changes on planet earth and among the plant and animal life that earth gave rise to. As I have already said, with hominisation Man moved from nature to culture and history, and sin was an accompaniment of this transition. Sin is not part of the universe immediately created by God; it is a human phenomenon and belongs to human history. Sin is an historical event.

The objection against the goodness of God, however, can be pressed further with the claim that in creating the evolutionary process that would lead to the emergence of a creature capable of doing evil, God must be held responsible for the moral evil that exists in the world. Simply by coupling the divine creative action with an evolutionary framework does not relieve God of responsibility for the moral evil brought about by one of the creatures to evolve within that framework, since God must be held responsible for the existence of the framework itself.

That is a telling point, but I believe that the existence of the evolutionary framework within which creation occurs provides God with a form of protection from the charge made against his goodness which would not obtain if this framework were absent. The evolutionary framework which I have linked to the divine creative action overcomes, I believe, the charge that God is responsible for human sinning. For the theory of evolution casts God as the creator of a process that would allow different species to evolve and originate over time. That one of these creatures should evolve into a being that is rationally free is in no way evil, but is rather good since this is an ascent from a lower to a higher form of life, a living being closer in nature to God himself. It was this freedom that enabled Man, like God, to become a creative being and hence made invention, civilisation and human development possible. Without such freedom human action would simply have followed the routines and predetermined patterns followed by the other, non-human animals.[55] Nature alone would have determined the course of the universe's development. It was the breakthrough to an intelligent life form that put Man in the driving seat and made history and culture possible. It also made it possible for Man to enter into a relationship with God and hence made it possible for salvation history to occur. All of these developments are only possible because Man is an intelligent and free being.

However, it might be argued that alongside all these positive developments and what we might consider to be human gains, there occurred the conditions which made moral evil possible, and hence that in bringing about these conditions or at the very least enabling them to come about, God must take ultimate responsibility for the fact of human sin.

Such an argument has a certain *prima facie* plausibility, but it overlooks one essential fact. For intelligence and freedom by themselves do not make sin inevitable. Intelligent and free beings are not of necessity sinful beings; they are quite capable of using their gifts of intelligence and freedom in non-sinful activities or for choosing good over evil. Intelligence and freedom make possible merit as well as demerit; or to put the point negatively, without intelligence and freedom it would not be possible for Man to cooperate with God's grace and merit the reward of eternal life. And this is a great good. God is not beholden to us, his creatures, and hence we have no claim to union with God as of right. God is under no obligation to share his life with us, and for this reason he is perfectly free to create the process which will result in Man emerging as free and rational but separated or distanced from him. This will doubtless create a void in Man and Man is free to attempt to fill this void by self-centred actions linked to such things as fame, money, power, pleasure, and so forth; or to fill it by turning to God and asking for God's blessing and the power to resist evil. He is free to be self-centred and so create the conditions in which sin can thrive; he is also free to turn to God to fulfil his needs.

In the evolutionary explanation of how moral evil entered the world, there is some logical or causal space between God and sin. The reason is because in this version sin is not the "primordial fact." Rather, the "primordial fact" lies in the conditions that make sin possible but only possible as a potential by-product of what is essentially and in its totality a good, namely Man's graduation to the status of a rational creature. Sin in this interpretation is something that God permits for the sake of a higher good, not something he positively wills. By enabling the evolution of Man to this higher status, by enabling hominid Man to partake of the divine attribute of knowledge, God has created the human condition— Man as free, rational, self-determining but essentially incomplete—and this is a condition in which Man can either grow or decline morally and spiritually. Man can attempt to overcome, in cooperation with the divine initiative, the distance between himself and God, or he can reinforce and extend this distance by putting other things at the centre of his life.

The evolutionary explanation, unlike the traditional explanation, brings together a range of conditions making possible the moral and spiritual drama that constitutes human history. In the traditional explanation, there is no space between God and sin, since the only breakthrough that occurs is from innocence to sin—and I have argued that Man on his own in a state of perfect innocence is incapable of making such a breakthrough, and some other factor or agency must be at work, such as pride or an inclination to sin. In the evolutionary explanation, there is space between God and sin since the breakthrough is to a new and higher order of being, and sin is only one possibility within this new order, an order that also makes possible human creativity, human self-transcendence and human fulfilment through Man's response to a covenantal relationship with God. Augustine's account of the origin of sin in *The City of God* appears to lack the conditions that make possible sin in a sinless world without implicating God in Man's sinning. The evolutionary explanation puts in place the conditions needed for sinning but since those are also the conditions for life lived at the rational level, a level of life above that of plants and all other animals without exception, and one that makes it possible for God to call Man to a yet higher form of existence, namely a life of union with him, it can be argued that in order for this level of life to exist sin is permitted but not directly willed. What God directly wills is that human beings are saved by finding fulfilment and completion through sharing in his life and the bond of love that he makes possible. Man is called to fulfil his humanity by responding freely to God's invitation to become divine. Sin, in this account, is simply part of a larger whole—the economy of salvation—and the larger whole is good, and it is this good that God wills. It is in this way that the existence of moral evil or sin can be shown to be compatible with God's goodness. I am, of course, aware that everything I have said in this section is at an intellectual level and that no amount of intellectual theorising or agonising can alleviate the very real suffering and pain that human wrongdoing causes in the world. There is a great deal of Christian wisdom and insight in the comment that what we should do about the evil in the world is not to talk about it but to take action to overcome it. Evil is there to be overcome with God's help. So it is that my argument in this sub-section seems to have come round to agreeing with another comment of Augustine's, that God "judged it better to bring good out of evil than not to permit evil to exist at all."[56]

It would be my contention, however, that to present God's creative action as taking place within an evolutionary framework lends this remarkable statement of Augustine's greater significance and a richer intelligibility than it had within the more static conceptual framework entertained by Augustine himself. For the evolutionary framework makes for a clear demarcation in time between the world of nature and the world of human history and human culture—"clear" in the sense that there is such a division, not that anyone would be able to specify when exactly this division occurred or even that there was an exact moment in time when it took place. Now sin, wrongdoing and salvation belong not to the world of nature but to the world of human history and culture. It is upon the emergence of this human world that God forms a covenantal relationship with Man and it is in the arena of human history that the drama of sin and redemption, of wrongdoing and salvation, understood as divinisation, takes place. God responds to the problem of human evil by taking action through the covenant. The amazing ascent of a hominid animal, of a mere animal, to full human status through the natural process of evolution is followed by the even more amazing invitation to all men and women, mere members of sinful and mortal humanity, to ascend to the status of Godlike, divine beings through God's extension of his covenantal relationship to all of humankind. The human evil attendant on the evolutionary creation of humankind is more than compensated for by the new creation begun with Noah and culminating in Christ Jesus: the new creation begun with Noah is subsumed and elevated in the most surprising fashion in the final new creation that is Christ. Through our union with Christ by the indwelling of his Spirit, we are made worthy of friendship and union with God, our Father and creator. Here the telling word is "friendship." Our relationship with God is not that of any other creature for no other creature can be considered God's friend; we, however, are now capable of being truly God's friends. This is what is "new" in the "new creation" initiated by Jesus. "But you are a chosen race, a royal priesthood, a holy nation, God's own people, that you may declare the wonderful deeds of him who called you out of darkness into his marvellous light. Once you were no people but now you are God's people." (1 Peter 2: 9-10)

THE IRENAEAN VISION

Writing more than a century before Augustine, in the second half of the second century AD, St Irenaeus, an Eastern church father who became the bishop of Lyon in the West, presented an interpretation of the story of Adam and Eve in Eden that differs in many important respects from that developed later by Augustine. Irenaeus believed that the human race as created by God was essentially immature and only at the beginning of a long process of development necessary for growth in humanity and likeness to God.[57] In the garden of Eden Adam and Eve were mere children whose transgression, for that reason, was not some defiant act of rebellion, deserving of punishment, but an act of weakness and vulnerability that summoned forth God's merciful love and compassion. For Irenaeus, human life—created by the Father, redeemed by the Son and nourished by the Holy Spirit—was a process of growth and development. He distinguishes between "image" and "likeness": made in the image (*imago*) of God, Man gradually attains to the likeness (*similitudo*) of God by means of his experience of good and evil, and adherence to the former under the guidance of the Spirit.

Time is central to Irenaeus's thinking. Time is needed for God to prepare humankind for perfection; human beings have to be developed in order to become like God: "The Father decides and commands, the Son carries out and forms, the Spirit nourishes and gives life."[58] God's providence is tutorial, preparing women and men through education, and in particular through the trials and tribulations encountered in this life, to be worthy of eternal life.[59] Irenaeus takes literally St Paul's text in Galatians 4: 4: "But when the time had fully come, God sent forth his Son, born of woman, born under the law, to redeem those who were under the law, so that we might receive adoption as sons." All the history of salvation, including the prophets and the coming of Christ, are placed by Irenaeus within a developmental framework—"when the time had fully come." Irenaeus is forward-looking: paradise lies in the future rather than in the past, and the evils of life, even our sins, are growing pains preparing us for the glory to come.

The contrasts with Augustine's interpretation of the story of Adam and Eve in Eden are very evident. First and foremost, the act of transgression, though blameworthy, is more akin to the capricious action of children and there is no emphasis on the dreadful consequences, including the weakening and distortion of human nature, claimed by Augustine to follow from this act. There is no suggestion that Adam and Eve fell from some previous lofty spiritual state of being to some lower state, and hence the Irenaean interpretation is free of the difficulties stemming from the theory of evolution that Augustine's interpretation meets with on this account. It is perhaps not surprising that this more benign interpretation of Irenaeus has proved to be more influential in the Eastern church than in the West. In the fourth century, for example, such Eastern church figures as Methodius and St Gregory of Nanzianzus accepted that Adam was infantile and immature and the corollary belief that Man's perfection lay in the future rather in the past.[60] It is in this orientation to the future rather than to the past as well as in his refusal to consider that Adam's sin contaminated humankind with guilt that Irenaeus's vision most closely resembles the interpretation being put forward here—that and the fact that this relatively ancient interpretation, because of its emphasis on time and development, has the potentiality to be considered compatible with the scientific theory of evolution.[61] This Irenaean vision is widely shared in the Orthodox church and accounts for what N.P. Williams has referred to as the "sunny genius of Christian Hellenism" in contrast to the North African/Latin tradition that condemned "human nature as largely or entirely depraved."[62]

The grounds for the estrangement that took place in the Middle Ages between Eastern and Western Christianity are quite complex but the very fact of this division is regrettable and in conflict with the prayer of Jesus that his followers might be one as he is one with the Father (Jn 17: 11). At the doctrinal level, the main cause of the East-West split was undoubtedly the insertion by the Western Catholic church of the *Filioque* phrase into the creed drawn up by Eastern Bishops at the Council of Constantinople in 381 AD. The creed formulated at Constantinople (often referred to as the Nicene-Constantinopolitan Creed) came to be widely adopted in the West but was changed to include the statement that the Spirit proceeds from both the Father "and the Son" (*Filioque*), whereas the Council of Constantinople had affirmed only that the Spirit proceeds from the Father.[63] A thousand years later the question of *Filioque* continues to divide the Catholic from the Orthodox church. But another doctrinal source of estrangement between East and West has been the Catholic insistence, following Augustine, that all of us share in the guilt of Adam's original sin; the Orthodox church does not accept this.[64] If the Catholic church in the West were able to move towards the Orthodox view on this point by, for example, adopting a notion of original *sinfulness* in place of the traditional notion of an original *sin*, then this would help to patch up some parts at least of this ancient quarrel. We have seen how St Irenaeus's interpretation of Genesis 3 is much closer to the one put forward in this book than is that of Augustine, and is also well regarded in the East. It might be that advances made possible by Western scholarship, motivated by a respect for modern science and a renewed spirit of ecumenism, could lead the church in the West to move beyond Augustine on this question and in this way contribute towards the eventual healing of the East-West divide, which all Christians must hope for. Some such rapprochement between the Catholic church and the Orthodox church would be one of the biggest favours the churches could do for the world, which is becoming increasingly divided along East-West lines. It would require vision, courage and humility on both sides, but would be a wonderful example of Christian love in action in a world where love of this kind is in short supply.

CORRECTION OF THE TRADITION

At this point it might be worth looking to see how far my proposal that it would make more sense to speak of *original sinfulness* than of *original sin* makes for change within the Christian tradition. I believe that this proposal does not destroy the unity of the tradition but rather marks a correction of the tradition, helping to bring it into closer alignment on this question with scripture and the thinking of the ancient Hebrews as well as with Orthodox thinking. Such a correction of the tradition might also serve the cause of ecumenism not only by achieving closer unity between the Eastern church and the churches of the West but also by leading the churches in the West to a deeper understanding of their own ecclesiology as a function of the Holy Spirit. The correction, to be taken seriously, must be aimed at both the Catholic and the Protestant traditions, both of which have invested heavily in Augustinian theology. But first, to prevent things going too far, it is important to stress the points of great theological importance that remain the same in this new interpretation. These are:

- Everything in creation is a gift from God, the creator
- Human beings depend totally on God to be saved
- Human beings are strongly inclined to sin
- Salvation is essentially divinisation, the process of becoming like God
- The order of grace differs radically from the order of nature
- Grace is essentially a sharing in the life of God
- Salvation is holiness or wholeness, which only God can provide, making us fit to enjoy union with him
- Man is by nature predisposed to an end which can only be met supernaturally, as a gratuitous gift from God

In short, the correction suggested here would not require any alterations in the major Christian creeds or the early Christian confessions of faith.

Among the points of difference from the position established by Augustine are the following:

- The notion of some first or original sin, of a rebellion by the first humans against their creator, is the product of a mistaken interpretation of Genesis 3
- Man does not share in Adam's guilt since there was, historically, no original sin: human beings are not born guilty before God
- The default setting of humanity is not damnation
- Grace and salvation are not the counterpoint of sin and damnation: salvation is not essentially forgiveness or remediation but divinisation and wholeness
- Perfection lies in the future and not in the past
- The state of Adam before the "Fall," or before the event described in Genesis 3, a subject on which Augustine's followers have spilt

an ocean of ink[65], need not concern us, just as it appears not to
have concerned the authors of Genesis
- Like all members of the animal kingdom, Adam was created mortal, not immortal: the story told in Genesis 3 is in line with the scientific theory of evolution

There are other major points of similarity and difference that shall
emerge more coherently in the closing section of this book. To evaluate
how far the traditional understanding of original sin would have to be
amended in order to comply with the interpretation put forward here, it
would be useful in addition to undertake a more detailed comparison of
the similarities and differences between it and the notion of the "basic
human situation" argued for in this book. Such a comparison will, I believe, be assisted through engagement with a work that champions the
traditional doctrine against modern attempts at reinterpreting it. In chapter 2 of his book, *Bound to Sin*, Alistair McFadyen conducts a helpful
comparison of the Augustinian understanding of original sin with some
modern critiques of this ancient belief.[66] He works out some of the basic
characteristics of original sin according to Augustine only to find that
some modern interpretations omit some of them from their account and
in this way fall some way short of Augustine in accounting for human
sinfulness.

McFadyen considers that the doctrine of Original Sin "chafes against
modern assumptions and inbuilt ways of thinking" by, first, appearing to
be at odds with the evolutionary view of human origins, and, second, by
holding human beings to be morally accountable for something done by
others, to be deemed guilty for something over which they had absolutely no control. "This moral source of offence," McFadyen argues, "is
both the most powerful in contemporary culture and the most enduring."[67] These comments on the discomfort felt by many "modern" people
over the traditional doctrine of original sin would appear to underline the
value of the interpretation being put forward in this book which, as we
have seen, has no difficulty in endorsing the evolutionary account of the
origins of human beings and, in addition, repudiates with the same vigour as any so-called "modern" the notion that human beings born after
Adam and Eve inherit the guilt for their "original sin"—if there was no
such sin there can be no guilt, inherited or otherwise.

Dr McFadyen finds that the traditional, Augustinian notion of original sin has four outstanding characteristics, "four interrelated corollaries," and suggests that the explanatory force of the traditional doctrine lies in these characteristics: original sin is *contingent, radical, communicable and universal.*[68] The following is my summary of the points he makes:

> First, original sin is contingent in being the product of a free act; it was not inevitable but once it occurred it brought about a distortion in human nature.
> Second, it has a radical hold on human beings, referring to a condition we are in before it refers to individual acts.
> Third, it is communicated pre-personally—that is, it infects us prior to our achievement of personhood, resulting in a pre-personal distortion of our human nature that underlies all our personal acts, and is itself named sin.
> Fourth, it is universally extensive both as a condition and as a realized possibility: all of us are in a situation of sin. There is universal human solidarity in sin.[69]

McFadyen considers these four characteristics of original sin to be responsible for the profundity and explanatory force of the traditional doctrine, and it is by holding up modern attempts to reinterpret the doctrine against these characteristics that he finds them wanting in one or more respects. To choose but one of several examples put forward, he claims that the traditional doctrine's insistence that sin is biologically transmitted with our humanity, that it is a structural reality of human nature, places the doctrine beyond modern notions such as that of the "fundamental option" whereby one orients oneself or makes some fundamental option about the self, in existentialist fashion, with the result that the history of sinning is the history of oneself. On this view he comments, "This is an internal, *self*-binding in sin, not the impersonal inheritance and transmission of an external distortion, bondage and guilt."[70]

My reason for citing McFadyen's reasoning on this point is to see how well the interpretation put forward here copes with his critical comments. If a comparison is made with the explanatory force of the traditional doctrine on the basis of the four crucial characteristics of original sin he suggests, I think it can be said that the interpretation put forward in this work satisfies all four:

> First, the evolutionary interpretation I have argued for has as its outcome what I have termed "the basic human situation," and this is a *contingent* outcome since it is the product of human evolution; in so far as evolution is dependent on random variations, human evolution can be

seen to be a contingent event. If the objection is raised that God willed that humanity should evolve in this fashion, this should not be thought to imply that Man's ascent to full rational consciousness was necessitated, since clearly God willed it precisely as a contingent event.

Second, the basic human situation is *radical*, referring to a condition that cannot be avoided by any human being; it is part of the very condition of humanity.

Third, it is *communicable* in the sense that it underpins everything that is done by the individual and conditions the free actions of human beings.

Fourth, it is *universally extensive*, since no human being is exempted from this basic situation.

Because it meets each of the four crucial characteristics cited by McFadyen, the interpretation I have argued for in these pages can be seen to enjoy the same explanatory force that McFadyen celebrates in his reflections on the traditional doctrine of original sin. And because it complies with each of these four criteria, this interpretation, which might be thought of as a reinterpretation of the traditional doctrine, escapes the charges McFadyen brings against the reinterpretations he cites in his book. The reason is quite simple. My argument in this book has not been about the established doctrine of original sin but about the event described in Genesis 3 on which the established doctrine is based. By attending not to this or that feature of the traditional doctrine but to the event underlying it, to its very basis, it is clear that I am not attempting to critique original sin on the basis of "modernity"—and McFadyen's strictures are at heart dependent on the alliance he considers to exist between the alternative interpretations of original sin he examines and what he cites as the central tenets and assumptions of "modernity."[71] Rather, because the basic human situation I argue for is at heart about Man's relationship with God, his need for wholeness which translates into his need for God for his own completion, it shares the radical, pre-personal and universal characteristics that McFadyen attributes to the traditional doctrine.

There is, however, one area where this interpretation is at one with the modern objections to original sin and that is in its rebuttal of the traditional doctrine's insistence that all of us participate in the guilt of Adam's first sin. As McFadyen puts it, "In particular, it is the attribution—indeed, the transference—of guilt by natural or metaphysical means, rather than by free, personal action, which is a major sticking point."[72] McFadyen struggles heroically to show that modernity is wrong on this point but I have to say that modernity is right on it. It is offensive to brand as guilty those who took no part in the action to which the guilt accrues. As Gabriel Daly observes, "if the genetic model (i.e., the inheritance of sin "by generation") is pressed, it can offend against the most elementary sense of justice."[73] Guilt cannot be attributed in the absence of responsibility: where responsibility is completely absent, then so must guilt be completely absent. That may be a position shared by most "modern" people, but it is also one shared by people from earlier times.[74] As I have indicated already, McFadyen's overall argument is too dependent on Augustine's reflections on freedom which considered freedom to be incompatible with coercion but to be compatible with necessity. Believing this, he claims that human beings remain free even when they are necessitated to sin, bound to sin by virtue of their inheritance of the sin of Adam. McFadyen takes Augustine to be representative of the Christian tradition on this point[75], but unfortunately for his argument this is a mistaken assumption, since the notion that the will could be free but necessitated was strongly repudiated by Aquinas.[76] For Aquinas freedom of the will requires both freedom from coercion and freedom from necessity.

To sum up this section, my interpretation agrees with what McFadyen considers to be the central objection to the traditional doctrine of original sin; in that way it ought to be considered to have the merit of not repelling women and men on moral grounds, a distinct strength. On the other hand, in its depiction of the basic human situation it is still as radical and universal as an explanation of human behaviour as the traditional doctrine since it upholds "the inherent, antecedent sinfulness of men and women even before they have been exposed to bad example and have begun to sin personally."[77] What is more, the grounds of my objection to original sin are not any tendencies to accommodate traditional theology to modernity, but are strictly theological since my argument attempts to do more justice than the traditional interpretation to the data of scripture, helped by the insights of modern scholarship.

It should also be added that my interpretation has the distinct advantage of being not only compatible but in league with the scientific theory of evolution, in the sense that both the interpretation and the scientific theory claim that Man is an evolved creature. In that way the interpretation gets round one of the most serious problems confronting the traditional doctrine of original sin without in any way diluting the traditional Christian claim that human beings are inherently sinful. Dr McFadyen does not really come to terms with the difficulties raised against the traditional doctrine by evolution, referring to one of them, though not the one highlighted in this work, briefly in a footnote.[78] Moreover, the present interpretation does not incur the problem Augustine struggled with but never resolved, of explaining how sin and the guilt attached to it can be transmitted down through the generations; Augustine's failure to give a coherent account of how this transmission might be accomplished must be counted as a serious weakness in his argument. The notion of "the basic human situation" avoids all the difficulties attendant on the "mechanics of transmission" that afflict anyone who upholds the Augustinian view, since it holds quite simply that human beings are born in a state of needing God for their completion, in a state of *privatio Dei*, as explained at some length in Chapter Five. This is not a state resulting from some sinful act of rebellion by human creatures against their creator, nor is it transmitted by parents to their offspring; rather, it is a brute fact of human existence, the human way of being in the world, on which the whole history of salvation, as revealed in the bible, is predicated. In short, my interpretation avoids the objections, ancient and modern, raised against the doctrine of original sin while maintaining the doctrine's not inconsiderable strengths as an explanation of the human propensity to sin.

SUMMARY AND REVIEW OF METHODOLOGY

(1) THE BIG PICTURE

In this book I have argued against the Augustinian notion of original sin and against the interpretation of scripture that led Augustine to this notion. I have not denied that there is great moral evil in the world or that human beings are sinners but I have provided a different understanding of the cause of such evil and have supported my understanding by arguments from scripture that are in many ways different from and at variance with those of Augustine. Although like Augustine I have focused in particular on Genesis chapter 3, I have not centred my argument on the so-called deliberate "act of disobedience" of our first parents but have placed at the epicentre of my argument Man's eating from the tree of knowledge and failure, through God's deliberate intervention, to eat from the tree of life. What is more, unlike Augustine, I have not considered the situation that arose as a consequence of the actions described in Genesis 3 to be completely and utterly disastrous but to be thoroughly ambiguous: certainly Man lost his pre-rational innocence, becoming capable of sinning and indeed strongly inclined to sin, but, in addition to that, Man became knowledgeable and creative, capable of becoming civilised and capable of being called into a covenantal relationship with God in the course of history.

This is a relationship that God graciously chose to cultivate with the aim of educating Man in the use of the very divine attribute, the acquisition of which had caused Man to become an anomaly of nature, a hybrid of divinity and animality, a danger to himself and the rest of nature. God chose to give Man the opportunity to become once more a complete being, whole and entire, by enabling him to become divine like himself, and to do this by completing the work of divinisation that had begun with his acquisition of the knowledge of good and evil. Under God's tutelage, over time by means of covenant, law, kingship and prophecy, and finally through the cultivation of Wisdom, Man's knowledge of good and evil became ever more refined and developed, and Man was provided with the means to draw ever closer into union with God.[79] This is what I have deemed to be the divinisation of Man through history. However, to effect true union with God, to convert knowledge into life, something more was needed and that something arrived with God's entry into human history in the person of Jesus, the Christ, the divine Logos. Through his witness to the Father and his death on the cross Christ completed the translation of knowledge into life so that by the action of the Spirit of Christ on the human spirit Man could become by means of self-sacrificing love once more whole and complete, albeit quite different from what he was at the point of creation, and worthy of being admitted to fellowship with God.

That in summary outline has been the core of the argument I have put forward in these pages. In the course of developing my case I have at various points focused on the reflections of some twentieth century thinkers and theologians in order to show how well supported their reflections are by the thesis I have argued for. I have also offered reflections on some traditional aspects of Christian theology, such as Christology and Redemption. My comments on these topics clearly favour what has been called the "bottom up" approach to theology, one that begins with human existence and the words we find in scripture, as opposed to the "top down" approach that begins with a theological formula from some past Church Council. The "bottom up" approach has had many strong exponents among Catholic theologians since the Second Vatican Council; but while there have been many Catholic biblical scholars and

theologians who have recognised the shortcomings of the traditional interpretation of the Fall, there has been lacking a convincing interpretation to put in its place. It is my hope that this book will provide the missing piece of the jigsaw.

With regard to how I have organised the book, clearly one of the
more innovative things I have done, when comparison is made with the
usual treatments of original sin in works of Christian theology, is to
bring the work of an anthropologist to bear on Genesis 1-11. The insights
into the primitive outlook of the ancient Hebrews yielded by this approach fully justify its employment and provide a much needed correc-
tive of how Genesis 1-11 should be read as well as crucial insights into
the meaning of the story of Adam and Eve in Genesis 3. Without the
support of Mary Douglas's work, which was cited at some length in
Chapter Three, I might have felt constrained to read the myth in Genesis
3, in the traditional way, as a tale about the sin committed by the first
Man; certainly it would have been a great deal more difficult to make the
interpretation I offered in Chapter Two carry conviction or stick. With
the benefit of this work, the traditional, Augustinian reading became not
only unnecessary but positively misleading. Instead, it became possible,
indeed necessary, to see the tale as being about Man transgressing the
boundary separating creation from God and, in addition, about God's
gracious mercy in making accommodation for this transgression by
changing all of creation to fit with the new situation Man found himself
in. This provided the context for grasping the meaning of the words spoken by the Lord God at the end of Genesis 3, since they clearly reflected
the fact that Man had crossed one line and that God was determined to
take action to ensure that he did not cross another, at least not without his
permission and in a way that he sanctioned and, in its essential outline,
planned. The story then came to be seen as one about Man crossing one
line but being prevented from crossing another—about Man becoming in
part divine (through his achievement of knowledge) but being prevented
from completing this process (by achieving eternal life).

It was this fine balance between achieving so much but being prevented from achieving fullness and completion that constituted the basic
ingredient of my account: the fact that Man was essentially incomplete
and broken off became the explanatory framework for his tendency to
sin: it is this incompleteness that is referred to in the phrase "the basic
human situation." On this showing, sin flows from Man's attempt to
complete himself when in fact such completion can only be the work of
God, or the work of Man when cooperating with God's plan.

The accommodation made by the Lord God to Man's sinful nature then came into view as the concession he made to Man for frustrating the human attempt at achieving divinisation "on the cheap," as we might say—the history of salvation would become the history of God's empowering Man to fill out and complete the process of divinisation begun in Eden, but this would be the stuff of human history and not something Man would simply reach out and effortlessly grab for himself. It became necessary at this point for Man to "leave Eden" behind him. What is more, the main means by which Man would make progress in this process would be through the opportunities afforded in the course of history for him to enhance, refine and develop the divine attribute of knowledge and wisdom he had acquired in Eden, which had in fact made him into the strange, anomalous creature that the Yahwist storytellers of Genesis knew. Here "knowledge and wisdom" should not be interpreted in some narrow "intellectual" sense—although the triumphs of the human intellect should in no way be excluded from this account since they vividly illustrate the divinity of humanity—but should relate to the Hebrew word *leb* and include all of the traditional human and Christian virtues as well as the education of the feelings. God's infinite intelligence is accompanied by his holiness, his wholeness, and human growth in holiness and wholeness,[80] human maturation, is achieved through the trials and challenges that life throws up and is never an easy or totally comfortable experience. It requires effort, perseverance and repentance on the part of the human subject and, Christians believe, will be greatly assisted by prayer, self-denying love and the gifts of the Spirit indwelling in us.

In this way the "Primitive Tradition" furnished the basic shape and framework for the interpretation that was developed in the remainder of the book. It provided a convincing seal of approval for the interpretation, presented in Chapter Two, of Genesis 3 within the broader context of Genesis 1-11. As far as thematic content was concerned, it provided the main ingredients of boundary transgression, incompleteness and the efforts at completion that make up most of the rest of the book. One of these efforts was with a view to the achievement of immortality. This was the theme of Chapter Four and took us a certain distance along the road of interpretation. In dealing with this theme, I commented on the parallels between the story of Enkidu as related in the ancient Babylonian epic poem, *Gilgamesh*, and the story of Adam and Eve in Genesis. Enkidu's sexual seduction by the temple love-priestess, Shamhat, has the character of a sacral activity symbolising some deep communion with and participation in the divine, as understood by the Babylonians. It is this activity that results in Enkidu becoming human—he becomes human by partaking of the divine, by becoming "as if a god," in the words of Shamhat. And in becoming human he is distanced from his former companions, the other animals, who now flee from him in fear. There is little room for doubting the parallels between the story of Enkidu and the story of Adam and Eve in the garden of Eden. And since there is no doubt at all among commentators that by succumbing to her blandishments and having sexual intercourse with Shamhat Enkidu passes from the animal to the human state,[81] from a feral type of existence to a world of culture and civilisation, *Gilgamesh* can be seen to provide evidence for the occurrence of a similar transition or passage in the case of the man and the woman in the Genesis story. In this way the *Gilgamesh* epic provides strong evidence for the accuracy of the central element, and the most controversial, of the interpretation of Genesis 3 argued for in this book. Indeed, by showing clearly that the central episode in the Shamhat-Enkidu encounter concerns the *transformation* or *elevation* of the latter, I would go so far as to say that the *Gilgamesh* evidence promotes the interpretation of Genesis 3 presented here from being likely or probable to being highly likely or highly probable.

However, notwithstanding the thematic link between the story of the humanising of Enkidu in the *Gilgamesh* epic and the story of the humanising of the woman and the man (in that order) in Genesis, immortality was always only a subsidiary theme in Genesis, since in Hebrew thought, unlike that of the Babylonians and Egyptians, it could only be achieved through union with the one and only God and such union could only possibly be received by Man as a gift from God. Chapter Five sought to use all the insights gathered up to that point to set out the position on Man's nature and his inclination to sin in clear and forthright terms; in this chapter I provided an alternative understanding of the source of sinning to that suggested by Augustine in his interpretation of the events in Genesis 3. This was then completed in Chapter Six, where it was seen how the Wisdom Tradition, which came late in the Old Testament literature, linked back to Genesis 3 and illustrated just how ambiguous Man's achievement of the divine attribute of knowledge had proved to be since, in addition to explaining the human capacity for sin, it also became an instrument for God's teaching of Man through history and hence a means of his salvation, as confirmed by the OT and NT references to knowledge of good and evil as a gift to humankind from God.

Chapter Six also sought to reconnect with Genesis 3: Paul's theology of redemption, the account of Jesus's mission in the Gospel of John, and what the Book of Revelation tells us about the last things. I believe that the enrichment of our understanding of these later biblical events or discourses brought about by the work of reconnection with Genesis 3 should convince us that Augustine's interpretation of the story told there amounts to an impoverishment of the tale and stands in the way of it being recognised for what it is—the beginning of a truly wonderful and generous history of salvation that gradually but visibly is played out over long periods of time and comes to its final fruition in the mission and teaching of Jesus. The fact that Augustine's interpretation has endured for so long is testimony to his authority and greatness; for only the interpretation of a genius of the stature of Augustine could have had a chance of standing in the way of what must surely, I believe, be recognised as a more satisfactory and theologically fruitful understanding of the meaning of Genesis 3.

I also believe that the approach I have taken, while it acknowledges the diversity of the Jewish and Christian scriptures and the individuality of the different books and episodes within these books, has also brought out the unity of the scriptures and, from a Christian perspective, has illustrated how the Christian scriptures fit with and indeed complement the books of the bible which Christians call the Old Testament, to the extent of forming an integrated unit with them. But if my work of exploration has left me happy at finding how well integrated the Christian scriptures appear to be with certain themes and tendencies found in the books of the Old Testament, they have also left me in awe before the grandeur of our Jewish literary heritage. For the Christian scriptures can only be understood when considered as part of this great heritage and their riches and depth can only be revealed and appreciated when brought into contact with it. That is why I think it is important that we arrive at a deeper and more comprehensive understanding of the first chapters of Genesis, for unless we do so our tradition, the Christian Tradition, will be the poorer. For there is a "logic" or cast of mind in both the gospels and the epistles that has its roots or its basic premises in Genesis 3 and, in particular, in the speech of the Lord God at the conclusion of that chapter. That speech points the way forward for all the rest of the bible, it indicates the central theme and it drives the narrative core that runs through everything that follows: God's desire for loving union with Man and Man's need and desire for loving union with God.

(2) A CLOSER LOOK AT THE ARGUMENT

It is the rich mixture, the weaving together of different modes of thought and the different mindsets of peoples at different periods of their history that makes the story in Genesis 1-11 so fascinating and powerful.[82] It is a tale that reveals us to ourselves by revealing the basic set of relationships that structure the human personality. In addition, it bears the imprint of different periods in Hebrew history. It is a rich multi-faceted tale that eludes neat classification and causes us to ponder and think long after we have read it.

First, the primitive way of thinking gives us the basic plan or outline: Man as a hybrid, part God and part animal, a danger to himself and to others; Man as an anomaly of nature, who cannot be neatly classified along with the other members of the animal kingdom; Man as only half finished, broken off, in need of completion. The primitive mentality of the authors of the literary unit of Genesis 1-11 can also be traced in what I can only term the "literary form" of this piece of writing. For the basic pattern of the central episode described there, the episode of the eating of the fruit from the tree of knowledge of good and evil, is prescribed by the notion of a rite of passage, a passage from one state of being to another: a passage from the proto-human to the human; from childhood to adulthood; from nature to culture and history. From innocence to sinfulness, yes, certainly; but the reading achieved in this book by means of a more strictly literary approach to the task of interpretation points to dimensions of meaning and significance that the traditional Augustinian tradition, with its black-and-white emphasis on human depravity and sin, is in danger of losing altogether. Augustine fails completely to do justice to the superb artistry of the Genesis story.

Living and working at the time he did, what Augustine perforce lacked most of all was any true insight into what I have called the primitive way of thinking. The primitive way of thinking, present also in the *Gilgamesh* epic, is basic to a true and accurate understanding of Genesis 3 and the whole of Genesis 1-11; and it is the impact that the primitive way of thinking has on our understanding of Genesis 1-11 that leads eventually to the new understanding of the course and shape of salvation history presented in this book. It is by grasping the primitive outlook of the authors of the early chapters of Genesis that we grasp the true narrative structure of these chapters, and the purpose or intention that lies behind them. So it is that the primitive layer of meaning is normative and the other dimensions of the tale told in Genesis 3 are relatively superficial refinements added later. For example, once we have grasped the *primitive* thought patterns present in Genesis 1-11, the whole of Genesis 4-8 becomes clearer, for we can see that this section concerns a dangerous interlude or period of transition stretching from the period immediately after Man's eating from the tree of knowledge up till the end of Flood, when there occurs the re-birth of Man and the inauguration of the covenant. Genesis 4-8 is an account of the second of the three stages, the dangerous interim period characteristic of rites of passage. Also clearer is the strange incident, which James Barr informs us that commentators from the various Christian traditions have tended to ignore, considering that it explained nothing in our experience and "strained belief," namely the episode of the sexual liaisons of the sons of God with the daughters of men, described at the beginning of Genesis 6.[83] When viewed within the context of primitive thinking, this rather bizarre episode begins to make new sense since it can be seen to belong to this dangerous interlude and to constitute another breaching of the boundaries separating the divine from the created realm, effectively conveying the magnitude of the breakdown of order unleashed by the episode in Genesis 3. To view Genesis 1-11 through the lens of the primitive way of thinking is to grasp its meaning with a subtlety and force not otherwise possible.

The theme of immortality is also present in Genesis 3 since it is raised as a threatening possibility by the Lord God in his closing speech in that chapter. The immortality theme reveals how, with the onset of reflective intelligence, Man becomes a question to himself and at the heart of this question is the issue of his death. Man's self-understanding as a creature who must die is yet another point of division between himself and the rest of the animal kingdom: all animals instinctively fear danger and death but only Man knows he is mortal. The quest for immortality, which the Hebrews shared with most ancient peoples, reveals Man's aspiring nature, his inability to accept death as the final answer to life's mystery and his search for some form of eternal life and happiness. This quest is itself correlative with the divine dimension of the human personality and Man's unrestricted longing—hence its universality across cultures and continents; hence also the cross-grained struggle of modern atheism in its attempts to suppress this natural human aspiration and explain it away. The distinctive characteristic of Hebrew thinking on this question is the conviction that immortality cannot be earned or won by human effort or human cunning, and that it is simply not possible for Man to achieve immortality outside of union with God, and such union is strictly in the gift of God.

Finally, by addressing the wisdom tradition in the context of a reading of the early chapters of Genesis, it was possible to plot the connection between the emergence of Wisdom as something deeply venerated in Hebrew culture and the event described in Genesis 3 of Man eating from the tree of knowledge of good and evil. It was possible to restore the true meaning of the phrase "knowledge of good and evil" by reference to a range of passages in the Old Testament and one important passage in the New Testament, and thereby to establish its association with knowledge of a mature, adult kind, with knowledge gained from experience, knowledge that can be passed on to one's descendants; this is at the root of cultural evolution and in many ways is what the Hebrews understood by wisdom; and this made it possible in turn to restore the profoundly positive symbolism of the tree of knowledge of good and evil, something that is quite lost within Augustine's interpretation. Augustine has thoughts only for what he believes Man loses by eating from the tree, whereas the present interpretation points to what Man has acquired or gained, the knowledge of good and evil which in various passages of the bible is seen to be synonymous with wisdom, an attribute of God, celebrated as among the greatest of the gifts that God has bestowed on humankind.

The wisdom tradition marks a further refinement in human development, the acquisition of a refined moral sensibility, the search for the conditions that make for the good life, the virtues and modes of conduct that make life happy and rewarding. Sin makes its most potent appearance within this version of the story: it is not longer simply defilement but sin—personal guilt before God—for which Man must accept responsibility. Viewed in the context of the wisdom tradition, the central episode in Genesis 3 appears to be a sinful action, a deliberate act of disobedience of God's explicit command. It is my proposal, however, that the style of writing in this chapter (not least the appearance of a talking snake) suggests that we are dealing here not with an actual incident, an historical occurrence, but with the product of the human imagination; this view is reinforced by the evidence of a strong literary influence by the Babylonian epic poem *Gilgamesh* and other Near Eastern works of fiction on several of the episodes described in the first chapters of Genesis. Rather than seeing Genesis 3 as an account of some historical event, it makes more sense to view this episode as illustrative and not causative, as a parable or commentary about the newly emerged human species and, as such, as an action that is a type, or prototype, of the many sinful actions that will unfold in the historical narrative of the remainder of the

Bible. This effectively neuters or negates the force of this episode, which for Augustine is the catastrophic original sin in human history, the guilt for which is shared by all of humankind, from which flow all of the devastating consequences listed in Chapter One.

To these reflections it should be added that if I am correct in viewing Genesis 3 as only the first stage in the tale of rite of passage, then it is mistaken to treat it in isolation. We are much more likely to grasp the true narrative intention of the tale if we see it as integral to the larger narrative that unfolds from Genesis 3 through Genesis 4-8 and reaches its completion and denouement with the Flood and the inauguration of the covenant in Genesis 9. From a literary artistic point of view, that seems to be a much more satisfying way of viewing these early sections of Genesis. Genesis 3-9 needs to be grasped as a literary unit in its own right; we only see it aright if we grasp it in its totality; to concentrate on only one incident from this totality is to damage the tale's narrative structure. When seen as the opening part of a three-part tale or story, the focus of Genesis 3 can be seen to be on the change or transformation that occurs in the couple who cross the line separating the created realm from the divine. It is this transformation that leads on to the next stage in the rite of passage, the tale of disorientation and disorder related in chapters 4-8, when God decides to wipe out humankind, and then to the final stage of re-integration and renewal when God reverses his decision, that is symbolised by the Flood and the introduction of the covenant with Noah. To wrench the story in Genesis 3 from the larger narrative whole recounted in chapters 3-9 is to damage the artistic integrity and coherence of these chapters, the surest way to a mistaken understanding of their meaning.

THE PROBLEM POSED BY PAUL

James Barr considers that it was under the influence of Greek thought, which by Paul's day had penetrated the Jewish Wisdom tradition, that Paul wrote as he did in both Romans 5 and 1 Corinthians 15 about sin entering the world with Adam and about how with sin came death. The two texts Barr considers to have been regulative for Paul's thinking on this matter are Wisdom 2: 23 and IV Ezra 7: 116-118[84]: both are from what Barr refers to as the "later strata" of the Old Testament strongly influenced by Greek thought. The first of these suggests that Man was created immortal and that it was only because of Adam's sin that he was rendered mortal, while the second suggests that Adam's fall is shared by all of humanity. In discussing these issues in both Chapter Four and Chapter Six we noted that the Hebrew Old Testament makes no mention of Adam's fall and, despite being highly conscious of the sinfulness of human beings, it nowhere attempts to explain this sinfulness by reference to the events described in Genesis 3; we also observed that in ancient Hebrew thought death not associated with violence was considered normal and natural, and that there was no suggestion that death was something imposed on humanity as a punishment for sin. References to the sin of Adam and its consequences for humanity are confined to the later strata of the bible, those sections influenced by Greek ideas about death. We also stressed the fact that in making the Adam-Christ comparisons in Romans 5 and 1 Corinthians 15, Paul is chiefly concerned with illustrating the scope of Christ's redemptive activity and finds the comparison with Adam serves his purposes in this matter—in other words, it is not his intention to comment on Adam's trespass so much as to highlight the fact that Christ is the new head of the human race, and in that sense the new Adam.

This is perhaps even clearer in the case of 1 Corinthians 15 than of Romans 5, for in the former Paul stresses the point that Christ is the first of many and introduces the Adam-Christ comparison with the words, "But in fact Christ has been raised from the dead, the first fruits of those who have fallen asleep." (1 Cor. 15: 20) He discourses on the themes of life and death and, like the great religious orator he is, Paul plays on the words, extending their meaning well beyond their literal reference to physical life and death to include their spiritual reference respectively to union with God (life) or alienation from God (death): "For as in Adam all die, so also in Christ shall all be made alive." (1 Cor 15: 22) In Paul's hands the word "life" begins to take on the associations with God, freedom and wholeness that it has in the gospel of John. For Paul death and life have strong spiritual associations; but behind these associations stands the literal claim that death, death as a universal phenomenon of human existence, came into the world because of Adam's sin. This, as we say, shows the influence of Greek thought on the religious tradition on which Paul draws; these ideas were circulating widely in the Hellenized Hebrew culture of Paul's age. Paul, it would appear, simply takes these Greek inspired views for granted, as providing a useful analogy for describing the mission of Christ, and, as we have argued, Augustine takes them over from Paul but interprets them more strictly and more literally, finding that they appear to answer the persistent, unrelenting question—*Whence comes evil?*—that puzzled him for many years. So bold and confident is Augustine that there is the distinct likelihood that he simply incorporates Paul's words into his own anxious search for an answer to that question, taking them out of context and exaggerating their significance.

The question then arises: which of these two strands of interpretation ought we to endorse—that of the Hebrew Old Testament, which makes no mention of Adam's sin nor of death being the result of such sin, or that of some texts in the Greek Old Testament, which do? That is the acute problem faced by the Church in the West, though I would hope that it is not insuperable; after all, the doctrine of original sin has never been part of any of the great Christian creeds. However, the issue of the Church's problem is really extraneous to the work I am carrying forward in this book, which is to provide a convincing interpretation of Genesis 3 based on the biblical text itself and assisted by whatever conceptual tools modern scholarship can provide. I am concerned to answer the question: what is the meaning that was meant by the authors of this tale? Nothing more and nothing less than that. In light of that concern, it is clear that I must go along with the Hebrew understanding of the Hebrew bible, and not with some later understanding shaped by foreign influences.

CONCLUSION

Returning to Paul and the general direction of his thought, I hope to have shown that at its deepest level Paul's religious vision is quite consistent with the most ancient and primitive religious thinking of the Hebrew tradition, the Hebrew myths, and that he interprets the meaning and impact of the life and death of Jesus in terms taken from that tradition. By reference to a broad range of his writings, I have argued that Paul builds on and advances from the most basic and central concepts found in the Book of Genesis, that he grasps firmly the idea that mere knowledge or wisdom is not on its own sufficient to convey or deliver life. He presents Christ's crucifixion as introducing a new conception of wisdom, one that stands traditional Hebrew wisdom on its head, and his resurrection as converting wisdom into life by ushering in the reign of the Spirit in the human heart, and holding out the promise of resurrection from the dead for all of those bonded to Christ through the Spirit.

This is well summarised in this passage from the Letter to Titus, long thought to share Paul's theological vision:

> But when the goodness and loving kindness of God our Saviour ap-
> peared, he saved us, not because of deeds done by us in righteousness,
> but in virtue of his own mercy, by the washing of regeneration and re-
> newal in the Holy Spirit, which he poured out upon us richly through
> Jesus Christ our Saviour, so that we might be justified by his grace and
> become heirs in hope of eternal life. (Titus, 3: 4-7)

The mission of the Spirit of God, the Spirit of Christ, is the completion of Christ's mission on earth, the realization of God's plan of salvation, since the reign of the Spirit is, through Man's free consent and submission, the mastery by the Divine Spirit of the spirit of Man, that spirit which the creator God first breathed into Man and which developed and blossomed over time into the human intellectual and spiritual capacity we learn about in Genesis 3, when proto-humans mutated into *homo sapiens*. Man, the strange hybrid, is organic to nature, the product of the gradual evolution of forms of life over millions of years, but also an "anomaly of nature" who stands somewhat apart from the rest of creation, a creature with something of the divine in him. His life has a goal and a purpose that transcends the biological level of his existence and he is drawn to live by values that rise above the mere struggle for survival.

The need for wholeness that human beings experience does not equate with a search for ego-bound self-sufficiency. Like divine wholeness, human wholeness is relational. Humans are not and cannot be self-sufficient: even at the biological level, from infancy we depend on others for our very survival; we are dependent beings, social beings. And what applies at the level of biology is even more apparent at the level of cultural progress, intellectual development and moral and spiritual growth—we are dependent on the contributions, achievements and gifts of many others in all of these areas. As Philip Sheldrake observes, we can only become whole by receiving from others.[85] The point is eloquently made by the seventeenth century English "Metaphysical Poet," John Donne, in his famous lines: "No man is an Island, entire of itself; every man is a piece of the Continent, a part of the main..."[86]

Jesus expressed a similar point forcefully in what he described as the two commandments on which depend all the law and the prophets, referring to the Jewish *shema* of Deuteronomy 6: 5 but, significantly, coupling with it a reference about love of neighbour from Leviticus 19:18:

You shall love the Lord your God with all your heart, and with all your soul, and with all your mind. This is the first and the great commandment. And a second is like it, You shall love your neighbour as yourself. (Mt 22: 37-40; Mk 12: 28-34; Lk 10: 25-28).

These words of Jesus are not just commandments, they go to the very heart of the commandments and are a programme for human living—as Jesus says in Luke's version, "Do this, and you will live." Human wholeness cannot be achieved without relationship. And we cannot achieve successful relationship without self-giving and self-transcendence, and we cannot achieve that by ourselves; to achieve and sustain it we stand in need of God. It is a two-way process and, as in all things pertaining to salvation, which is a gift from God, in the final analysis the initiative, the initial impulse, must come from God. What is required of us is to yield, submit, give way to the divine impulse in order to break out of our self-absorbed selfhood. The state of being in love with God, the gift of the Spirit, reveals itself in us through acts of self-giving, when we reach out beyond ourselves in love, joy, peace, patience, kindness, goodness, faithfulness, gentleness, and self-control. (Galatians 5: 22) The action of the Spirit in us causes us to overcome our natural egotism, to allow God's Spirit to take command of our lives, and to grow as human beings by "spilling out" beyond ourselves, by truly loving our neighbour and in this way bridging the gap between knowledge and life. It is by being taken up and divinized by the Spirit of God that Man reaches the final stages of that process of divinisation/hominisation first set in motion in Eden when he first broke free of the confines of his animal nature and tasted the fruit of the tree of knowledge of good and evil. By loving our neighbour in all her or his humanity, we make God present in the world since we give true and authentic expression to the divinity we share with God, who is love (1 Jn 4: 8, 16); we show what is best in us, we realize ourselves as human beings. It is in this way that hybrid Man at last attains wholeness and integrity, and the danger unleashed by his crossing the line between divinity and creation is finally overcome. That danger, which is all too real, is overcome not through some reduction of Man or the repression of his gifts but, in line with God's purposes and promises, through the expansion of what he has become; in a word, through his divinisation.

The trajectory of salvation history ought not to be defined by the fall of Adam and the redeeming action of Christ. In the West, under the influence of Augustine, Christianity has tended to define the course and

shape of salvation history as, "Adam fell; Christ saved; we are redeemed." On this understanding, "redemption" is literally a "buying
back" by Christ of what was lost by Adam, a reopening of the gates of
heaven that were shut by the sin of Adam. While such a crude concept of
redemption doubtless appealed to people in an age when prisoners could
literally be bought back in exchange for money or gold, it has less appeal
in the changed circumstances of today and it does less than justice to the
Hebrew notion of the "life motif" that stands at the heart of the God-Man
relationship. Where Augustine, believing he is following Paul in this,
contrasts Adam, the bringer of death and sin, with Christ, the bringer of
life and redemption, I would suggest that this Adam-Christ polarity fails
to do justice to the totality of Paul's thought on redemption, which demands a more trinitarian response to the problem posed by the human
need for wholeness. For according to Paul, the completion of Man can
only be achieved through his union with God. And this is accomplished
when Man is annexed to Christ, his fellow human, through the indwelling of Christ's Spirit in him, and in this way becomes by adoption what
Christ is by nature, at one with the Father. It is mistaken, I believe, to
consider that Paul's understanding of redemption is predicated on the so-
called "original sin" of Adam or that redemption makes no sense unless
there is an original sin. Rather, Paul's understanding of redemption is
predicated on humanity's basic sinfulness, the fact that, as he says in
Romans, all of us have sinned (Romans 5: 12). Paul's understanding of
redemption can be more accurately conveyed in these terms: "We are
sinners, incomplete, lacking in wholeness; Christ's Spirit, the spirit of
love, is the source of true wholeness given to us; we are redeemed by
being made whole in Christ through the power of his Spirit and united
with him to the Father."

Paul in his writings gives trinitarian expression to the highly developed Hebrew sense of the human need for holiness, which stresses human wholeness, integrity and fulfilment through our response to God's
creative and sustaining action: instead of redemption being understood as
the *undoing* of the sin of Adam and its dreadful consequences, Paul sees
redemption as the *answer* to Man's need for wholeness by his participation in the trinitarian life of God. It is not a restoration to some state that
preceded the Fall but an ascent or elevation to a new and unmerited, divine level of being. It is the acquisition of the spirit of love, of divine
life—divinisation—that frees us from the tyranny of false gods and the
slavery of sin by empowering us to exercise our reason and freedom in
the service of the one true God. Sin, by contrast, is the refusal of God's

offer of the gift of life, of love, a selfish prizing of some aspect of creation above life with God. Likewise the Church, the communion Christians are called to form, is the extension over time of the mission of God's Son and the mission of the Spirit. "Communion with the Triune God is the very life of the Church; communion with the mission of God's Son and Spirit is the very mission of the Church."[87] We are formed into a single Church because of the one Spirit that dwells in each of us. As Paul says, "For by one Spirit we were all baptized into one body—Jews or Greeks, slaves or free—and all were made to drink of one Spirit." (1 Cor. 12: 13) We fulfil our vocation as members of the Church by continuing the mission of Christ in the world with the aid of the Holy Spirit.

Paul's thoughts on redemption as on so much else are *trinitarian* and ought not to be defined by some supposed *polar* relationship between Adam and Christ. Paul wrote ten epistles, if we exclude the three so-called "pastoral epistles." These ten epistles consist of some 74 chapters, and in only two of these is there a comparison between Adam and Christ. Yet this comparison, not found elsewhere in the New Testament and totally absent from the gospels, has been allowed to dominate the theology of redemption in the West, but significantly not in the East. There is surely good reason to believe that the Western preoccupation with the Adam-Christ polarity has been disproportionate.

The polarity[88] at the centre of Paul's thinking is that between *two contrasting states*: slavery to sin, or idolatry, and the liberation from such slavery earned by Christ's death and resurrection with which we are conjoined by the power of his Spirit. The state of idolatry is countered and answered by the state brought about in us by the indwelling of the Holy Spirit. By dying and rising with Christ we are empowered to leave behind our enslavement to sin and all forms of idol-worship. Christ's role in our redemption is not defined by what Adam did or did not do at the beginning of history; it is defined by his trinitarian role, as the divine human being in and through whom, by the power of his Spirit, we are adopted as sons and daughters of the Father. Adam's role, so often considered to have been the introduction of the blight of sin from which Christ redeemed us, should be completely re-cast and presented in a totally new light. For from the perspective of salvation, the history of humankind is mainly shaped by two episodes of transformation. The first, which is the product of nature (and most probably the product of natural selection), took place when hominid creatures moved beyond their merely animal existence and achieved full rational consciousness. The second, which is the redemptive work of God alone, was begun by God with the introduction of the covenant and reached its end-point when Jesus was raised from the dead, thereby enabling each of us to achieve human wholeness by becoming enjoined with him by the agency of the Holy Spirit and being raised with him to a new life of joyful, loving union with the Father.

This understanding is more in line with Paul's comparison of Adam and Christ in 1 Corinthians 15:

> The first man Adam became a living being; the last Adam became a life-giving spirit. But it is not the spiritual which is first but the physical, and then the spiritual.
>
> The first man was from the earth, a man of dust; the second man is from heaven. As was the man of dust, so are those who are of the dust; and as is the man of heaven, so are those who are of heaven. Just as we have borne the image of the man of dust, we shall also bear the image of the man of heaven. I tell you this, brethren: flesh and blood cannot inherit the kingdom of God, nor does the perishable inherit the imperishable.
>
> Lo! I tell you a mystery. We shall not all sleep, but we shall all be changed, in a moment, in the twinkling of an eye, at the last trumpet. For the trumpet will sound, and the dead will be raised imperishable, and we shall be changed. For this perishable nature must put on the imperishable, and this mortal nature must put on immortality. When the perishable puts on the imperishable, and the mortal puts on immortality, then shall come to pass the saying that is written:
> "Death is swallowed up in victory."
> "O death, where is thy victory?
> O death, where is thy sting?"   (1 Cor. 15:45-55)

The first Adam became a living *nephesh* (Gen. 2: 7)—a purely natural occurrence; but the second Adam is a life-giving spirit because his work of redemption, opening up for us the possibility of being granted eternal life, pertains to the supernatural order which is the exclusive domain of God. It is by receiving the gift of the Spirit, the gift of love, that we become capable of union with the Father, who is love (1 Jn 4: 8; 4: 16). One outcome of moving away from the notion that redemption is about undoing the sin of Adam would be a renewed appreciation among Western theologians of the role of the Spirit in the divinisation and salvation of human beings.

In order to challenge adequately the Augustinian interpretation of Genesis 3, which has such deep roots in Christian culture and theology and such a strong hold on both the Christian and the popular imagination, at least in the West, it has not been enough simply to point out the weaknesses in Augustine's account. Nor has it been sufficient even to offer a new interpretation of Genesis 3. Such are the theological ramifications of the Augustinian interpretation that it has been necessary, in addition, to place the new interpretation of Genesis 3 in the context of a new interpretation of Genesis 1-11 and, more generally, of a new understanding of the history of salvation, one in which the image of the tree of life is seen to frame the Judaeo-Christian narrative.

It is my hope that in this book I have been able to indicate, however inadequately, the general nature and the broad characteristics of this particular understanding of salvation history. The history of salvation I have put forward in these pages is the story of God's transformative gifting of himself to Man over time: this presents, I believe, a vision of salvation history, of God's dealings with human beings over time, more extravagantly generous, more positive and more joyful than the Augustinian vision. It is also more coherent and in keeping with the vision of the Orthodox wing of the Christian church. Augustine's interpretation of Genesis 3 puts the emphasis on a deed, on a sin, but I have been at pains to shift the emphasis from a deed to a relationship—or more precisely to "relationship," since the nature of that relationship awaits determination. It is a relationship conditioned by the basic human situation, the need Man has for union with God. God has offered Man the answer to his need and Man can either accept or refuse God's offer. But the God-Man relationship itself was made possible by the profound and dramatic changes that took place when humanity was born.

NOTES

1. Martin Luther, *Commentary on Epistle to the Romans*, quoted in *Original Sin: The Patristic and Theological Background* by Henri Rondet, translated by Cajetan Finegan OP (Los Angeles: Ecclesia Press, 1972).

2. John Calvin, *Institutes of the Christian Religion* 2.3.2, quoted by Marguerite Shuster, op. cit., p. 160. On Augustine's relationship with the Reformers, see John Hick, *Evil and the God of Love* (London: Fontana Library, 1968) pp. 121-3.

3. Eugene Portalie, op. cit., p. 212.

4. See, for example, *Confessions*, 6, XVI.

5. Joseph Ratzinger, op. cit.

6. Joseph Ratzinger, op. cit., 62-71.

7. Augustine, *De natura et gratia*, 62.

8. Matthew Fox discusses some of the unfortunate consequences of the doctrine, quoting a variety of authorities, op. cit., p. 51.

9. These words are written the day after the publication of a 2,600 page report describing the systematic abuse of children by priests and religious in Ireland's care institutions over 60 years. In *The Irish Times*, the religious affairs correspondent, Patsy McGarry, wrote, "a dark theology of fallen human nature with a propensity to evil allowed a climate where such viciousness could constantly be visited on children." Quoted in the article by Daniel O'Leary, "Painful, slow redemption," The Tablet, (London) 6 June 2009, p 14.

10. Other Old Testament examples of this belief and of the "ontological link" between God and Man can be found in Joseph Blenkinsopp, op. cit., p. 96

11. It is worth pointing out that, notwithstanding the belief disseminated by some anti-religious polemicists that Darwin dealt a mortal blow to Christian theism, religious responses to Darwin's theory were quite diverse and not all contemporary Christian theologians or thinkers stood out against evolution, just as not all scientists fell in behind it. Frederick Temple, for example, espoused evolution and went on to become the Archbishop of Canterbury. See "Darwin and Victorian Christianity" by John Hedley Brooke in *The Cambridge Companion to Darwin*, edited by Jonathan Hodge and Gregory Raddick , Second Edition, (Cambridge: Cambridge University Press, 2009).

12. Bill Price, *Charles Darwin: Origins and Arguments* (Harpenden: Pocket Essentials, 2008) p. 78-9.

13. I am aware that in philosophy "intentionality" refers to mental or intellectual operations that are conscious as well as being spontaneous, whereas in biology there are many goal-directed instinctive operations that are spontaneous but not conscious. I use the word "intentionality" in the context of biology in an analogous sense in order to point up the contrast I wish to draw between spontaneous goal-directed biological operations and spontaneous goal-directed intellectual operations.

14. Gabriel Daly O.S.A., op. cit., p. 32-33.

15. Augustine's opinion on this matter is shared by Pope John Paul II in his reflections on *The Theology of the Body: Human Love in the Divine Plan* (Boston, MA: Pauline Books, 1997); see the references to that in Fergus Kerr, op. cit., p. 178. James Barr tells us that the Hebrew word for the "shame" referred to in Genesis 3 has nothing to do with guilt or wrongdoing or loss of innocence.

16. Ludwig Wittgenstein, *Philosophical Investigations*, trans. G.E.M. Anscombe (Oxford: Basil Blackwell, 1953) Pt 2, p. 178.

17. Bernard Lonergan, "Dimensions of Meaning" in *Collection* (London: Darton, Longman and Todd, 1967), p. 264.

18. Bernard Lonergan, "Healing and Creating in History" in *A Third Collection: Papers by Bernard J. F. Lonergan S.J.*, edited by Frederick E. Crowe S.J., (London: Geoffrey Chapman, 1985) p 106.

19. Ibid., p 107-8.

20. Ibid., in "Mission and the Spirit," p. 26.

21. Plato, *Phaedo* 64c and 85-95.

22. Serge Lancel, op. cit., p. 363.

23. *Humani Generis*, 36. I am indebted to the article by William Charlton, "Two Theories of Soul," *New Blackfriars*, Vol 90 No 1028, July 2009, for much of the factual information in this paragraph, including the references to Plato, as well as for several elements of the argument I put forward in this section.

24. See Nicholas Lash, "Are We Born and do We Die?" *New Blackfriars*, Vol 90 No 1028, July 2009, p. 406 f.

25. See Bernard Lonergan SJ, *Verbum: Word and Idea in Aquinas*, edited by David Burrell, (London: Darton, Longman and Todd, 1968) p. 112, p. 134.

26. See Aquinas's much quoted observation, *Anima mea non est ego* ("My soul is not me," or, "I am not my soul," or, more literally, "My soul is not I"), referred to by Nicholas Lash, op. cit., p. 409. Indeed Aquinas is insistent that any composite of matter and form is, first and foremost, a body: see *Summa Theologiae* 1, q 3, a. 2, where he writes *Omne compositum ex materia et forma est corpus* ("Everything composed of matter and form is a body").

27. It may appear an irrelevance to introduce epistemology at this point, but how we come to know is often the best route into the philosophy of mind, and the philosophy of mind is often the best route into our understanding of the human being.

28. See Joseph Fitzpatrick, *Philosophical Encounters: Lonergan and the Analytical Tradition*, (Toronto: University of Toronto Press, 2005) p. 159.

29. Ibid.

30. Ibid., p 135.

31. Anthony Kenny considers Descartes' dualistic view of mind to be the most widespread among educated people who are not professional philosophers, and his philosophical inheritance to be "the single most substantial obstacle to a correct philosophical understanding of the nature of the human mind." See Anthony Kenny, *The Metaphysics of Mind*, (Oxford: Oxford University Press, 1989) pp. 2 and vii. Kenny proposes that Wittgenstein's *Philosophical Investigations* provides "therapy" for overcoming this understanding of mind.

32. Serge Lancel, op. cit., p. 355.

33. Joseph Blenkinsopp, op. cit., Chapter XII, "On Saving one's Soul."

34. James Barr, op. cit., p. 112.

35. Bernard Lonergan, *Insight: A Study of Human Understanding*, (London: Longmans, Green and Co, 1957); also Joseph Fitzpatrick, op. cit., Chapter 1, "The Structure of Cognition."

36. This freedom from the constraints of time and place forms part of the intellectual intentionality denoted by the activities of reasoning, deciding, acting etc. with which human beings are familiar. "Free" does not mean "arbitrary," "at random" or "at will."

37. Gabriel Daly O.S.A., op. cit., p. 29. The author attributes these views to Karl Rahner.

38. The list of such problems could go on and on. William Charlton lists other problems confronting dualism in the article referred to above, as does Nicholas Lash in the other. The title of Lash's article is instructive.

39. Augustine, *City of God*, Book XIV, chapter 11, p 331.

40. See James L. Kugel, op. cit., chapter 3.

41. For example, see chapter 7, entitled "Adam and Eve," in Erich Auerbach, op. cit., where Auerbach discusses the twelfth century Christmas play, *Mystere d'Adam*, in which he claims (p. 147), "There is no moral consciousness in her (Eve) as there is in Adam; in its place she has a naïve, childishly hardy, and unreflectingly sinful curiosity." More recently, former US President Jimmy Carter has told how he parted company with the Southern Baptist Convention after an association of sixty years, citing as one of the reasons the convention leaders' claim that women must be subservient to their husbands and prohibited from serving as deacons and pastors because Eve was responsible for Original Sin! See the article, "For too many women, faith is the basis for cruelty," (*The Observer*, London, 12 July 2009. p.23).

42. Hilary Mantel, *Wolf Hall* (London: Fourth Estate, 2009) p. 362.

43. Bernard Lonergan SJ, *The Triune God: Systematics*, The Collected Works of Bernard Lonergan, Volume 12, (Toronto: University of Toronto Press, 2007) p. 559, n. 1.

44. It is worth noting how in scripture the conferring of the Spirit, the breathing of the Spirit on someone or on a group, is often linked to the inception of some event or enterprise before it is fully formed or before it has taken shape in history: compare the action described in Genesis 2: 7 with that described in John 20: 22.

45. See John J. O'Donnell, *The Mystery of the Triune God*, (London: Sheed and Ward, 1988) p. 160.

46. The nearest human analogy is most probably a couple who are deeply in love and because they are in love are of one mind and one heart: we might say that they share the same spirit. As the poet Francis Quarles expresses it, "Our firm-united souls did more than twine;/ So I my Best-beloved's am; so He is mine."

47. See John J. O'Donnell, op. cit., p. 153.

48. John J. O'Donnell, op. cit., p. 147.

49. It might be more appropriate to describe the episode of Noah's ark as the *final phase* of the rite of passage that begins with the eating of the fruit from the tree of knowledge and concludes with the ending of the Flood; similarly the death and resurrection of Jesus constitute the final phase of Jesus's saving mission on earth and the beginning of the mission of the Spirit to humankind. In both cases the passage results in a transformation of the divine-human relationship, in what scripture terms "a new creation." In each case the transformation is an elevation to a higher state of being.

50. Gabriel Daly, op. cit., p. 108.

51. See the commentary of Harvey D. Egan in *Karl Rahner: Mystic of Everyday Life* (New York: The Crossroad Publishing Co, 1998) pp. 134-6.

52. Gabriel Daly, op. cit., p. 116.

53. Gabriel Daly, ibid.

54. See Nicholas Lash, "The God of Man's Future," a paper read to the Aquinas Society, Cambridge, March 1968, (published in *Irish Theological Quarterly*).

55. There are strong sensitivities in this area with a tendency among some scientists to see animal and human consciousness and intelligence as continuous rather than markedly different. I would simply add that, notwithstanding the developments that have come about in understanding the different levels of intelligence in the animal kingdom and the sophisticated communication systems and complex social structures in many animal groups, human beings are different on account of their endowment with the two types of intentionality, the intellectual as well as the biological, described above.

56. Augustine, *Enchiridion*, VIII, 27. Quoted in Gabriel Daly, op. cit., p. 161.

57. Much of this section is indebted to John Hick, op. cit., p. 217 f.

58. St Irenaeus, *Adversus Haereses*, IV, 38, 1-2, quoted in Henri Rondet, op. cit., p 40.

59. Ibid., p 41.

60. John Hick, op. cit., p. 222.

61. This fact together with the discovery of one of Irenaeus's works, *Proof of the Apostolic Preaching*, at the beginning of the twentieth century earned Irenaeus a considerable amount of attention from a succession of mainly Protestant theologians keen to argue the compatibility of Christian salvation history with evolution. However, the strong strain of utopianism underpinning most of these accounts, the belief that Man was evolving into a better and spiritually more perfect creature, suffered a fatal setback with the onset of the First World War, and in consequence the interest in Irenaeus tended to evaporate. See John Hick, op. cit., p. 245.

62. N.P. Williams, op. cit., p. 450.

63. David L. Edwards, op. cit., p. 120.

64. Ibid., p. 120-1.

65. On this, see Henri de Lubac SJ, *Augustinianism and Modern Theology*, (New York: Crossroad Publishing Company, New Edition, 2000) chapter 6, "Pure Nature and Natural Desire."

66. Alistair McFadyen, *Bound to Sin: Abuse, Holocaust and the Christian Doctrine of Sin*, (Cambridge: Cambridge University Press, 2000) pp. 14-42.

67. Ibid., p. 19.

68. Ibid., p. 16.

69. Ibid., p. 17.

70. Ibid., p. 34.

71. Ibid., Chapter 2, *passim*.

72. Ibid., p. 26.

73. Gabriel Daly, op. cit., p. 117.

74. For example, Aquinas regarded freedom of action to be essential to the notions of merit and demerit (sin). See Bernard Lonergan, *Grace and Freedom: Operative Grace in the Thought of St Thomas Aquinas* (Toronto: University of Toronto Press, 2000) p. 317, n. 3.

75. Alistair McFadyen, op. cit., p. 167.

76. In *De Malo*, q. 6, a. 1.

77. Gabriel Daly, op. cit., p. 122.

78. McFadyen, op. cit., p. 18, n. 4. The problem of monogenism (descent from a single pair of ancestors), which he refers to, fails to arise in my interpretation of Genesis 3, since this interpretation is free of any need to maintain that Adam and Eve were historical people let alone the originating ancestors of the entire human race.

79. Clearly there are close similarities between this view and that of St Irenaeus, cited above.

80. The centrality of the notion of "wholeness" and "becoming whole" in Catholic spirituality is well developed by Philip Sheldrake. See his article, "Becoming Catholic Persons" in *Receptive Ecumenism and the Call to Catholic Learning*, edited by Paul D. Murray, (Oxford: Oxford University Press, 2008) p. 52 ff.

81. *The Epic of Giglamesh*, op. cit., Introduction by Robert D. Biggs, p. XVII.

82. On this, see David M. Carr, op. cit.

83. James Barr, op. cit., p 84.

84. James Barr, op. cit., pp 16-18.

85. Philip Sheldrake, op. cit., p. 54.

86. John Donne, *Devotions upon Emergent Occasions* (1624).

87. M-C Seoul, 74; document resulting from the International Dialogue between the Roman Catholic Church and the World Methodist Church; quoted in Walter Kasper, *Harvesting the Fruits*, (London: Continuum, 2009) p. 19.

88. By "polarity" or "polar relationship" I mean a relationship between each of a pair, A and B, in which A's role or function is determined by B's, and/or B's role or function is determined by A's.

Index

Printed in Great Britain
by Amazon.co.uk, Ltd.,
Marston Gate.